D0406917

THE PATRIOTS

ALSO BY WINSTON GROOM

Nonfiction

Conversations with the Enemy (1982, with Duncan Spencer)
Shrouds of Glory (1995)
The Crimson Tide (2002)
A Storm in Flanders (2002)
1942 (2004)
Patriotic Fire (2006)
Vicksburg, 1863 (2009)
Kearny's March (2011)
Shiloh, 1862 (2012)
The Aviators (2013)
The Generals (2015)
The Allies (2018)

Fiction

Better Times Than These (1978)
As Summers Die (1980)
Only (1984)
Forrest Gump (1986)
Gone the Sun (1988)
Gump and Co. (1995)
Such a Pretty, Pretty Girl (1998)
El Paso (2016)

THE PATRIOTS

Alexander Hamilton, Thomas Jefferson, John Adams, *and the* Making of America

WINSTON GROOM

WASHINGTON, D.C.

Published by National Geographic Partners, LLC
1145 17th Street NW Washington, DC 20036

ISBN: 978-1-4262-2149-1

Since 1888, the National Geographic Society has funded more than 13,000 research, exploration, and preservation projects around the world. National Geographic Partners distributes a portion of the funds it receives from your purchase to National Geographic Society to support programs including the conservation of animals and their habitats.

Get closer to National Geographic explorers and photographers, and connect with our global community. Join us today at nationalgeographic.com/join

Interior design: Nicole Miller

Printed in the United States of America

20/MP-CG/1

To Susan, without whose help,
love, and constant consideration
I could not have written this book.

CONTENTS

THE PATRIOTS

PROLOGUE

America's Founding Fathers were never quite sure that democracy would work, especially during their revolution. The British, for their part, were absolutely convinced that it wouldn't; their very Englishness had instilled in them a heightened sense of the rightness and superiority of their monarchical ways, and had provoked a fear and hatred of such outlandish notions as "democracy" and "republics."

The British redcoat was the epitome of the professional soldier: highly trained, impressively outfitted, well-armed, and merciless. There was never any doubt, at least in the early days of the war, that they would defeat the rebellious colonists. But history is strewn with stern and often peculiar endings. At the eleventh hour the British army was defeated by an army of ragged American soldiers and their allies.

From that revolutionary moment of history three men emerged, as unalike one another as it was possible to be. Alexander Hamilton was the illegitimate son of a mother from the West Indies and a wayward, penniless father from the Scottish nobility. Hamilton grew up working as a shipping clerk on the island of St. Croix and came to America as a student just before the Revolutionary

War began. Thomas Jefferson was, first, a farmer—a slaveholding planter (who hated slavery), a Virginia aristocrat, polymath, Renaissance man, and Enlightenment thinker. John Adams was an eccentric, Harvard-educated lawyer from Massachusetts, who became deeply involved with the early revolutionaries in Boston. Both he and Jefferson would become presidents of the United States, and Hamilton would become the nation's first secretary of the treasury. As such, he saved the fledgling country from bankruptcy and gave it the foundations of the financial system that has existed for more than two centuries.

Despite their mutual concerns during the Revolution, as the new country took form these three developed an abiding hatred of each other so intense that at times it threatened to bring down the fragile young republic. Yet each reached the very pinnacle of his own power and genius in the formative years of the nation, and each had a consuming patriotism. These three founders loved their embryonic country and were ready to lay down their lives for it. They were present at the creation of America's critical founding documents, and their high-minded ideals and policies have resonated for nearly 250 years.

Those 250 years have not always been easy. In his famous farewell address at the end of his presidency, George Washington warned against "foreign entanglements" and the growth of political factions, which he saw as malignantly divisive forces that could tear the nation apart. His fears were prescient but his warning went unheeded.

As the newly minted United States attempted to create a viable federal system, the country began to split politically into two main factions. The Federalists, led by Hamilton (by then a New Yorker), argued for a strong central government modeled loosely on the

British system. The other faction, the Republicans, led by Jefferson the Virginian, demanded a much weaker central government, emphasized states' rights, and generally favored the French over the British model.

As the tempest brewed, the press entered the fray. Newspapers not only informed but deliberately inflamed political opinion, inspiring fistfights and duels and sometimes tearing family and friends apart. Personal attacks were the order of the day, with stories written on the flimsiest of evidence.

Into this toxic climate the three founders plunged themselves, each believing that the political notions of the others would lead the country into dangerous chaos and ruin. They were, after all, floundering in the unknown: nothing like the American experiment had ever been tried on such a scale and with such a diverse population, both ethnically and regionally.

If Hamilton, Jefferson, and Adams were intemperate in their political passions, it was most likely out of fear of squandering the exquisite main chance they had acquired with the revolutionary victory. None of the three wished to dispel it; they wanted to see America prosper and live on through history as an enlightened model of self-government among men. It is a sad irony of history that at one time they were on such friendly terms—particularly Jefferson and Adams—and that their divergence in political thought led first to discomfort, then distrust, then mistrust, and at last hatred.

The arguments they engaged in have not ended, and Americans continue to enjoy the liberty to indulge in sometimes fractious disagreements. If the revolutionary victory was something of a miracle, it remains a wonder that the democracy it spawned has survived at all. That it does so is a twist of fate for which all Americans should be eternally grateful.

CHAPTER ONE

A man of striking intelligence, remarkable presence, and driving ambition, Alexander Hamilton tried to outrun his unpropitious beginnings most of his life. His birthplace, the tiny West Indian island of Nevis, was an unlikely setting for a man who would change the course of history: no more than a volcanic cone protruding from the Caribbean, its peak eternally covered in clouds. Hamilton's mother, Rachel Faucette, was half British and half French Huguenot, the daughter of a prosperous Caribbean planter. Alexander's father, James Hamilton, was the fourth son of a Scottish laird. When Alexander was born on January 11, 1755, the two were not married—and never would be.

The heiress of what Alexander called a "snug" fortune, Rachel had been pushed years before by her mother into marrying Johann Michael Lavien, a Danish merchant nearly twice her age. She and Lavien lived on her father's former estate on the Danish-controlled island of St. Croix. Abusive and determined to cow his willful young wife, Lavien managed to have her imprisoned for several months in the island's dreaded Christiansted dungeon.

After five years of brutal marriage, Rachel fled St. Croix, leaving behind her young son, Peter. She and her mother settled on nearby

St. Kitts, where she met James Hamilton, a failed seeker of fortune. The two settled on Nevis, as Rachel owned inherited land there in the capital, Charlestown. Lavien later claimed in court that Rachel had gone to "an English island" (Nevis) when she abandoned him and "begot two illegitimate children."[1] He filed for divorce, apparently intimating that his wife was also a prostitute, and obtained a court order stating that Rachel was to have "no rights whatsoever" in any of his properties. Furthermore, the court decreed that under Danish law Rachel was forevermore forbidden to remarry—although Lavien was free to do so.

Rachel and Hamilton were living on St. Croix with their two sons in the mid-1760s when Hamilton deserted the family; Rachel was left to raise twelve-year-old James and ten-year-old Alexander on her own. She opened a small store, selling such supplies as soap, threads, salt pork, butter, and other provisions, and supplemented her income by renting out five slaves—three adults and two children—inherited from her mother. The Hamilton boys were denied entry into the church school, because they were born "out of wedlock," but Rachel had them tutored by a Jewish schoolmistress. Then, in February 1768, Rachel died after only two days of an illness that was likely yellow fever. Her teenage boys looked on as their mother, only thirty-nine, was given a Christian burial in a plot of land owned by her relatives. For all intents and purposes, the boys were now orphans.

The vengeful Lavien appeared on the scene as Rachel's estate was being settled to claim the entire amount as his own—in the end, Rachel's son with Lavien, Peter, received the proceeds from the sale of her slaves, a dozen or so pieces of silverware, and some books that were put up at auction. Peter Lytton, a cousin by marriage of the Hamilton children and now their guardian, purchased the books—among them Machiavelli's *The Prince*, the works of Alexander Pope, and some volumes of sermons. Lytton returned them to Alexander and James. For Alexander, at least, these volumes marked the beginning of his self-education.[2]

The boys were expected to earn their keep, so James was apprenticed to a carpenter and Alexander was put to work for a merchant, Nicholas Cruger. He began as an errand boy and clerk but quickly moved upward to handle correspondence and accounts. Cruger's business was exporting island products, such as sugar, molasses, and rum, and importing plantation implements and provisions—plows, lumber, livestock—from the American colonies. When Cruger put Alexander in charge of all shipping trade, the boy received a critical, practical education in economic affairs.

Around that time Alexander was befriended by an Irish-born, Princeton-educated Presbyterian minister named Hugh Knox. In 1772 the most violent hurricane in memory smashed into St. Croix, killing dozens, wrecking homes and businesses, and tossing large boats onto the city streets. The seventeen-year-old Alexander wrote such a colorful account of the storm that Knox arranged for it to be published in the local English-language newspaper.

Knox became Alexander's literary patron. He recognized the boy's raw intellectual talent and was determined to coax it into fruition. It would be a sin, in Reverend Knox's opinion, if this youth were to live a life of obscurity on a small Caribbean island. He lent Alexander books and engaged him in worldly conversations regarding the state of politics, science, philosophy, economics, and literature. Led by the Reverend Knox, other benefactors eventually championed Alexander, including his boss Cruger, several wealthy merchants, and a prosperous cousin, Ann Lytton Venton. They decided to send Alexander to mainland America, where he could receive a college education. Years afterward, Knox wrote to Hamilton, "I have always had a just & secret pride in having advised you to go to America, and in having recommended you to some [of] my old friends there."

History doesn't tell us if Knox, Cruger, and the others went to the dock at St. Croix in the autumn of 1772 to see off their grateful ward—but a good guess would be that they did. It was Alexander's farewell to the West Indies. Once he reached America, he would never return.

Hamilton's schooner sailed north out of the Caribbean, and then along the Atlantic coast to Boston. Only 150 years earlier the land had been the domain of native tribes— but in the intervening decades English and other European settlers had taken over the coast, importing slaves to work their lands, especially in the South and along the Chesapeake Bay. By the time Hamilton set sail, slavery existed in every one of the thirteen American colonies. The rude houses that early settlers had built had been replaced by homes, some of them palatial; roadways and riverways connected the large port cities of New York, Philadelphia, Baltimore, and Boston.

By today's standards, transportation and communication were rudimentary. Railroads and steamboats were in the future, and most travel was powered by horse or by sail. It took a month to get a message from New York to New Orleans. Newspapers, broadsheets, and pamphlets were the principal means of communication. (For deeper reading, there were Voltaire, Fielding, Swift, Pope, and Defoe—and always Shakespeare.) City streets were dark at night. Among the wealthier classes, most furnishings, clothes, and other high-end items were imported from England. The less affluent purchased some cheap local goods but often made their own.

Americans ate pancakes, which had been around since the ancient Egyptians, and mayonnaise—but no tomatoes, because they were widely regarded as poisonous. Much of the table fare remained wild game or seafood, both of which were abundant. The colonists drank tea or coffee and hot chocolate when they could get it, and washed down their meals with wine, cider, whiskey, or water. Sudden death was an omnipresent reality, as medicine had not made appreciable inroads since the Middle Ages (bleeding a patient, for example, was still a widely accepted medical practice, as was using bloodsucking leeches). As a general cure-all, people were often given mercury, one of the most poisonous elements on earth. The average American life span was less than forty years; frightful epidemics of typhoid and yellow fever ravaged the country nearly every year, as did scourges of cholera, typhus, diphtheria, tuberculosis, influenza, smallpox, dysentery, measles, and uncontrollable staph infections. And then there were the dangers of shipwreck; horse throws or kicks; house fires; and the sudden and unpredictable arrival of natural disasters, such as hurricanes. If you lived in more remote areas, there was always the possibility of Indian attack or getting mauled by bears or panthers. Complications from pregnancy and childbirth were the leading causes of death for women of childbearing age, and most families lost a heartbreaking number of children before they could reach adulthood.

Nevertheless, a majority of British Americans were proud to be part of a land of bounty and promise. Yet in the years just before Hamilton's arrival, a dark shadow had appeared over the land, and many colonists had begun to question the monarchical and parliamentary system of governing that they had accepted just a few years before.

WHEN ALEXANDER HAMILTON'S SCHOONER reached Boston in October 1772, he found a city that had become an armed camp garrisoned by British redcoats and overseen by a military governor. Townspeople had rioted over British taxes, and two years earlier the so-called Boston Massacre had taken place when British troops opened fire on a rowdy group of Americans. Hamilton did not tarry. He moved south to New York, where similar passions were at large (while not as ardent).

At seventeen Hamilton had developed a warm, cheery disposition despite his broken upbringing—but he "craved legitimacy in all its forms." He had also developed an abhorrence for disorder, as well as a kind of mistrust of human nature that ran against his "veneer of lively charm." He was beginning to acquire a very high sense of personal honor, and had determined to become known in this new country as something other than the bastard son of an accused prostitute and a runaway father. He was to hone this sense of honor until, in time, it became a major feature of his character.

Luckily for the young Hamilton, Reverend Knox had friends in high places: among them the wealthy and well-connected William Livingston, son of one of the most prestigious colonial families of the lower Hudson River Valley. Livingston was a brilliant satirist and eventually served as a nine-time governor of New Jersey, as well as a member of the Continental Congress and delegate to the Constitutional Convention. Livingston despised the practices of the British Crown, but he was also an eccentric aristocrat who knew the rich and powerful. He welcomed Hamilton into his large family and home, Liberty Hall, in Elizabethtown, New Jersey. At last, the young Alexander found himself in a happy home.

After studying briefly at a Presbyterian academy near Elizabethtown, Hamilton enrolled at King's College (later Columbia) in Manhattan, but he continued to live at Liberty Hall. He was a good student who took his work seriously. His first year he studied math, Latin, and anatomy and formed a debating club with several other students. He became friends with numerous classmates, most of whom were members of New York society. Preparing for debates, he developed a lifelong practice of pacing back and forth while talking to himself or delivering his oratory. He read voraciously and well. He was a good houseguest and a good neighbor. When the infant daughter of a nearby neighbor in Elizabethtown died, he wrote a poem for the parents, and before her funeral he "stayed up all night to watch the tiny corpse."[3]

Sometime in mid-December 1773, word reached Liberty Hall that a band of several hundred furious Bostonians, dressed as Indians, had boarded British ships in Boston Harbor and chucked thousands of pounds of British tea into the water to protest a new British tax on tea. Not long after this "Boston Tea Party," the colonies were convulsed by news that Boston had been put under total British occupation: the first of the so-called Intolerable Acts that included a British blockade of Boston Harbor.

With his distaste for disorder, these events created a profound dilemma for nineteen-year-old Hamilton. Revolution—a rising up of an entire people against constituted authority—was the very essence of disorder. But many Americans had had enough. Though Livingston and most of Hamilton's friends joined in the rebellious spirit, he remained conflicted. Then he began turning his reasoning into writing and saw a different picture of the stakes involved. Hamilton had read John Locke, whose principal theory was that government was a contract between the leaders and the subjects—and that the contract could be canceled if it was abused. Taxation without representation, Hamilton concluded, was abuse.

In September 1774, the First Continental Congress convened in Philadelphia in response to the British Parliament's "intolerable" acts. Representatives from twelve of the thirteen colonies attended; Georgia alone did not send delegates, because those elected could not agree on what actions to take regarding the British and refused to go to Philadelphia. Congress urged each of the colonies to raise, strengthen, and train their own militia. It also debated, and then agreed upon, a list of grievances to present to George III; they included a call to repeal these Intolerable Acts under the threat of an American boycott of British goods.

In December 1774, two months after the First Continental Congress ended, Hamilton published a widely read pamphlet entitled "A Full Vindication of the Measures of Congress," arguing that Americans, who had no vote in Parliament, should not be subject to its laws. He did not accuse King George of tyranny but instead blamed Parliament itself, which, he wrote, consisted of men who had no "interest" in the American colonies and therefore were tyrannical in the treatment of them. Still, he could not bring himself to favor spontaneous acts of rebellion. When a group of Patriot night riders wrecked a press with a known allegiance to the British Crown, Hamilton, then in his second year at King's College, told his friend John Jay, "I am more or less alarmed at every thing that is done as mere will and pleasure, without proper authority. Irregularities I know are to be expected, but they are dangerous and ought to be checked by every prudent and moderate means."[4]

THE AMERICAN POPULATION OF EUROPEAN EXTRACTION in 1774 has been estimated at around 2.5 million. Politically, about half a million were Tories, or Loyalists, who remained faithful to the British Crown. At the outbreak of fighting, many of them fled to Canada or England. But some remained in the colonies and joined with the British to fight the rebellious Americans. Others tried to maintain an uncomfortable neutrality that would protect their lives and property, while still others engaged in acts of espionage or terrorism against the so-called Patriots, who returned the favor.

In time, Hamilton was able to rationalize his passion for order with the huge disruption that a revolution would cause; he simply denied it was a revolution. Years later he explained, "Our separation from the mother country cannot be called a revolution. There have been no changes in the laws, no one's interests have been interfered with . . . All that is altered is that the seat of government has changed."[5]

Hamilton's equivocating aside, by April 1775, with the Battles of Lexington and Concord, revolution against Britain had become a reality. In May, word got around King's College that a large party of New York Patriots intended to seize the Reverend Myles Cooper, the Tory president of the college, and tar and feather him. When a hundreds-strong mob tore down the college gates and made for Cooper's sleeping quarters, Hamilton's distaste for mobs and disorder overcame his revolutionary ardor. He and a friend and fellow student, Robert Troup, ran ahead to the steps of the president's chambers. From there, they began to harangue the mob, giving the reverend time to get away and board a British warship.

When word of the fighting in Massachusetts reached New York, Hamilton knew he was bound for the army. Bravery and military glory became his passions, and he was anxious to prove himself. He was in fact a natural soldier; he stood like one, moved like one, had the voice of a commander. In August he, along with Troup and several other fellow students, joined a training company that drilled every morning in a churchyard. They wore green jackets and leather caps, and Hamilton quickly learned the manual of arms and drill commands. Drill was highly important in armies in those times. Since there were no radios, troop movements had to be timed by commanders to place a unit on a battlefield in exactly the right place at exactly the right time to bring collective fire on an enemy. The facing movements, echelons, cadence, and speed of steps all needed to be performed with precision. From the beginning, Hamilton not only excelled in but thrived on these martial exercises.

After five months of training, instruction, and personal study, Hamilton was given an oral examination by an American officer who certified that the young man was qualified to become a captain of artillery. The appointment was made March 4, 1776. Initially, Hamilton served as an officer in the newly raised New York State artillery company, which contained a battery of three six-pounder guns. New York did not furnish its military units with uniforms, and so Hamilton took it upon himself to purchase his men's outfits from a New York tailor. He bought seventy-five pairs of buckskin breeches and blue coats with buff cuffs and facing; the purchase cost him the last draw of the remittance provided by his benefactors in St. Croix.

Against all odds, George Washington had chased the British from Boston in March, soon after Hamilton received his captain's appointment. In early April, Washington marched his army to New York and ordered an immediate shoring up of the city's defenses, expecting the British to attack the city as soon as their reinforcements arrived. Hamilton's company of sixty-eight men was set to work building a large heptagonal artillery redoubt on Bayard's Hill at the tip of Manhattan Island. This was a stupendous undertaking for a young captain, but Hamilton still found time early in the mornings to conduct drill and gunnery exercises.

Among those observing Hamilton's smartly conducted drill was Nathanael Greene, one of Washington's most trusted generals. Greene invited the young officer to dinner. There is some suggestion that Greene offered Hamilton a spot as aide on his staff and that Hamilton respectfully turned him down, preferring the more challenging and glamorous job of a field command.

In mid-July, a Royal Navy battleship and frigate broke through obstructions in the Hudson River and sailed northward, blasting American positions and houses and buildings all along the way. Hamilton's battery, in the line of fire, commenced a sharp return on the two enemy ships, but one of his cannons burst, killing as many as half a dozen of his men. In the days afterward, a kind of panic set in through the city, and all but about 5,000 of New York's 25,000 residents fled. Many of those who stayed were Tories.

In August the British landed unopposed on Staten Island and began transferring as many as 25,000 redcoats across to Long

Island, where they vastly outnumbered the Continental defenders. On the night of August 26 they advanced north toward Brooklyn Heights, plowing through the thin Continental defenses. They soon had the American forces on the heights hemmed in, with the East River at their back. Washington's army put up a fierce fight, but to no avail. Seeing his remaining force about to be destroyed, Washington managed to ferry his men silently across the river in a dead-of-night retreat in heavy fog, but his losses were catastrophic: some 1,300 men killed or taken prisoner.

After losing Long Island, Washington set up strong defenses on Harlem Heights in northwest Manhattan. Hamilton's men built a redoubt in a forward position that was intended to slow the enemy down and confuse his attack. There were other such American positions in Lower Manhattan, but on September 15 British general William Howe landed a large force at Kip's Bay, on the East River in mid-Manhattan. The force of American militia defending Kip's Bay ran away when British warships entered the East River and began to bombard them. Washington, seeing the fiasco from the heights above, galloped down to stop the rout, but the panic that had set in with the militia was too great.

When news of this reached Hamilton, he and Col. Henry Knox went in search of Gen. Israel Putnam, who was in charge of lower Manhattan's defenses. The younger officers pleaded to make a last stand, but Putnam's aide Maj. Aaron Burr instead told them to escape to Harlem Heights via the Bloomingdale Road. Armed with this plan, Hamilton returned to the redoubt in time to save all his guns. He began a sharp rearguard action, blasting the oncoming British troops, slowing them to wait for cannons of their own, then moving quickly rearward to repeat the practice from suitable positions along the eight-mile retreat. It was well after nightfall when Hamilton and his exhausted men finally arrived at the Harlem Heights defenses. Next morning the British attacked but were ingloriously driven off the heights. Apparently Hamilton was not involved in this action, but Washington learned of his heroism the day before and commended him and his men for throwing up excellent breastworks for their guns.

Following this sharp repulse, General Howe did not attack the Americans again for three weeks, though British soldiers descended on New York in a carnival of boiling vengeance, looting, burning, and pillaging the city. They destroyed all the library books in King's College and turned it into a hospital. British officers rounded up hundreds of suspected Patriots and hanged Nathan Hale, who had volunteered for the dangerous job of spying on behalf of the Patriots. Sometime during this period, Washington "invited [Hamilton] to his tent and entered into conversation [regarding] his military talent."[6]

On October 9, 1776, several British frigates again forced past obstructions in the Hudson River. Three days later a fleet of British troopships put ashore at Throggs Neck, depositing half of Howe's army. Caught in a pincer, Washington reacted by withdrawing his army north to White Plains. Following several weeks of desultory fighting, some of which involved Hamilton's artillery, a battle broke out at Chatterton's Hill, in which Hamilton dearly earned his keep.

He had posted his guns on the hill, which overlooked the shallow Bronx River. The British marched down to the river's edge with brass bands playing and bayonets flashing, a tide of redcoats who smelled victory. As the column struggled to wade across the river, Hamilton unleashed his cannons, spraying the enemy with grape and canister shot in a fearful loss of life. The enemy recoiled but came on again, only to suffer the same result. At length they began a flanking movement that caused Washington to order a withdrawal, but the British had suffered far greater losses. For a change, the Americans could claim victory.

Washington decided to abandon New York and cross the Hudson into New Jersey. He suspected that the next British objective would be Philadelphia, where the Continental Congress sat. Even though he was outnumbered more than two to one, he hoped an opportunity would arise to surprise and defeat the British onslaught. The British pursued Washington but not before capturing Fort Washington, with its garrison of nearly 3,000 American soldiers and critical artillery, weapons, powder, and other supplies. A similar catastrophe nearly befell Fort Lee in the Jersey Palisades—but there, at least, the garrison managed to escape, though again an enormous amount of material was lost to the enemy.

These events were so dispiriting that troops began deserting in appalling numbers. The desertions, along with casualties and the capture of the garrison, had reduced the size of Washington's army by more than half. The American Revolution was beginning to look like a terrible mistake; only men of high resolve believed otherwise. Hamilton was one of these.

The British army, led by the redoubtable general Lord Charles Cornwallis, relentlessly pursued Washington. Just as his army crossed the Raritan River into New Brunswick, New Jersey, the British reached the bluffs Washington had just left on the New York side. Once more, Hamilton was called on to perform rearguard action, playing two of his cannons on the enemy as they began crossing the river. The rearguard fighting slowed Cornwallis's forces long enough for Washington to reach Princeton.

Here one of the strangest and most egregious events of the war took place: the treachery of Gen. Charles Lee. In desperate need of reinforcements, Washington had ordered Lee, his second in command, to bring men up from his command immediately to buttress Washington's own troops. Instead Lee—a former British officer and soldier of fortune who had also served in the Polish army—dawdled and wrote letters to congressmen advocating himself as the overall commander of the Continental Army instead of Washington. He was in fact captured in the act of writing such letters—in his nightshirt, miles from his command at a tavern in Basking Ridge, New Jersey.

Despite Lee's ineptitude, the American forces managed to cross New Jersey and escape into Pennsylvania. But by this point Washington was so concerned with the condition and morale of his army that he wrote to warn Congress on December 20, 1776, that "Ten days more will put an end to the existence of our army."[7]

What saved the revolution was the arrival at last of the tardy reinforcements from Lee's command. Washington decided that something had to be done to restore the morale of his soldiers. That, he knew, required a victory. Thus was born a scheme that turned into one of the most celebrated events of the Revolutionary War.

One of his cavalry patrols had discovered a brigade of Hessian mercenaries serving under the British encamped on the east bank of the Delaware River. Washington determined to try for the victory he so desperately needed. On Christmas night 1776, in a howling blizzard, his army boarded various boats and barges and polled across the semi-frozen Delaware after midnight. With snow muffling their footfalls, the Americans marched eight miles in a snowstorm to the enemy encampment and thoroughly surprised the Hessians, who were sleeping off their Christmas festivities. When the Hessians realized what had happened, they put up a spirited defense, but Washington had them cornered. Hamilton commanded two guns, which, with the surprise attack, forced the surrender of more than a thousand enemy soldiers and all their weapons and supplies.

Not content to rest on his laurels, Washington recrossed the Delaware on January 2 and marched his army back toward Princeton, where Cornwallis had assembled 9,000 men. The British general had gotten word from patrols that the Americans were in the neighborhood, so he had marched his army some miles south. Washington gave him the slip by setting up dummy watchmen and campfires, then doubling back on Princeton by a new road. The Americans found 1,400 redcoats holding the town, and sharp fighting ensued. The British detachment was thoroughly defeated after Washington arrived to rally his troops. Again, Hamilton's two cannons played a role by forcing the surrender of nearly 200 British troops fighting from inside Princeton College's main building, Nassau Hall. Hamilton's actions sparked a legend that one of his shots went through a window and blasted a portrait of George II hanging in the chapel. If true, it was a delicious irony, because Princeton had rejected Hamilton's application to attend school there.

Here were two American victories, one on top of the other. Neither was significant militarily, but they were significant nevertheless. Not only did they provide a critical boost to Patriotic spirits and the spirit of the soldiers, but they also showed that Washington had learned an invaluable strategic lesson: in the future, he would not face off against a superior British force, but would instead go after smaller, detached enemy forces that he outnumbered. Until more troops were gathered and the Continental Army built up into a major fighting machine, these tactics would have to suffice. Hamilton defended it this way in a letter to New York friends: "I know the comments that people will make on our Fabian conduct. It will be imputed to cowardice or weakness. But it proceeds from the truest policy. The liberties of America are at stake. We should not put it upon a single cast of the die. The loss of one general engagement may effectually ruin us."

Throughout the long and dreary defeats in New York and New Jersey, the infant revolution seemed doomed. But a new spirit had instilled itself in the American character—the Spirit of '76—a force that somehow reached down into the deepest wellsprings of human fortitude and conjured the courage to go on. With that new spirit ringing in his mind, Washington took the army, with Alexander Hamilton's artillery in tow, into winter quarters at Morristown, New Jersey.

HAMILTON AND HIS TROOPS SPENT THAT WINTER on instruction, performing maintenance on guns, wagons, and other equipment, as well as drilling. Hamilton spent his spare time reading. He waded through Plutarch's *Lives,* a study of famous Roman emperors, Spartans, and Greeks that revealed the various facets of their characters. And he made a careful study of economics by an Englishman named Malachy Postlethwayt, who had published *The Universal Dictionary of Trade and Commerce* about twenty years earlier. Although the "father of economics," Adam Smith, had published his now celebrated *Wealth of Nations* the previous year, Hamilton apparently couldn't locate a copy of it.

The Continental Army had been in winter quarters less than a month when George Washington asked Hamilton to become his aide-de-camp with the rank of lieutenant colonel. It was one thing to be an aide to some other general, and Hamilton was truly satisfied with having a fighting command. But Washington was—different. He was not only the commanding general of the entire army; he was a man with great personal charm and powers of persuasion. His physical presence was impressive: six-foot-two—quite tall for that era—and with great physical bearing. To Washington, his thirty-two-man staff command was his "family"; they regularly dined together and enjoyed mutual comradeship.

With his joint fluency in English and French, both learned in his Caribbean boyhood, Hamilton quickly rose to be one of Washington's most respected aides, and at length he became his top aide bar none. It wasn't only his writing ability but his *reasoning* ability that allowed Hamilton to achieve what Washington described as "thinking as one." Washington would tell Hamilton to write an order or a letter on one of many subjects, and he would soon produce a document that appeared to have been written by the commander in chief himself. Hamilton also had responsibilities as a riding aide, who on the battlefield could be depended upon by Washington to see that his wishes and his orders were carried out. There was danger in this, but Hamilton seemed oblivious to it.

That Morristown winter, wives of the senior officers would often visit the camp, bringing their daughters. Dances were arranged as well as other social events—carriage rides, dinners, teas. Winter quarters lasted until well into the spring, because the muddy condition of roads did not support artillery. The British general

Howe was likewise a great believer in long restful winter quarters, and he gave no trouble to the Americans until summer.

Howe had made either an attempt or a feint at marching from New York toward Philadelphia in July 1777, but Washington moved his army forward to some low mountains in the Poconos and blocked the passes. Then, in mid-July, Howe moved his army north to the New York area. Washington assumed Howe was going to move it up the Hudson to support Gen. John "Gentleman Johnny" Burgoyne's army, then marching on Albany from Canada. But he was wrong. Soon word came from American lookouts that Howe's army was headed south down the Atlantic coast. Washington then assumed Howe would turn off toward Delaware Bay and continue up the Delaware River, but again he was wrong. Howe continued south. Washington guessed Howe was aiming for Charleston, but once more he was wrong. Lookouts soon reported a British fleet in the Chesapeake Bay. Now Washington realized the truth. Howe had been aiming for Philadelphia all along. Washington began strengthening the city's defenses.

On August 25, 1777, a British force of 15,000 redcoats landed near what is now Elkton, Maryland, and marched north. Washington marshaled his army of 10,000 bluecoats near Chadds Ford, where he calculated Howe would strike. Instead, Howe posted a large force opposite Chadds Ford to menace the Americans, while Howe and Cornwallis crossed above them at Brandywine Creek. On September 11, the British struck the right flank of Washington's army and forced a retreat.

The road to Philadelphia was now open to the British. As the enemy neared the city, Washington ordered Hamilton to take a cavalry party under Capt. Henry Lee and destroy the flour in a number of mills along the Schuylkill River to prevent it from falling into British hands. The order nearly became Hamilton's undoing.

He and four companions had just finished firing the last mill when a troop of British cavalry pitched into them. The Americans sprang onto a waiting barge with bullets ripping all around them and began rowing out of range; one of Hamilton's companions was shot dead and another wounded. When he landed on the other side of the river, Hamilton dispatched a message to John Hancock, president of the Continental Congress: "If Congress have not yet left Philadelphia, they ought to do it immediately without fail; for the [British] have the means of throwing a party this night into the city."[8]

Hamilton was also charged with removing all the public stores from the city and requisitioning such necessary items as blankets, clothing, food, shoes, horses. He got little of the latter but was successful in retrieving the critical military stores. Poor scouting by the Americans had led to the defeat: Washington had lost 1,300 men, the British only 500. It was a major setback for the Continentals, but not a catastrophe. In fact, it may have been a blessing in disguise.

There was little of value the British could claim in taking Philadelphia. The Continental Congress had moved to Lancaster after Hamilton's initial warnings and continued to function. Occupying the city tied up Howe and Cornwallis for more than a year; General Burgoyne, coming from Canada without Howe's support, found himself surrounded by the forces of American general Horatio Gates at the Battle of Saratoga. Burgoyne was forced to surrender a month after Howe took Philadelphia, his entire 7,200-man army lost as a fighting force.

If Howe had moved up the Hudson to support him, Burgoyne's defeat likely wouldn't have happened. But jealous squabbles among British generals were no less common than they were among American generals. The victory at Saratoga—the greatest and most decisive American victory thus far in the war—had a further ramification even more important than the military event itself. It convinced France that Americans could fight and win. The French Empire was now ready to ally with the Patriots in a war against Britain, its own longtime enemy.

EVEN AFTER THE LOSS OF PHILADELPHIA, Washington was not ready to concede defeat. He immediately began planning for another battle, and on October 4 it began. Four American columns had set out in a morning fog. Howe had left 3,000 troops to garrison Philadelphia and sent the rest of his army to Germantown, north of the city. Washington's force was heading for the larger force at Germantown.

Things were going tolerably well, and the attack seemed to be succeeding. The British were either driven back or scattered, but about 200 of them had holed up in the three-story home of one Benjamin Chew and began firing on an American column coming into the fight. Henry Knox, now a brigadier general, insisted on subduing the soldiers in the house on grounds that it was a violation of military principle to leave such an enemy garrison in his rear.

The firing grew more intense, and the thick fog complicated matters. A flag of truce was sent over by the Americans; its bearer was immediately shot dead. A six-pound gun was brought up, but the balls rebounded off the heavy masonry of the house. Hamilton's good friend John Laurens tried to set the house afire and was shot for his troubles. The firing was so intense that other American commanders assumed it came from the main area of battle, which was half a mile south, so they diverted their troops away from there. Meanwhile, the British took this diversion for a retreat and began a spirited pursuit, which ended in an American debacle.

Washington held a war council and was advised by his generals that if Howe were to be evicted from Philadelphia, a large portion of Horatio Gates's victorious army in New York would have to be combined with Washington's dwindled force. Alexander Hamilton was selected by Washington for the delicate assignment of soliciting Gates.

Gates at that point was at the top of his game. He wasn't serving directly under Washington but had been chosen by Congress to command independently in the Hudson River Valley. And he had already begun angling to replace Washington as overall commander of the Continental Army.

Washington had given the twenty-two-year-old Hamilton explicit instructions, but also a high degree of discretion. He was to explain to General Gates in the "clearest and fullest manner" the military situation and the "absolute necessity" of his detaching a large part of his army south to Philadelphia. If, however, Gates had plans for some other expedition "in which the common cause will be expedited," then Hamilton was given the discretion of whether or not to order Gates to detach his troops in Washington's name. It was a tremendous responsibility to place on someone of Hamilton's age and status, but Washington had come to rely on Hamilton's judgment and abilities. The fate of the country could quite literally depend on it.

Hamilton set out for New York on horseback on October 30, as the leaves were turning. Legend says he rode 60 miles a day to reach Albany, 250 miles away. Along the way he encountered Col. Daniel Morgan and his regiment of riflemen headed for Washington's camp. At Fishkill he encountered Gen. Israel Putnam, who was watching the British at New York City; Hamilton ordered him to send Washington two brigades of men and keep the militia. In Albany Hamilton found that Gates was obstreperously opposed to sending Washington reinforcements. After lengthy efforts at persuasion, Hamilton managed to get a concession that Gates would send one of his three brigades—but it turned out to be the smallest and worst in Gates's army. In the end, after much wheedling, he was able to secure two of Gates's brigades.

When he rode back downriver, Hamilton discovered that Putnam had not sent off the troops as ordered because, he said, they had mutinied over lack of pay. Hamilton then arranged with New York's governor George Clinton for a $6,000 loan. The men were paid off and set marching south, but Hamilton told Washington later that he was "disgusted" with Putnam's behavior in the matter.

All of these issues took a toll on Hamilton, whose health had been fragile since boyhood; among other problems, he suffered bouts of malaria throughout his life. His friend and benefactor Hugh Knox understood this when, in a letter, he had cautioned his young ward against going into the fighting service for fear his constitution would fail him. Those fears were realized as Hamilton made his way back to Washington. The young officer came down with a fever and serious rheumatic pains; the doctor who examined him in Peekskill, New York, believed Hamilton was "drawing nigh his last."

But that was not to be. A few days later the fever broke and after a few more days' rest Hamilton was on his way again, highly annoyed to learn that one of the brigades promised by General Gates was delayed because it was receiving treatment "for the itch,"[9] a mild venereal disease.

While Washington heartily approved of Hamilton's handling of the reinforcements matter, the troops dispatched would arrive too late. General Howe had received reinforcements of his own from New York and was stronger than ever. The British Navy had sailed up the Delaware and bombarded all the American fortifications there into matchwood, thus allowing Howe to resupply from New York by water. Washington saw no other course but to take his army into winter quarters. The spot he chose was a secure but desolate area known as Valley Forge, about 20 miles northwest of Philadelphia on the Schuylkill River.

Presently General Gates departed on a trip to address Congress, which was in session at York, Pennsylvania. His supporters thought he should be given command of the army over Washington, and so did Gates, whose reputation after Saratoga had risen meteorically. But then a kerfuffle arose that caused Gates's reputation to go up in flames.

Riding ahead of the general, Gates's aide Col. James Wilkinson—who later proved a crook and a traitor in the pay of the Spanish government—stopped for an evening at a roadhouse in Reading, Pennsylvania. Also staying there was the staff of Lord Stirling, a British subject turned Patriot from New Jersey. Wilkinson, after sufficiently imbibing, revealed to Lord Stirling's aide the contents of a letter that Gates had received from Gen. Thomas Conway, stating that "Heaven has been determined to save your country, or a weak Gen. [Washington] and bad Councellors would have ruined it." Hamilton had this to say about the Irish-born Conway, a loudmouthed and boastful soldier of fortune: "There does not exist a more villainous calumniator or incendiary."

Meanwhile, Stirling, incensed at this demeaning slap at his commander in chief, quickly passed the slur on to Washington. In an extremely curt letter, Washington confronted Conway about his comment, thus touching off a military scandal that became known as the Conway Cabal. Conway responded by showing Washington's letter to a friend of Gates, who warned Gates that Washington apparently had access to all of his letters. Gates went on offense and sent letters to Congress blaming Alexander Hamilton for pilfering his mail during the period Hamilton had been in Gates's headquarters on the reinforcements mission. Washington fired Conway from his command, then made a fool of Gates by revealing that the source of his information was not Hamilton but Gates's own drunken aide-de-camp.

Thus ended the scandal. Most of the players were exposed in the press, and the movement to sack General Washington faded with the dreadful winter of Valley Forge.

ALMOST FROM THE BEGINNING OF THE WAR, it had become apparent that American military volunteers and colonial militia were no match for the professional redcoats of the British regular army in open field fights or other classical battle formations. The redcoats were simply too skilled in tactics, strategy, and firepower. But it was good fortune for the Patriots that, unlike Europe where the land was heavily deforested, the American countryside was covered in woodland. The quick hit-and-run tactics Washington had used at Trenton and Princeton had paid off handsomely. In his war councils, his officers agreed that until the Continental Army could be brought up in both numbers and martial excellence, these small-scale harassing strategies would have to do. As Hamilton put it in a letter to the Reverend Knox, "Our hopes are not placed in [holding] any city or spot of ground but in preserving the army to take advantage of favorable opportunities, and waste and defeat the enemy piecemeal."[10]

There were about 12,000 men in the Continental Army at Valley Forge. Up to a third of the men did not speak English as their first language; their native tongues included German, Irish, Spanish, and Dutch. About 10 percent of the army was black, either already freed blacks or former slaves given their freedom in exchange for joining up (their owners were reimbursed with government funds). Some of the soldiers included a band of Iroquois Indians.

The winter of 1777–78 was not especially harsh, but in that part of Pennsylvania there was always an abundant amount of snow on the ground. Provisions were often spare to nonexistent. Many of the men were shoeless and in rags. Two days before Christmas, Washington wrote to Henry Laurens, now president of the Continental Congress (and father of Hamilton's friend John), that the army now faced three choices: "Starve, dissolve, or disburse."

A month after Washington's letter to Laurens, a committee of five congressmen arrived at Valley Forge to see the conditions for themselves. They were taken aback by the tattered scarecrows living in unsanitary conditions in scores of rude log huts. Their report to Congress spurred an immediate improvement in the supply of food and clothing to the soldiers. The quartermaster general Thomas Mifflin (one of the Conway Cabalists) had reportedly been selling army food and goods to the highest bidder in Philadelphia and elsewhere. He was replaced by one of Washington's most trusted generals, Nathanael Greene, and provisions for the troops began to flow more smoothly.

Two important foreigners also arrived on the scene that winter. One was the Marquis de Lafayette, scion of an aristocratic French military dynasty. He was nineteen years old when he came to America to join the revolution of "people seeking liberty." Lafayette had entered the military at the age of fourteen and was an accomplished young officer. When he offered his services for free to the American cause, Congress voted to make him a major general. In Philadelphia he had met Washington, who was much taken with the enthusiastic young Frenchman and invited him to join his staff. There the young marquis met Alexander Hamilton—who also spoke flawless French—and a fast and lasting friendship was formed. Lafayette made himself useful in many ways during the terrible winter at Valley Forge by organizing training drills for bayonet practice, marksmanship, gunnery, and other military arts. It was Lafayette who had recruited the Iroquois band to fight on the side of the Patriots.

The other significant foreigner in camp that winter was Baron Friedrich von Steuben, a forty-eight-year-old Prussian who had served as an aide-de-camp to Frederick the Great and with the army of the Russian czar. His highest rank had been that of a captain, but after meeting him in Paris Benjamin Franklin wrote to Washington and the Congress that Steuben was a lieutenant general and wished to serve in the Continental Army. His arrival was a godsend to Washington, who made him his inspector general with the rank of major general (to be paid after the war).

Steuben immediately set about reorganizing the sloppy and unsanitary Valley Forge encampment and, like Lafayette, training the men in drill, riflery, tactics, and other military skills. Morale began to improve almost immediately. The baron, who spoke no English, came immensely into the debt of the French-speaking Hamilton.

In early summer, as Washington was trying to figure out ways to get at Howe, a new British commander, Gen. Sir Henry Clinton, solved the problem for him by evacuating Philadelphia on June 17 and withdrawing his army to New York. After the British failure at Saratoga, Clinton feared the Americans might come at the main British base in New York City with armies from both north and south and overwhelm it. Moreover, the French were now in the war on the American side, and Clinton worried that a French fleet could blockade the Delaware and cut off his provisions.

Clinton's surprise move to New York immediately presented Washington with the opportunity to harass and "waste and defeat" the redcoats piecemeal, as Hamilton had earlier described. Clinton's army contained 2,000 fewer men than Washington's, but it was superior in cavalry. Its main disadvantage was that the redcoats would be slowed down by some 1,500 wagons, many carrying loot, as well as by the carriages of several thousand Tories who were fleeing the City of Brotherly Love.

Before breaking camp at Valley Forge, Washington called for a council of war to discuss options. If the Continental Army overtook the British army, would it be "prudent" to attack, and if so, should it be a full or a partial attack? Three of the generals present—Charles Lee (back from British imprisonment); Steuben; and Louis DuPortail, the army's chief engineer—were against bringing on a large-scale battle. Generals Lafayette, Anthony Wayne, John Cadwalader, and Nathanael Greene favored total engagement.

Detachments of several thousand Patriots were already vexing Clinton's left flank and rear when the main body of the Continental Army outstripped him by 25 miles on June 23 and came to rest for a day near Princeton. Again a council of war was called, and another vote taken as to whether the Continentals should allow the British to cross New Jersey relatively unmolested, and then make a full-scale attack on the redcoats when the French fleet arrived. This time, the majority recommended waiting. Hamilton wrote a friend indignantly, referring to these generals as "mid-wives."

Washington signed an order written by Hamilton sending an additional detachment of 1,500 men to join the two brigades already harassing Clinton's army. That would make for a total of 4,000 American infantry. To lead them, he selected Lafayette instead of the senior major general, Charles Lee, who disdainfully remarked that Lafayette was "more suited" to such a small command. There then followed an absurdist comedy of vacillations on Lee's part in which he changed his mind about commanding half a dozen times before at last telling an exasperated Washington that he would lead the command with Lafayette as his second. Hamilton would go along as Lafayette's liaison.

On June 26, Hamilton dispatched information to Washington that Clinton, who was near Monmouth, had moved his baggage to the front of his train. At the rear, where the Americans had been hitting and running, he had placed his best troops; a quarter mile beyond the main body was a special guard of 1,000 redcoats. Washington decided that the opportunity to strike the British army was now at hand. He ordered Lee to deliver the first blow at eight on the morning of June 27. A little before nine, Hamilton, reconnoitering, found Lee in a state of confusion still several miles west of Monmouth. Hamilton counseled Lee to have Lafayette attack the British train immediately. Then he went to find Washington, who was riding at the head of the main body of the army not far from what would soon be the battlefield.

Hamilton recommended that General Greene and Lord Stirling, commanding the army's right and left wings, go to support General Lee's attack. But no sooner had the order been made than Washington's party encountered a breathless fife player from Lee's command who told them that all was lost. Washington was stunned. He had heard only desultory firing, while a pitched battle should have made a racket that filled the air. He rode forward and encountered Lee's command in full retreat, for what reason the retreaters knew not, except that they had been told to withdraw and were now being pursued by enemy infantry and grenadiers.

By a church on the edge of the battlefield Washington found a confused and muddled General Lee, with whom he had some brief choice words. He then galloped out onto the open field and personally rallied Lee's disordered troops, ordering them to fire on the enemy and check the redcoats' advance. Hamilton galloped up to Lee, shouting, "I will stay here with you, my dear general, and die with you! Let us all die rather than retreat!" Washington then rushed back to the main army and drew them up on high ground to prepare for an assault. He had personally brought order out of disorder.[11]

The summer morning was hot and heavy with clouds and rain. The temperature was in the high 90s. The battle broke out when the British came within range. Numerous volleys were exchanged.

In the end the British force withdrew back to their wagon train and moved on, leaving the Patriots in possession of the field of battle. It was technically an American victory, but Washington's intention of doing great harm to Clinton's army went unfulfilled and the redcoats marched on to New York.

Lee was court-martialed the week after the battle. He testified that when he found he was facing not a motley rear guard but a powerful enemy force, he determined that his men could not stand up to British regulars. He was found guilty of disobeying of orders, misbehavior before the enemy, and disrespect of the commanding officer and sentenced to a year's suspension from command.

Hamilton's horse had been shot from under him during the fight at Monmouth; he was badly bruised and bedridden for several days. But he wrote to a friend in Congress, "Our troops, after the first impulse of mismanagement, behaved with more spirit and moved with greater order than the British troops." Then he added, "You know my way of thinking about our army, and that I am not apt to flatter it. I assure you I was never pleased with it until this day." Of Lee, Hamilton wrote, "This man is either a driveler in the business of soldiership or something worse . . . I shall continue to believe and say—his conduct was monstrous and unpardonable."[12]

IN JULY 1778, A FRENCH FLEET under Vice Admiral Comte d'Estaing anchored off Sandy Hook, New Jersey. Washington sent Hamilton to the French with a proposition that they sail to New York, sink the British fleet at its anchorage, then bombard the city while Washington and the Continental Army came in from

New Jersey. The French admiral demurred, on grounds that the water was too shallow. His fleet, he told Hamilton, drew 27 feet, while the British drew only 20. Furthermore, d'Estaing said, a powerful British fleet was now headed to New York; when combined with the present British fleet, the enemy would outnumber him. That said, d'Estaing marshaled his ships and sailed them off into the Atlantic.

The combined British troops in America—the Manhattan area, Rhode Island, and Canada—numbered 30,000 soldiers. But after the defeat at the Battle of Saratoga and the French-American alliance, King George gave up any notions of sending more troops, especially because Britain was now mixed up in a European war with France, and would soon be engaged with Spain and Holland as well. A British commission was sent to negotiate directly with the Continental Congress. The commissioners offered acceptance of all the demands the Americans had made before the war started—but Congress refused to meet the delegation unless it acknowledged America's right to independence and withdrew British armies. The delegation went home.

The British then pursued a policy of smaller operations, including persuading various Indian tribes to massacre white men and launching small raids against American positions. They also concocted a Southern Strategy to bring to Georgia and the Carolinas. In December 1778 Savannah fell to the British.

The following February, Lafayette sailed for France to garner more support for the Patriots. At Versailles, he told the king and military leaders that a powerful fleet was needed in American waters and an army of at least 6,000 to go with it. After due consideration, these requests were promised—and with no time to spare for the Americans.

In 1779 and 1780, the British Southern Strategy had cost the Continentals dearly. At the end of 1779, General Clinton had boarded much of his army onto a waiting armada and sailed out of New York to the South. By early spring Charleston was under siege and in early May it fell. Among those sent south to combat the British threat was Gen. Horatio Gates, the hero of Saratoga—but in August, he was badly defeated at the Battle of Camden, South Carolina. In fact, it was said that he ran away at the beginning of the fight. Hamilton, who despised Gates for his machinations against Washington, was prompted to remark sarcastically to a friend serving in Congress, "Was there ever an instance of a general running away, as Gates has done, from his whole army? It does admirable credit to a man at his time of life."[13]

Gates's defeat only stiffened Hamilton's conviction that the war should not be fought with militia, as the Americans had done at Camden, but with regular soldiers under long terms of enlistments. Only Congress could achieve this, and so Hamilton began a letter-writing campaign to convince them to do so.

Meanwhile, Washington had moved his army to White Plains to keep close watch on the British in New York. As winter approached, he put it in quarters at Middlebrook, New Jersey, about 20 miles west of the city. With no large-scale fighting on the horizon in the northern theater of war, Hamilton sought other means of assisting the revolution. Around that time, he and his close friend Col. John Laurens of South Carolina devised a scheme to fill the army's ranks with black soldiers—slaves— in exchange for their freedom. Both men had been raised in slave societies and both found the institution distasteful if not abominable. "In the current shortage of troops, what more suitable than to enlist slaves and give freedom to those who survive the war?" Laurens wrote to his father, Henry.[14]

Laurens headed to South Carolina, hoping to bring the scheme into fruition. He stopped on the way to ask Congress for its blessing. Hamilton gave Laurens a letter addressed to the current president of the Continental Congress, John Jay, intended to persuade the members to agree to the plan. "I frequently heard it objected to the scheme of embodying negroes, that they are too stupid to make soldiers," Hamilton said. "This is so far from appearing to me valid objection, that I think their want of cultivation . . . joined to [their] habit of subordination . . . will enable them sooner to become soldiers than our white inhabitants."[15]

Hamilton's argument worked. Congress recommended that Georgia and South Carolina, presently under British occupation, raise 3,000 slave troops officered by whites. They should be taken from plantations on a proportional basis. The government would recompense slave owners for the slaves who were serving and who would be freed at the end of the war.

The scheme was doomed to failure. The South Carolina legislature—of which Laurens himself was a member—killed the notion on grounds that slaves could not be made into soldiers. The way the Continental Congress had been set up was pitifully deficient in exerting power over the colonies; it had no taxing power nor any real authority. Hamilton had understood and lamented this ever since joining Washington's inner circle, writing friends in Congress that a "strong executive" was needed—meaning some form of what is now known as the presidency, as opposed to a government where most power rested with individual states that for all intents acted as individual countries. But that was not immediately in the cards. Each state had been established in the previous centuries as a colony with a charter from the British king, and each thought itself autonomous. Rectifying this would be a recurring theme in Hamilton's life from those revolutionary days onward.

He set all his thoughts out in a now famous letter that has been noted by historians for its canny prescience. It was written to New York congressman James Duane while Hamilton was in winter quarters in Morristown, New Jersey. That grim season of 1779–80 was even harsher than the winter at Valley Forge; several feet of snow covered the ground, mounding to 12-foot drifts in places. Ink froze on writers' pens. The troops were in pitiable condition, going for days without pay and provisions, shoeless, wearing rags for clothes. Washington again feared the army might dissolve.

In his letter to Duane, Hamilton laid the blame for these appalling conditions squarely on Congress—and in particular on its weak governing document, the Articles of Confederation. He suggested that Congress scrap the "namby-pamby" Articles and instead produce a full, permanent constitution laying out all of the powers held by a federal government and others that would be held by the states. The powers that Hamilton recommended for the federal government were vast: it should be provided with "perpetual revenues . . . have complete sovereignty in all that relates to war, peace, trade, finance, and to the management of foreign affairs, the right of declaring war, of raising armies . . . paying them, directing their motions . . . building fortifications . . . coining money, establishing banks on such terms, and with such privileges as they think proper . . . making alliances offensive and defensive, treaties of commerce, etc. etc."[16]

One recurring problem with supplying the army was that hyperinflation had overtaken the currency, as the colonies had been remiss in sending payments to the government for the conduct of the war. The purchase of a $200 horse, for instance, required nearly $20,000 in Continental paper money. Hamilton damned the Congress for letting soldiers barely survive "in this land of plenty." He recommended that the government secure a foreign loan—from the French perhaps, or the Dutch. He was also strongly in favor of a national bank, backed by government money, similar to the Bank of England, which could make loans both public and private. Scholars have noted that nearly all these things came to pass, including the Bank of the United States, though none would happen in the time frame that Hamilton had envisioned.

IT WAS DURING THE LONG, BITTER WINTER of 1779–80 in Morristown that Hamilton found his life's companion. She was Elizabeth "Eliza" Schuyler, second daughter of the wealthy and politically powerful general and congressman Philip Schuyler, a Hudson Valley aristocrat. Two years earlier Hamilton, in uniform, had paid a visit to the Schuylers' Albany home and was afterward described thusly by Eliza's younger sister Catherine: He "exhibited a natural yet unassuming superiority. A high, expansive forehead, a nose of the Grecian mold, a dark bright eye, and the line of a mouth expressing decision and courage completed the contour of a face never to be forgotten."[17]

On her way to Philadelphia in February of 1780, Eliza had appeared at Washington's winter quarters at Morristown to deliver a letter from her father to Baron von Steuben, and she stayed on. Despite the miserable weather, ruination of the currency, lack of food and other provisions, the officers managed to amuse themselves from time to time by staging cotillions, assemblies, sleigh rides, and other social events where there might be a punch bowl to spike. Eliza was twenty-two, Hamilton twenty-five. He wrote of her that she was "most unmercifully handsome and so perverse that she has none of those pretty affectations which are the prerogatives of beauty. She has good nature, affability and vivacity . . ."

The feeling was mutual. They fell in love and after seven weeks were engaged. Schuyler himself was pleased by the match. Even though Hamilton was a penniless "bastard" from the islands, Schuyler saw something in the youth that told him Hamilton would go far in life. The fact that Washington had chosen him as an aide and that now he was effectively serving the commander as chief of staff could not have hurt. After the wedding, Schuyler wrote Hamilton, "You cannot, my dear sir, be more happy at the connection you have made with my family than I am. Until a child has made a judicious choice, the heart of a parent is in continuous anxiety." He went on to say that Hamilton was as judicious a choice as imaginable.[18]

As the cruel winter of 1780 turned to spring, Washington kept a watchful eye on the British army in New York. With Clinton in the South, the enemy forces holding New York amounted to no more than some 4,000 Hessians. Had the Americans known that, they might have gone in and captured it. But they never found out.

Word had reached Washington that Clinton and most of the British forces were returning from their siege and capture of Charleston and should arrive in New York in the late spring of 1780. Washington, fearing that Clinton would do what he himself would do in Clinton's situation, immediately set out to secure and refortify the American fortress at West Point. Washington feared that Clinton might get past American forts downstream and sail directly for that strongpoint on the Hudson. If West Point fell, the entire river would be open for British traffic, and New England would be severed from the rest of the country.

In September 1780 Washington set off to visit the fort and its trusted commander, Benedict Arnold. He and his beautiful wife, Peggy, had taken a house on the east side of the Hudson just below West Point. Hamilton had been sent ahead and was breakfasting with Arnold when the commander received a message and excused himself, never to return to the table. In the meantime, Washington and Lafayette arrived, then continued on to inspect West Point. Hamilton, who had stayed behind to sort through dispatches that had arrived, kept hearing unnerving shrieks coming from a distraught Mrs. Arnold upstairs. When Washington returned, Hamilton gave the dispatch pouch to his commander in chief and then left him to his work.

When he returned, he found Washington standing with a paper in his trembling hand and tears in his eyes. "Arnold has betrayed us! Whom can we trust now?"[19]

Benedict Arnold had some time before gone over to the British. A hero of Saratoga and later commandant of Philadelphia, he felt he had not been accorded the promotions he deserved, and he no longer believed in the American cause. He was in a unique position to provide the British with the invaluable prize of West Point in exchange for £20,000 (about four million dollars in today's money). The man who was to conclude this treasonous transaction was the British adjutant and spymaster Maj. John André. But just before Hamilton arrived at the Arnold home, André had been caught in civilian clothing with a false pass, a map of West Point in his boot, and evidence pointing to Arnold as a traitor.

Hamilton began writing orders to Nathanael Greene to rush to West Point and guard it against the British when there commenced upstairs a dreadful screaming from the rooms of Mrs. Arnold. Washington and Hamilton rushed up and found her in a state of hysteria, sobbing, clutching her infant child and babbling that she knew nothing of the treason and feared that Washington would have the child murdered and that all of America would be against her. In fact, she was enacting a crazed fit that duped both Washington and Hamilton.

Peggy Shippen Arnold, the daughter of a prominent Tory family of Philadelphia, was in fact deeply involved in the British plot. But Hamilton was quite moved by her seemingly vulnerable state and spent so much time trying to calm her that he nearly neglected his duties. As thousands of American soldiers double-timed to Fortress West Point, Mrs. Arnold managed to have other Americans ferry her downriver to a waiting British frigate, where her execrable husband awaited her. They then set sail for the safety of New York City. Major André was hanged as a spy the week after his capture, though Hamilton had argued that he be shot instead—a more gentlemanly method of execution. Washington was obdurate, however, saying that all convicted spies would hang.

By sheer luck the plot to turn over West Point to the British had failed, and Arnold's treachery came to naught.

HAMILTON HAD BEEN WITH WASHINGTON for three years by 1780 and yearned for a field command. He had come to see his work on the general staff as menial, and he felt the opportunity for personal glory during wartime was passing him by. He was driven by a need to prove himself on the battlefield, to gain recognition by some feat that would demonstrate his bravery. Several times either he or others on his behalf had asked Washington to transfer him to a combat command, but each time the commander in chief refused on grounds that it would look like preferential treatment, and that Hamilton was too valuable in his staff role. The relationship between Hamilton and his revered commander was beginning to fray. The young man resolved to look for opportunities for a breach and when it happened "never to consent to an accommodation."

In the meantime, there was a marriage to conduct. The ceremony was held on a snowy December 14, 1780, in the great hall of the Pastures, the Schuyler mansion in Albany, and recorded in the books of the Dutch Reformed church there. The home was filled with Eliza's relatives and friends of the large Schuyler clan, but none of Hamilton's fellow aides from Washington's staff. The general had given Hamilton two weeks' leave—his first since joining the army—but could not spare his friends. Alexander Hamilton was now a welcomed member of one of the wealthiest and most powerful political families in the country, which provided him the security he had never before enjoyed. For their part, the Schuylers continued to see Hamilton as a man who would one day go far.

His quest for a battle assignment having failed, another avenue opened up. There was a desperate need for someone to go to France to plead the case for more munitions and French soldiers. Congress simply did not have the power to raise funds and recruits from the states under the weak Articles of Confederation, and the states would no longer furnish this assistance willingly. The war had dragged on for five long years, and everyone was weary of it. The Revolution, in fact, was on the verge of failure. The only hope was through the support of the French fleet and more help from France.

Two men—Lafayette and Hamilton's friend John Laurens—were nominated for the job as emissary to France, but neither wanted to go; they wanted to stay on with their field commands in the South. Both recommended Hamilton to Washington, but instead the general insisted on Laurens. Hamilton felt that he had been slighted, that he was nothing more than the clerk he'd been at Cruger's warehouse on St. Croix.[20]

The rupture Hamilton had been anticipating occurred on February 14, 1781. At winter quarters in New Windsor, on the Hudson about 50 miles north of Manhattan, Hamilton received a messenger who told him Washington wanted to see him. Hamilton told the messenger to reply that he had an important message to take to another of the aides, but that he would return rapidly. Then on the stairwell that led up to Washington's office, Hamilton encountered Lafayette, who insisted on talking. When they were finished, Hamilton hurried upstairs only to find Washington looming at the top of the steps. The commander in chief confronted him harshly.

"Colonel Hamilton . . . you have kept me waiting at the head of these stairs ten minutes . . . I must tell you sir, you treat me with disrespect." Hamilton responded just as abruptly. "I am not conscious of it, sir, but since you have felt it necessary to tell me so, we part." To which Washington replied, "Very well, sir, if it be your choice."

An hour later Washington sent an aide, one of Hamilton's close friends, Tench Tilghman, to Hamilton's quarters to say he had not meant to offend Hamilton and wanted to make amends. Hamilton replied that his decision to leave was "irrevocable," adding that he would neither make their quarrel public nor leave until Washington was satisfied that a suitable replacement had been found. Two days later, Hamilton wrote a letter to his father-in-law, which was filled with pent-up rage. He called down Washington for all manner of things, describing him as "selfish," "moody," and "wrong," and said he would "never forgive" the general or go back to his job. It was what the Hamilton biographer J. T. Flexner described as a "crackup."[21]

This was, of course, a serious matter. Washington was at the time the most powerful man in the nascent country, and Hamilton's only career was in the army. What had inspired this fury? Evidently, Hamilton had been smoldering for months, through all of Washington's refusals of his requests for a change of position. Somehow, Hamilton's frustration and pique had magnified Washington's faults in his mind until they had fashioned a twisted picture of the elder commander.

It was not entirely wrong. Washington could in fact be short-tempered and obdurate. Hamilton was evidently under an enormous strain at headquarters. The war seemed to be eternally stuck in a rut, and he with it. It all erupted at last in a hail of vituperation that was unworthy of Washington's most trusted aide.

Hamilton also wrote several influential friends, including Nathanael Greene—he had taken over command of the Southern Army from the disgraced General Gates—asking for employment in the field. But Washington's shadow loomed over him and nothing was done. He left headquarters in March, vowing that he was through with George Washington. But the next month he wrote him twice, saying that because he was no longer in the "family" he should now be eligible for the command of troops. Washington patiently responded that the only new regiments were to be raised from New England, and that they would demand New Englander commanders.

Through the summer of 1781 Hamilton sweated it out. He knew that a last-best-hope strategy to win the war had been formulated. Washington understood that any complete victory would probably have to involve the French fleet, which was presently based in the Caribbean. It was his plan to have the fleet attack the British at New York while his own army invaded the town from the north. But once more he was informed that a large sandbar protected Manhattan Island from the deep-draft French battleships. Then the French made a breathtaking recommendation.

Months earlier, in January 1781, at the Battle of Cowpens in South Carolina, an American force had all but wiped out a small British force under the despised and dreaded Bloody Ban—Col. Banastre Tarleton. From then until mid-summer, Nathanael Greene fought the British to a frazzle in a series of small battles and skirmishes against Cornwallis's command, causing him to move northward through North Carolina to Virginia, where he expected to unite with the rest of the British army or be evacuated by sea by the British fleet. In the spring Cornwallis wrote to his commander, Clinton, proposing that they bring their "whole force into Virginia," where "a successful battle may give us America."

Lafayette had taken his forces to Virginia that spring to deal with another British force under the traitorous Benedict Arnold, who had sailed up the James in late December 1780 and burned Richmond, as well as scores of plantations along the route of march. Now he had to deal with Cornwallis as well. Steuben was sent to reenforce him, but they were far outnumbered by the British.

At Clinton's behest, Cornwallis moved east, searching for a deepwater port near the Chesapeake. By August 1 he was in Yorktown, a small port on the York River near its confluence with the Chesapeake Bay. Lafayette felt Cornwallis and his 7,000-man British army were vulnerable in that position, but only if the French could get their fleet to Virginia before the British fleet arrived.

A dispatch boat was sent from Virginia and miraculously evaded the British blockade of the East Coast to deliver a plea to the French to bring their Caribbean fleet up to Virginia. Word soon came back (through the blockade, even more miraculously) from the French admiral François Joseph Paul de Grasse that he could have his fleet in the Chesapeake by August. It was now that the French unleashed their grand plan. If Washington's army in New York and the French forces in Newport, Rhode Island, marched to Virginia in time to coincide with the arrival of the French fleet, Cornwallis and his army could be destroyed.

It was a desperate gamble, but the war was wearing the Americans down. Washington agreed to the plan—but first, he needed to remove his army from in front of the British in New York without their knowledge. He concocted a complex scheme in which his troops and the allied French forces under General Jean-Baptiste Rochambeau would leave at different intervals and take different routes as they moved south some 400 miles from New York to Yorktown.

Alexander Hamilton recognized that this could be his last chance at a combat command. He wrote Washington once more, enclosing his officer's commission, which was tantamount to resigning, pleading for something, anything. This time, Washington came through. He responded affirmatively, saying that two light infantry companies would be joined with two new companies of New York draftees to form a battalion under the command of Col. Alexander Hamilton. They would march south with the army.

On August 22 Hamilton wrote Eliza, who was three months pregnant with their first child: "A part of the army my dear girl, is going to Virginia, and I of necessity must be separated from my beloved wife . . . It is ten to one that our views will be disappointed, by Cornwallis retiring to South Carolina."

Ten days later Clinton informed Cornwallis that "It would seem that Mr. Washington is moving an army southward." And four days after that, on September 10, he wrote again. "I can have no doubt that Mr. Washington is moving with at least 6,000 French and rebel troops against you."

But instead of ordering Cornwallis to evacuate or to move his army southward and inland, Clinton promised to send him reinforcements as well as a British fleet to protect his back.[22] Cornwallis fortified the British position with a series of redoubts—small earthwork forts designed to rain cannon and rifle fire down on anyone attacking the main British lines.

Through the heat of late August, the Continental cavalry rode, while the heavy infantry and artillery marched through Trenton, Philadelphia, Wilmington, Baltimore, south to Virginia. Light infantry, including Hamilton's command, boarded small boats and floated down the Delaware to the head of the Chesapeake, and down it also, where word arrived that the French fleet had reached the bay.

On the morning of September 5, lookouts in the French fleet under Comte de Grasse spied the British fleet in the Atlantic just outside the mouth of the bay. Battle stations were taken immediately and the fleet put under way to meet the enemy. An extraordinary amount of maneuvering took place before the first shots were fired around 4 p.m.

The two lines crossed each other with the French having a slight advantage in the number of its ships of the line and their position vis-à-vis the wind direction. By sundown the French had suffered 220 casualties and two ships damaged, the British 340 casualties—90 of them killed—two ships damaged, and a third so badly it had to be scuttled. Next day showed that the British had lost their taste for the fight, and soon they were back in harbor in New York.

On September 20, Hamilton and his battalion reached Williamsburg, Virginia, which had become a hive of military activity. He was assigned to the left wing of the army under his old friend Lafayette. On September 28, the Continental forces marched the 13 miles from Williamsburg to Yorktown. Washington now had a 17,600-man army and a powerful French fleet waiting offshore. Cornwallis's force of 8,300 men was heavily fortified behind earthworks and trenches, but the French had brought with them a large number of siege guns and other artillery—mostly mortars designed to fire into the lines of a besieged enemy. In order to use that artillery properly, Washington needed to get closer than he presently could to the fortified British positions. The Americans would need to dig their own entrenchments.

Time was of the essence as the digging commenced. Washington's greatest fear was that the British fleet might return and rescue Cornwallis's besieged army. Cornwallis was desperate— so desperate, in fact, that he had begun infecting slaves who had come to him for protection with smallpox, then prodded them out to the American lines to sicken enemy soldiers.

As it began to dawn on the American soldiers that they were quite possibly on the verge of a great victory, a devil-may-care atmosphere swept through the lines. A New York colonel paraded his men only a few hundred yards from the British positions "with flags flying and drums beating." Baron von Steuben mounted the parapet and put his men through drill in full view of the enemy gunners. Hamilton also got into the act. He ordered his battalion over the parapet in formation to go through the manual of arms.[23]

Washington's men had completed most of a line of parallel trenches fronting the British by mid-October, but two enemy redoubts stood in the way of completion and potential victory. A night bayonet attack was called for October 14, placing surprise over firepower. The eastern redoubt was to be stormed by French forces and the western one by Americans under Lafayette.

A French officer, a Colonel Gimat, who served as Lafayette's aide-de-camp, was designated to lead the attack. Hamilton pleaded with Lafayette to give him the honor instead, but despite their close personal friendship Lafayette declined, saying Gimat was already approved by Washington and that it was impossible to make changes this close to the action. Undeterred, Hamilton took his case directly to Washington, pointing out that because he would be serving as officer of the day at the time of the attack, the leadership was rightfully his. Washington agreed and so informed Lafayette.

On the night of October 14, Hamilton and his men crept over the parapet and ran swiftly and silently toward the redoubt, bayonets fixed. Only when they reached the enemy abatis were they challenged by a sentry, but he was silenced before he could spread the alarm. Not a shot was fired. Once at the redoubt, the Americans broke into a yell at the top of their lungs, helped one another over the spikes, and dropped into the British redoubt, their bayonets flashing. Hamilton was among the first men inside. Some of the British soldiers tried to put up a fight but others, utterly surprised and demoralized, quickly surrendered or tried to run away. It was all over in under thirty minutes. In the attack on the two redoubts, nine Americans were killed and fifteen wounded, including all three of the colonels besides Hamilton.

With both critical redoubts now in friendly hands, the siege artillery could be set up and brought to bear on the hapless redcoats. Cornwallis attempted to escape in ships across the York but bad weather prevented it. A 5,000-man army of relief sent by General Clinton arrived too late to help the British commander. After three days of heavy pounding by American guns, on October 17 a British drummer appeared with an officer waving a white flag, and the negotiations for surrender began next day.

On October 19 all the American and French forces lined the battlefield as the British surrender was taken. Alexander Hamilton stood at Washington's side, along with his other staff. Cornwallis had cravenly refused to attend the ceremony, saying he was sick and sending another general in his place. When the British officer offered Washington his sword, the American commander refused to take it. American bands played "Yankee Doodle" and other lively Continental tunes. The British band was said to have played "The World Turned Upside Down."

For all intents and purposes the Revolutionary War was won that day. Still, the fighting went on in the South and the British continued to occupy New York. It would be two more years before the Treaty of Paris officially ended the war. The first chapter of the history of the United States of America was complete. It remained to be seen what kind of government would evolve, and if the country could keep it.

Throughout the Revolution, Hamilton had been well known as Washington's brave aide-de-camp. But his role in the assault at Yorktown made him a legendary hero. He had already married into a wealthy and highly regarded New York family. Now he was poised to assume a role as one of the principal shapers of American policy, finance, and politics: a true Founding Father.

CHAPTER TWO

John Adams was obnoxious.[24] He said so himself.[25] He talked too much and wrote that he wished he didn't. He was irritable and wished he wasn't. He did not suffer fools gladly (and his notion of a fool was set at a very low bar). But he was brilliant and well-read and energetic to a fault—"a great-hearted, persevering man of uncommon ability and force . . . He was honest and everyone knew it."[26]

Adams's ancestors had lived in Braintree, Massachusetts, for a hundred years by the time he was born there on October 30, 1735. They had emigrated from England as Puritans, escaping persecution and the overarching dominance of the Church of England. John's father—also named John—was a farmer, as was his father's father. Generations of civic-minded Adams farmers had contributed to the well-being of their small community a dozen miles north of Boston. The senior John Adams was a deacon in the Congregational Church (the eighteenth-century iteration of the old Puritanism), a selectman on the town council, and a lieutenant in the colony's militia.

They were not wealthy, these New England farmers—nothing like the planter aristocracy of the southern colonies with their estates of tobacco and rice so vast that they were worked by scores of slaves. While there was some slavery in New England, a family farm with only a few stony fields and some fowl and livestock hardly required a force of enslaved labor to maintain it. Massachusetts farmers plowed their fields of corn, wheat, barley, and hay with a simple ash plow pulled by a horse or mule. But though they were not wealthy, they were proud, stubborn, and God-fearing people—and, in their own estimation, the equal of any other folk in America.

The Adams house was a fairly typical farmhouse. In the traditional "saltbox" style, it was built around a huge brick fireplace, with three rooms down and two up. A stone fence ran along the road in front; a brook meandered through the back of the property. John thought of his early years there as a golden time spent wandering fields and orchards; exploring creeks, rivers, and beaches; hunting, fishing, swimming, and playing with the other children.

When he was old enough, John helped his father with farm chores and went to the local school, where he studied *The New England Primer.* His father was determined that his first son be educated—in hopes, perhaps, of his becoming a minister. So when John was older, his father sent him to the Braintree Latin School. He did not fare well there, due to a personality clash with the master and because he initially eschewed education for farming. At length, his father found a new master under whom John prospered, learning Latin, math, logic, and rhetoric.

In 1751, when he was sixteen, John entered nearby Harvard College, studying Cicero, Tacitus, Plato, and other classics, as well as the various sciences taught at that time: rude versions of biology, chemistry, and mathematics. He graduated four years later with a bachelor of arts degree and taught for a while in a one-room school serving the children in Worcester, Massachusetts.

During his brief teaching career, John came to understand that it was esteem, reputation, and recognition that he craved above all else. Yet his Puritan upbringing was opposed to this, causing him to declare, "Vanity, I am sensible, is my cardinal Vice and my cardinal Folly."[27] Torn, he was unable to decide whether to join the clergy or study the law, on the premise that law might make him into a "great man,"[28] wrestling with his conscience until vanity won out.

In 1756 Adams contracted to read law under Worcester's leading attorney James Putnam. It was tough work, given that he had to continue teaching to support himself. But after two years Putnam pronounced him ready to practice law (there was no Massachusetts bar exam at the time). Putnam recommended him to several leading lawyers in Boston, who might be disposed to take a fledgling under their wing.

Boston was a huge metropolis compared with Braintree or Worcester. Adams had a few acquaintances with whom he played cards, went to concerts, and hoisted a glass of Madeira. By his own admission, he was "shy and uncomfortable" in the presence of women, but nevertheless became infatuated with Hannah Quincy, the attractive daughter of Col. Josiah Quincy. Over the long winter of 1758–59 Adams courted her and marriage was discussed, but he was unwilling to wed until he had established himself in the legal world. In time she got tired of waiting and began seeing someone else, whom she eventually wed. This threw Adams into a slough of despondence so deep that for a year he was unable to drink tea because it reminded him of Hannah, "that face, those eyes, that shape, that familiar friendly look."[29]

He continued in his diary to fight with himself over his vanity versus his Puritan reserve; mostly, he was merely disgusted that he had so little to be vain about. But slowly his legal caseload increased, and in the fall of 1760 he won his first jury trial. As his reputation grew, much of Adams's self-doubt evaporated, and the pages of his diary exuded a newfound confidence.

In May of 1761 Adams's father died—a particularly hard blow. John inherited a third of his father's estate, which, while not vast, was certainly a useful windfall to a young attorney. His quest for recognition continued; the notion of making a name for oneself had been quite elusive to anyone not born of the aristocracy prior to the eighteenth century, as the historian John Ferling has observed. But the advent of newspapers and the pamphlet offered a platform to those who could express themselves well; characters such as celebrated British author Samuel Johnson and Benjamin Franklin proved "that fame might be achieved by men born into a lesser social rank."[30]

IN 1759, AROUND THE TIME HANNAH QUINCY was breaking off with him, John Adams had met Abigail Smith, the daughter of a wealthy, slave-owning clergyman from Weymouth, a town neighboring Braintree. Abigail was barely fifteen years old then, and certainly no woman of the world. But two years later, Adams and Abigail became reacquainted. At seventeen she was graceful, if not quite a beauty, very intelligent, and more highly educated than many men and most women. She had read Shakespeare, Milton, and Pope with a private tutor and was both witty and charming.

By 1763 Adams and Abigail had become inseparable. They talked of all manner of things, and he praised her "fair Complexion, her Crimson Blushes, and her million charms and graces." Marriage was in the air, and they set a date for October 1764. That allowed time before the wedding for Adams to be inoculated against smallpox, a disease that ravaged the colonies in unrelenting epidemics. Because Adams had to travel for his law practice, he was more likely to be exposed.

The innovation of inoculations had come to New England via Africa. In 1721, during an epidemic in Boston, the great Puritan leader Cotton Mather learned from an African slave that in his native land, a small amount of infected material from a smallpox victim would be placed in a cut on a healthy person, who would then develop a mild form of smallpox for a few days and have to be quarantined for up to a month. After that, the person had some immunity to the disease, which killed a third of its victims in the American colonies and left most survivors scarred by pockmarks. Mather urged physicians in Boston to administer the inoculation but was met with much hostility. Yet gradually, over the ensuing decades, inoculation became accepted by many.

During Adams's month in the infirmary, he and Abigail corresponded daily, and on his discharge the two spent the rest of the spring and summer planning their wedding and furnishing their home to be. The century-old house on the Adams property was part of his inheritance from his father and sat next to the one in which he had been born. On October 25, 1764, John and Abigail were married by her father at her family home in Weymouth, surrounded by friends and relatives. She was twenty, he just turning twenty-nine. It was the beginning of a lifelong love affair and friendship, chronicled in extensive letters and diaries over the next sixty years.

When he wasn't riding the legal circuit, Adams cleared brush, dug ditches, spread manure, trimmed apple trees in the orchard, tended livestock on his 40 acres, and loved every minute of it. He and Abigail spent evenings talking in front of the fire, planning their lives, and discussing other matters pertaining to married life. By Christmas she was pregnant, which caused the normal anxiety of mother and child surviving childbirth. But those worries were laid to rest in July 1765, when Abigail gave birth to a baby girl. Named after her mother, a common practice at the time, she would for the rest of her life be called Nabby.

The joyous event of Nabby's arrival only added to the bliss Adams felt at this time. His law practice was thriving and the farm producing handsomely. There seemed to be no dark clouds on the horizon as the months rolled by—but barely a year after his marriage, a distasteful piece of news convulsed Massachusetts and the other colonies. Parliament had passed the so-called Stamp Act, requiring that all legal papers—wills, deeds, lawsuits, licenses—have a stamp affixed attesting that a hefty tax had been paid. A lawyer, for example, was required to buy a £10 tax stamp (equivalent to $1,530 in today's money) to affix to his law license. No document was admissible in court without paying stamp duties. Persons caught in violation were to be tried in British admiralty courts without a jury. It all went against the colonists' basic sense of fairness, and of their rights as British citizens.

The act hit Adams particularly hard, because his job revolved around producing legal documents. He lamented in his diary that he was "just getting under sail," when "this execrable Project was set on foot for my Ruin." Outraged colonists rioted and other protests ensued. Some stamp agents were beaten, threatened, tarred and feathered and their homes destroyed; many agents resigned.

Few people in those days had money to spare, and the Stamp Act was seen as a naked attempt to wring revenue from British subjects in America while their counterparts in England had no such obligations. Anti–Stamp Tax resolutions were introduced in various colonial governments. In newspapers and pamphlets, taverns and colonial legislatures, the jeremiad "no taxation without representation" was repeated. Movements were organized to boycott British goods and commodities. People were beginning for the first time to question the very relationship between Britain and its American colonies.

For their part, the British reacted with dismay and disgust. Parliament had justified the Stamp Act on grounds that Britain's victory in the Seven Years' War against France (called the French and Indian War in America) benefited the colonists more than it benefited Britain. (That was not particularly the case, since Britain had wrested much of Canada away from the French and added it to its own colonial empire.) But the war had also left Britain with a staggering debt and far more territory in North America to protect, which cost the Crown dearly. There was talk in Parliamentary circles of establishing a titled nobility in America to bring colonial leaders closer to the mother country; there was even talk of establishing the Anglican Church of England as the official church of all the colonies. But nothing came of it.

As word got back to England of the colonists' resistance to the Stamp Act, many members of Parliament insisted that its measures be enforced by Britain's military might. Benjamin Franklin, who was serving as the agent of the Pennsylvania Assembly in England, wrote a parody piece in a British newspaper under the pseudonym Pacificus in which he mocked any use of force against the Americans by Britain. He posited that the colonists could raise an army of 250,000 men, but "as one Englishman is sure as good as five Americans," England would have to transport and maintain an army of only 50,000 men in order to subdue the ungrateful Americans in a war that would take "three or four years," costing "ten or twelve million [pounds] per year." In the meantime, said Pacificus, France, Spain, and other European enemies would pounce on England "while engaged in this necessary work," against the Americans. Further, he suggested that "all the [American] capitals . . . be burned to the ground," the inhabitants scalped, and "the shipping . . . destroyed." And, he added, the colonies could be repopulated by "felons [in British] gaols" and the enormous number of English who would become unemployed as the result of such a war.[31]

Franklin's parody of the vast cost of conflict between the mother country and its American colonies was soon borne out. British merchants who had sent their goods across 3,000 miles of ocean found the goods were being returned before even being offloaded, as the colonists refused to pay the taxes on them. As a result, an estimated 100,000 British textile and other workers were unemployed and threatened to march on Parliament, and twenty-six mercantile towns in Britain protested the Stamp Act.

While acknowledging the unjustness of the Stamp Act, Adams himself was not in the frame of mind to advocate disorderly public protests. Like all colonists, Adams was a British subject, with strong emotional ties to the mother country. God Save the King—both the expression and the song—had been said or sung since the middle of the eighteenth century, and the newly crowned young king, George III, was still as popular in the colonies as in Great Britain. While Adams favored political and legal methods of dealing with Britain's newfound push to harness the American colonies for its own aggrandizement, his Boston cousin Samuel Adams was openly talking of a split with Britain. And the more he talked, the more he sounded like a revolutionary.

Samuel had been born to a family of some wealth. Like John, he was educated at Harvard but never managed to make much of himself. He had gone into several businesses in his forty-three years, all of which failed. Having frittered away his inheritance, he managed to supplement his wife and large family by becoming, of all things, a tax collector. Yet when the Stamp Act furor arose, Samuel Adams seized the opportunity to become a highly vocal opponent—not just of the act but of the Crown itself. In time he was a critical force behind the Sons of Liberty, which would take stands in ever more opposition to Britain's treatment of her American colonists. This Adams was not afraid of public demonstrations nor incitement-raising newspaper articles.[32] He regularly published incendiary pieces in the *Boston Gazette,* and his party included merchants, artisans, and unskilled laborers. Soon his followers came from towns and farmsteads all over Massachusetts, and his name was becoming well known on both sides of the Atlantic.

John felt great admiration for Samuel and considered him "a gentleman of Erudition and engaging manners." But he feared that his cousin sought disorder and discord, which could lead to no telling what end. As a lawyer, John favored harmony and genteel behavior and was dead set against the rough-and-tumble world of public politics conducted in city streets.[33]

In the face of immense public pressure, the British repealed the Stamp Act in 1766. The Massachusetts electorate showed its mood by sweeping out the old, entrenched members of the state legislature and installing instead men who had vociferously opposed the act, including Samuel Adams. He was elected clerk of the legislature, while John, like his father before him, was elected a selectman of Braintree.

In the summer of 1767 Abigail and John had their first son, John Quincy. As she had during her pregnancy with Nabby, Abigail went to stay at her family home in Weymouth, leaving John to tend the farm and concentrate on his legal practice. He was now comfortably well known as a respected, up-and-coming lawyer with a hefty caseload.

At almost the same time that John Quincy was coming into the world, so was Parliament's next insult to the American colonies: the Townshend Duties. Named for Chancellor of the Exchequer Charles Townshend, who had championed them, they put a tax on all tea, paints, glass, paper, and lead imported from Britain by the colonists. The Sons of Liberty—a secret group of agitators in various colonies that included Samuel Adams, Paul Revere, Benedict Arnold, John Hancock, and Patrick Henry—had disbanded after the Stamp Act was repealed. But now they regrouped to organize mass protest rallies against the duties, and again to urge the colonists to boycott all British goods.

About the same time, British customs agents seized one of the ships owned by the wealthy merchant and Son of Liberty John Hancock; the British agents claimed the *Liberty* was smuggling Madeira wine. A local crowd gathered at the customhouse, and in the ensuing riot two of the king's agents were beaten and British property damaged. The king's prosecutor filed for forfeiture of the *Liberty*, as well as imposing a fine of £9,000 sterling against Hancock for smuggling. Hancock retained John Adams to defend him, and Adams got the prosecutor to drop the charge of smuggling. But the *Liberty* was lost to Hancock and became a British revenue cutter.[34]

The British continued their provocations, and the Americans continued their protests. The general assembly sent a letter denouncing the Townshend Duties and petitioning for their repeal. This prompted the king's secretary for colonial American affairs, Lord Hillsborough, to attempt to isolate Boston, which he considered the hotbed of colonial dissent and impudence. In 1768 he sent a letter threatening to dissolve the general assembly of any colony that demanded repeal of the king's taxes and duties. To back this up, four regiments of British redcoats were dispatched to garrison the city of Boston.

The outrage this provoked was palpable. Newspaper accounts soon began retailing a litany of depredations allegedly committed by the British soldiers, and warned that colonial liberty was in jeopardy from these "redcoat dragoons." To add insult to injury, Parliament also passed the Quartering Act, forcing Bostonians to both shelter and feed the Crown troops.

The British soldiers proved a great nuisance. With 4,000 of them—nearly one for every four Bostonians—they seemed to be everywhere. Their favorite pastimes involved rum and prostitutes, offending the sensibilities of many Bostonians, who retained some of their ancestors' Puritan rigor. The soldiers bought up much of the available food and marched around with bands playing martial music as if they owned Boston.

Many of the redcoats were billeted near Brattle Square, where Adams had moved his family to be nearer the center of Boston and the courts (hired help ran the family's Quincy farm). The soldiers used the square for a parade ground and military base. One day ten soldiers were marched out, tied to posts, and publicly whipped in front of Abigail and the children; on another day a deserter was tied up and shot by firing squad at seven in the morning.[35]

In the months that followed, the kettle simmered; the next decade, which was fast approaching, would see it boil over. Adams remained cautious, unwilling to commit to a cause that might lead to disorder, let alone dishonor or disaster to his law practice. Some of the radicals, including his cousin Samuel, had become zealots. "That way madness lies," he told two prominent Bostonians who had asked him to address a mass meeting to remonstrate against the British troops.

But it was becoming apparent that peaceful and reasonable American pleas and protests were unmoving to Parliament, and that the British government intended to put as much pressure as was needed on their intractable colonies. Privately, John Adams was gravitating toward the cause of what were now called the "Patriots"—the need for an America free of British rule.

Two weeks before Christmas 1768, Abigail gave birth to another daughter, Susanna. The infant was pale and sickly, and despite everything that was done to keep her healthy she died the following February. It was hard on John, but it was devastating for Abigail, who seemed to be in a trance. John's brothers Peter and Elihu brought the large sled out from the barn at Braintree and retrieved the tiny coffin. The three men took it to the Adams burying ground beside the Braintree Meeting House. When the frozen ground proved too hard to dig, they covered the coffin with pine boughs. Elihu promised to watch over it until the thaw, and then dig the small grave.

AS THE 1770S BEGAN, John Adams could look back on the previous decade and see that his life had prospered. He had begun it as a lonely, fledgling attorney whose practice consisted mainly of wills, deeds, and issues with livestock, petty theft, and public drunkenness. Now he was a landed family man with a fine wife and children, one of the largest law practices in the colony, and considerable standing in the Boston community. He was thirty-five, well dressed, pudgy, going bald, and stood five-foot-seven. And he was, as he said, happy.

That contentment was not to last. The escalating tension between Bostonians and British troops occasionally erupted into physical violence, as it did at the end of February 1770. A British informer named Ebenezer Richardson was caught chopping down a sign that had been posted by his house containing the names of Bostonians who had been dealing in British goods against the American boycott. A group of boys began hurling snowballs and ice chunks at him. When he retreated inside, they threw brickbats and broke the glass panes of his windows. Richardson retrieved a gun and exclaimed, "By God I'll make a lane through you!" and fired once. When the boys withdrew, one of them lay dead on the ground. An enormous public funeral was held, and the line of mourners stretched a quarter mile. John Adams was one of them. Even though the incident had nothing to do with the British soldiers, a loose connection to them was nevertheless made, and the ill will grew.[36]

Monday, March 5, was bitterly cold, with a layer of ice covering the ground. It snowed that day but by evening the skies had cleared and a moon appeared over Beacon Hill. There were taunts and jeers between a crowd of citizens and a file of British soldiers "out for a stroll," and a great deal of muttering and mumbling among the throng. About eight in the evening, a boy said something impudent to the British sentinel on guard in front of the customhouse. The soldier chased him down and gave him a whack with the butt of his musket. "The boy set up a howl calculated to raise the dead," and this set the crowd, which had grown, to scuffling and pelting the soldiers with ice and snowballs. A British officer intervened and ordered the soldiers back inside their compound. It seemed like the end of the matter. But it wasn't.

Someone hoisted a boy through the window of a nearby church and instructed him to climb to the steeple and begin ringing the bell, which was a signal that a fire had broken out. People poured into the streets with buckets, wanting to know where the fire was. When no fire was reported, the street began to clear. The British sentinel guarding the customhouse marched back and forth. But one street down someone was heard shouting, addressing a crowd. He was said to have worn a white wig and a red cloak. At the same time another large crowd appeared in King Street, and at the customhouse a man shouted, "Here's the soldier that struck the boy!"

Some in the crowd called, "Kill the soldier. Kill the damn coward. Kill him. Knock him down." Men and boys began pelting the sentinel with heavy pieces of ice, chunks of wood, and snowballs. He backed up on the customhouse steps and frantically began loading his gun and shouting for help. Captain of the Guard Thomas Preston heard him from the barracks and ordered a file of seven men to cross the square on the double. They were in shirtsleeves but with bayonets drawn. Parting the crowd, they joined the frightened sentinel on the steps of the customhouse.

The eight soldiers and Captain Preston now confronted a mob of more than a hundred, taunting, whistling, shouting, pelting the British with ice, wood, and snowballs. "Let's see you fire . . . you dare not fire . . . lobsters [so the redcoats were sometimes called], bloody backs . . . Let's burn the sentry box . . . come on, boys!" Some kind of missile knocked down one of the soldiers and he lost his gun. No one heard the order to fire, but suddenly the eight soldiers began to discharge their weapons into the mob, which shrank back. As the smoke cleared, five men lay dead or dying on the snow. For a brief moment a silence took hold as the crowd absorbed what had happened. The soldiers quickly began to reload.[37]

Captain Preston then led the men back toward the barracks, shouldering their way with bayonets through the horrified crowd. Within the barracks drums began to beat and several platoons of armed soldiers soon poured into Brattle Square, taking up firing positions. Bells began to ring in the city streets, spreading alarm, and the cry "to arms!" was raised. Men arrived with weapons—knives, guns, cudgels, cutlasses—and the air filled with shouts and curses.[38]

The Crown's governor arrived on the balcony of the statehouse and appeared silhouetted in the moonshine above the "seething, roaring, angry mass that filled the square and street." "Go home!" he shouted. "Let the law settle this thing. Let the law take its course . . . blood has been shed . . . tomorrow there will be an inquiry." "Tonight!" the crowd responded, shouting for Captain Preston to be arrested. The colonel commanding the Boston troops appeared suddenly at the governor's side and whispered into his ear. Preston and the eight soldiers would be taken to jail, he said, and the soldiers ordered back to their barracks. Slowly, noisily, the throng began to disperse; the issue was defused for the time being, but it was far from over.[39]

John Adams was at the other end of town at his club when he heard the alarm bells ringing. He and the others, supposing a fire, left immediately to help. Along the way Adams learned what had happened, that soldiers had fired on citizens. His first worry was for Abigail and the children, who would have been near enough at their home to be in the line of musket fire. At Brattle Square he saw the soldiers with their bayonets fixed and the seething crowd opposite them.[40]

Arriving home, John found his family safe, and they settled in for what was left of the night. Next morning the streets were filled with angry citizens, some from the country carrying muskets. At his office Adams found a frantic Mr. Forester, a man known to befriend British officers. He was disheveled and appeared to be crying. He beseeched Adams to defend Captain Preston, "who has no one to defend him." Forester had already approached the Crown's lawyers who, fearing reprisals from the mob, would not get near the case. Two other lawyers said they would consider defending Preston, but only if John Adams agreed to come aboard.

"Captain Preston is innocent," Forester pleaded. "Before God in heaven, he acted in self-defense." Adams was filled with conflicting thoughts. He knew the case was highly explosive, filled with hatred and fire and politics and sorrow. He knew the risks he would be taking for himself, his family, and his law practice. He weighed them all against his long-standing conviction that every man was entitled to proper representation before a court of law, especially when faced with a hanging offense. Adams addressed

Forester, who was wringing his hands. "If Captain Preston doesn't think he can have a fair trial without my help, then he shall have it," John Adams said, adding that he would defend the eight enlisted soldiers too.

Preston's trial began October 24, 1770, almost seven months after it was originally scheduled. Adams had pleaded for and received this postponement, citing his heavy caseload, but in reality he believed that if the trial had been held just two weeks after what had become known as the Boston Massacre, the jury would have been much more likely to convict.

Adams's two co-councils were Josiah Quincy and Robert Auchmuty. Quincy was only twenty-six, but he was a sharp, quick thinker. Auchmuty was loyal to the Crown. He'd not gone to college, and Adams didn't think much of his legal expertise. The defending legal team spent two days picking the jury, with Adams carefully striking any Bostonian. In the end, all the jurors came from small outlying country towns.

The prosecution presented witnesses who testified that Preston gave the soldiers the order to fire into the crowd, though Preston had insisted to Adams privately that he hadn't. It didn't matter. Adams's skillful defense presented English case law stating that any officer or soldier who felt his life threatened while doing his duty was justified in using deadly force. It was enough for the jury. Preston was acquitted.

Next came the trial of the eight enlisted soldiers. Adams argued the same legal basis as he had with Preston. His team presented thirty-six witnesses who testified to the missiles thrown at the sentinel and the soldiers, and the threats hurled at them by the mob. Knowing that the trial would be followed carefully in Britain, Adams was extremely careful when examining the witnesses not to portray Boston as a riot-prone mobocracy. But he did capture the hysterical mood of the crowd that night. "Place yourselves in the position of [the soldiers]," Adams told the jury, "with the bells ringing—and you know well there is no fire—the people shouting, huzzaing, and making the mob whistle as they call it. Let a boy make this whistle in the street and it is no formidable thing, but when made by a multitude it is a most hideous shriek, almost as terrible as an Indian yell.

"People are crying, Kill them! Kill them!—and throwing snowballs, oyster shells, ice, clubs—white birch sticks three inches in diameter—consider yourselves in this situation and then judge if a reasonable man would not consider you were going to kill him."

Adams read aloud from a law book on self-defense. "He who in an assault retreats to the wall beyond which he can go no further before he kills the other, is judged by the law to act on unavoidable necessity. And an officer who kills one that insults him in the execution of his office may justify the fact."

When the verdict came in, six of the soldiers were acquitted and two were convicted of manslaughter, a much lesser charge than capital murder.[41] Although there was some grumbling, the citizens of Boston, if not exactly satisfied, seemed reasonably resigned to the verdicts and did not, as Adams had feared, make him into a pariah.

IRONICALLY, IN PARLIAMENT, on the very day of the Boston Massacre, the British government responded to persistent American protests and boycotts and repealed the Townshend Duties, except for the one on tea. Many members of Parliament wanted to repeal that, too, but Lord North, the new prime minister, said it was needed to remind the American colonists that the British government had the right to tax them.

Adams became convinced that the colonists, by resolutions, protests, boycott, and mediation, could deal with Great Britain in matters of taxes and tariffs. This greatly relieved him, because he felt certain that any attempt by the colonies to break away from Britain would result in war. Until the enactment of the Stamp Act, Adams reasoned, America's relationship with the mother country had been free, open, and tolerant. Now his hopes were high that that relationship would be restored.

But during this same period his cousin Samuel and another Son of Liberty—Maj. Joseph Hawley, a lawyer, powerful assemblyman, and veteran of the French and Indian War—persisted in trying to convince Adams to join their cause. John was now greatly admired for his balanced approach to the British, and Samuel and Hawley thought he would be a perfect addition to the American patriotic movement. They and other men, from New England to the Carolinas, had not given up their dream of American independence, and they felt the time for it was coming.

Whether Adams was manipulated or not remains an open question, but over the next several years he unquestionably began to believe that the relationship with Great Britain was unfair, unbalanced, and in the end probably could not hold. These conclusions were drawn from yet more provocations by Parliament.

First, it was decreed that the salaries of judges in the Massachusetts superior court would be paid by the British government, thus wiping out local control. Adams attacked the measure with a series of articles in a Boston newspaper in early 1773, and mass protest meetings were again convened; at one of them Joseph Hawley gave an explosive speech saying that the colony must either bow to Parliament or declare independence. "No middle ground existed," he exclaimed.[42] To cap it off, Samuel Adams privately showed John a series of stolen letters from a British minister to the Massachusetts royal governor Thomas Hutchinson, considered a British stooge. In the letter the minister warned that if the Americans refused to bend to the British, their liberties would be taken away—by force if necessary. These events so alarmed Adams that he came to believe Samuel had been correct from the outset—American independence was the only reasonable answer.

After the trials of the Boston Massacre soldiers, the rest of the British troops were marched to the town's Long Wharf and ferried to Castle William, site of a hundred-year-old fort in Boston Harbor. This development brought great merriment for what had become known as the liberty boys, the group of urchins who gathered perpetually in the streets of the city and marched alongside the soldiers, taunting them. With the redcoats thus confined, an uneasy peace descended on Boston, as it had in other colonies. But there remained a new sense of destiny among large segments of the American public. Britain was no longer regarded as a friendly, benevolent force presiding over her colonies. She was viewed more as a tyrannical ruler, uncaring of the Americans except to the extent she could wring money out of them.

This dissatisfaction predictably resulted in action, in a magnificent incident familiar to every American schoolchild. At the end of 1773 the British government, seeking to revive a near-bankrupt East India Company, decided to cut in half the price of several tons of Indian tea leaves that were rotting in London warehouses. British thinking went that the Americans, whose boycott of British tea had remained since the Townshend Duties, would not be able to resist half-price tea, and the British would put a threepence-a-pound duty on it, finally getting their tea tax money.

When word of this arrangement reached Boston, a cry went out that the tea must not be landed. When the three British tea ships arrived in early December, there was some legal wrangling about duty, but at length the ships were tied up to a wharf in the inner harbor. Such a ruckus developed over not unloading the tea that Abigail Adams wrote to a friend that the "flame is kindled and like lightning it reaches from soul to soul." "I dare not openly express my fears," she said in another letter, but spoke of "direful consequences," as if the tea business might start a war with England.[43]

A meeting was called for December 16 by Samuel Adams. At it he addressed several hundred Sons of Liberty, some dressed as Mohawk Indians in war paint and feathers and carrying hatchets. "This meeting can do no more to save the country," Adams concluded. This was the signal, and the audience jumped up and began to shout, "To the docks! To the docks!"

At Griffin's Wharf the "Indians" boarded the tea ships and, after overpowering their crews, dumped 342 chests of English tea into Boston Harbor. By morning there was a "tea-tide" all the way to Nantasket, a beachfront area at Quincy. No one had put so much as a handful of tea into his pockets, though one "Indian" found that his shoes were full of tea when he reached home; he scraped some out and put it in a jar for a souvenir.[44]

John Adams's reaction to the tea escapade is somewhat surprising given his penchant for law and order: "This is the most

Magnificent movement of all. There is a dignity, a Majesty, a Sublimity, in this last effort of the Patriots that I admire . . . This Destruction of the tea is so bold, so daring, so firm, intrepid and inflexible and it must have so important Consequences, and so lasting that I cannot but Consider it as an Epocha in History."[45]

Adams probably did not know how right he was. When word of the event reached England, it set off a furious uproar throughout the land—but especially in the halls of Parliament. After considering various punishments, the members voted on four measures that came to be known as the Coercive Acts, aimed at Boston in particular and the Massachusetts Bay Colony in general. Americans would know them as the Intolerable Acts. They stipulated that Boston Harbor would be blockaded by British warships to all commerce until the cost of the destroyed tea (£18,000 sterling) was repaid; that Boston's fishing fleet was banned from tapping into the bounteous Grand Banks fishing ground; that the Massachusetts government would be solely appointed by agents of the Crown, even down to juries (the colony's house of representatives was retained, but its functions were strictly limited); that mass meetings were forbidden; that any British officials, including soldiers, accused of capital offenses would be shipped to England for a fair trial, as would be any British subjects accused of being "disturbers of the King's peace"; that an additional five regiments of redcoats, commanded by the Massachusetts military governor—Maj. Gen. Thomas Gage, commander in chief of British forces in America—would be camped on Boston Common, as well as the soldiers that had been quartered in Castle William. Essentially, Bostonians were put under martial law and, with the closing of the port, exposed to starvation.

The Massachusetts colonists did not find out about these measures until mid-May 1774, when Gage and his redcoats arrived. Other colonies were infuriated by the measures against Massachusetts and responded by sending food: rice from South Carolina and wheat, flour, sugar, and a herd of hundreds of sheep from Connecticut and New York, which promised to send enough food to Boston to "withstand a ten-year siege." In the house of representatives, which had been banished to nearby Salem, Samuel Adams read a motion he had prepared: "That a General Congress of deputies meet at Philadelphia to consult together on the state of the colonies and to deliberate and determine upon wise and proper measures for the recovery of their just rights and liberties, civil and religious." It passed overwhelmingly, setting into motion an eventual meeting of the First Continental Congress.

The Intolerable Acts had set off the furor, but all of the British coercions over the past decade, from the Stamp Act to the Townshend Duties, had fueled the fire. For the first time, twelve of the thirteen colonies would be represented in one deliberative body. Whatever it decided would have to be ratified by the various colonial legislatures, but one thing was sure: any actions adopted by the forty-odd delegates would probably be considered treasonous in British eyes, and thus a hanging offense.

ON AN AUGUST MORNING IN 1774 John Adams prepared to set out for Philadelphia and the meeting of that first congress. With him were Thomas Cushing, Samuel Adams, and Robert Paine. John Hancock, Josiah Quincy, and a number of Sons of Liberty were there to see them off. Abigail of course was there as well. After a mid-morning feast, the delegates boarded Cushing's fancy coach, and his coachman shook the reins. The four chestnut horses danced into action and the coach lurched westward. Besides the drivers, two black servants in livery perched on the back of the vehicle and four black outriders carrying flintlock pistols accompanied the party of delegates. As an act of pure defiance, the coach did not take a roundabout way out of town but drove right past the thousands of redcoats camped on Boston Common.[46]

The trip took more than a week. John Adams had never been out of New England before, and he absorbed the sights during stops in New Jersey and New York—including the giant whirlpool at Hell's Gate on the East River. Once in the City of Brotherly Love, he was engulfed in the largest city in colonial America, home to roughly 30,000 people.

Adams and his party had arrived a few days early and got to know many of the other delegates—in particular the Virginia men. Among them was the imposing Col. George Washington and Patrick Henry, a member of Virginia's House of Burgesses and a fiery orator for Patriot causes. The delegates decided to meet in Carpenters' Hall instead of the larger, more formal State House.

Not all delegates were as radical as Samuel Adams; some were actually British sympathizers—Tories (or at least quasi-Tories). This group included Joseph Galloway, a wealthy Philadelphia politician to whom Adams took an immediate dislike. Galloway seemed particularly aggrieved when they voted for Carpenters' Hall, presumably because he would have assumed more personal prestige in the chambers of the state government, where he was speaker of the house.

New York's delegates also seemed to Adams to be men "whose weather vane pointed always to their private interests." They were wealthy and generally self-satisfied; most were proud British subjects who adored the royal government. They were in attendance to help iron out the growing differences between the colonies and Britain—and, above all else, to maintain harmony, rather than encourage controversy, let alone confrontation.[47]

The first order of business was how voting in the congress would work. Would it be by delegate (one vote each) or by colony or by the wealth of the colony? Some felt a vote by colony was unfair, because smaller colonies, like Rhode Island and Delaware, would have the same voting power as larger ones, such as Virginia and Pennsylvania. But to receive votes based on wealth would be difficult, because there was no sure means of determining it. In the end, it was decided each colony would have one vote, which meant the delegates representing a given colony would have to come to an agreement among themselves.

Another order of business was a nonimportation/nonconsumption agreement among all of the colonies—a promise to neither buy from nor sell to the British. Many of the delegates from Pennsylvania and New York were against such a measure, because it would be hard to enforce and extremely costly to farmers and merchants whose main business was selling to the mother country. Also on the agenda was a petition to the king, including a list of the colonists' rights and demands. This required finesse, because most delegates wanted to strike a balance between asserting what they felt were their rights and not making the king so angry that he would turn them down outright or even declare war with the colonies. Adams noted some of the remarks of various delegates in his diary.

"Negotiation, suspension of commerce, and war are the only three things. War is, by general consent, to be waved at present."

"A non-exportation at a future day cannot avail us."

"Sugar carries the greatest revenue—rum a great deal."

"I am inclined to think the present measures lead to war."

"I am one of those who hold the position that Parliament has a right to make Laws for us in some cases—to regulate trade."

"We ought to consider the consequences possible as well as probable of every resolution we make."

"There are numbers of Men who will risk their all. I shudder at the thought of the blood which will be spilled, and would be glad to avoid it."[48]

Most of the delegates to the Continental Congress were men of wealth, and after the business of the day ended they were fond of dining sumptuously in the evening (which began at 4 p.m.). Feasts were spread across large tables at City Tavern or wherever the gracious hosts of Philadelphia had opened their homes and mansions to the delegates. Adams told his cousin Samuel that his skin was turning green from eating turtle [soup] and that the amount of Madeira he had consumed would make a Rhode Island smuggler squint-eyed.[49]

Delegates from all twelve colonies eventually agreed to passage of the non–importation/exportation measure, with a provision that men would be stationed at wharves up and down the East Coast to enforce it. It was also decided that the petition to the king was to be drawn asserting American rights, including no taxation without representation.

Paul Revere had arrived on horseback, after riding hard, to deliver to the congress a set of resolutions drawn up by the Massachusetts legislature that bore directly on any petition to King George. Adams was on the committee that worked on the petition, though Patrick Henry wrote the first draft, which read in part, "Had we been permitted to enjoy in quiet the inheritance left us by our forefathers, we should [have] at this time been peacefully, cheerfully, and usefully employed in recommending ourselves by every testimony of devotion to Your Majesty, and of veneration of the state from which we derive our origin."

In addition to the petition and the nonimportation measures, Congress also voted to encourage colonies to strengthen significantly their various militias. This was a bold and hazardous step, for if British authorities learned of it, they might take military action to thwart it, starting war. But war seemed right below the horizon in any case.

John Adams was satisfied with what the congress had accomplished, but he was also terribly homesick. He had been gone from Abigail and the children for two months and longed for the peaceful autumn splendor of Braintree. At last, on October 28, a stormy morning, Cushing's coach arrived to bear the Massachusetts group home. "I now take leave of the elegant, the hospitable, and polite city of Philadelphia," Adams wrote. "It is not very likely I will ever see this part of the world again." How wrong he was.[50]

When Adams arrived in Boston, his friends threw a great party in his honor. Copies of the petition to the king had been printed and were being distributed by the newspapers. The colony was up in arms over General Gage's sorties out from Boston with his troops, searching for gunpowder or other military stores acquired by the colonists. Frowning militias would assemble and watch the redcoats at their grim tasks. Tempers were growing shorter every day.

Winter came on, and with it a slowdown in Gage's raids through the countryside. But Boston and the whole of the Massachusetts Bay Colony were in utter disarray. The government had essentially ceased to function, owing to threats to and intimidation of officials appointed by the Crown under the recent decrees from London; courts were closed and little was being done otherwise. But the colonists had formed a "provincial congress" with John Hancock as its president, and a Patriots' "committee of safety" to cope with the present emergency. Both had been outlawed by General Gage, but they continued to operate nevertheless.

Gage had written to the prime minister, Lord North, that the intimidation of royal officials was coming "from men of property and influence" and "not by the mob," as had been the case during the Stamp Act protests. He recommended that the British government pull back and suspend the Coercive Acts until order was restored.

When Lord North showed Gage's letter to George III, the king called the suggestion "absurd."[51] "Nothing could be more provoking than the conduct of the inhabitants of Massachusetts Bay," the king told his minister for the American colonies. "Some measures must undoubtedly be adopted after Christmas to curb them, and . . . bring them to a due obedience to the mother country." The king then told his prime minister, in what was nearly a declaration of war, "The New England governments are in a State of Rebellion. *Blows must decide* whether they are to be subject to this country or be independent."[52]

In London Benjamin Franklin was feverishly working back channels to avert a war, but to little avail. He had friends in high places, but this time it was the king himself calling the tune—and he was not a friend of Franklin and his support for the obstreperous colonists.

As spring began its annual thaw General Gage, at the urging of George III and his secretary of state, decided to renew raids on the American military stores. Word had come to him that ample military supplies, including brass cannons, were being stored secretly by militia in Concord, a town some 20 miles northwest of Boston.

John Adams had resumed his essays in the *Boston Gazette* in response to Tory essays debunking the continued defiance of the king. He had moved Abigail and their four children permanently back to Braintree after finding Boston "too dangerous." The courts remained closed and his law business was at a standstill. But he found himself serving on various patriotic committees and institutions, including the provincial congress.

In the meantime the Americans knew that something was up. Paul Revere rode out to Lexington, a village near Concord, where Samuel Adams and John Hancock had been hiding, for fear the British had plans to arrest them. Revere told the two Patriot leaders that if the British began marching out of their bivouac, he was going to put signal lanterns in the nearly 200-foot-tall belfry of North Church in Boston. A single lantern would mean the British were marching by land, two lanterns meant they were being rowed across the Charles River to Charlestown.[53]

By April 18 British spies had confirmed that colonial military stores were hidden in a farmhouse on the far side of the Concord River. Around 9 p.m. a force of 700 British regulars, comprising light infantry and grenadier guards, were assembled on Boston Common. Soon two lanterns appeared in the tower of North Church, while Revere rode hell-for-leather to Lexington to warn Adams and Hancock.

Along the way Revere had to elude British officers whom Gage had sent out earlier to take posts along the route, so that Concord could not be alerted. Adams and Hancock ordered the bell in the

Lexington Meetinghouse rung and by 2 a.m. more than a hundred members of the local militia had assembled in the cold April night on the village green. These were mostly the "minutemen," militia members who had promised to be ready at a minute's notice.

There being no word of the British advance from scouts, the American leaders dismissed the men with orders for them to reassemble on a minute's notice at the sound of a drum. Some went home but most went to a nearby tavern to get out of the cold and perhaps have a drink or two. By 5 a.m. Adams and Hancock were headed away from Lexington. Hancock had wanted to stay with the militia and fight the British, but Adams talked him out of it, saying, "We're cabinet."

In the meantime, one of the colonial scouts returned with the alarming word that the redcoats were just minutes away from Lexington.[54] The military drummer beat the call for assembly, but by the time the redcoats reached the Lexington village green only about 70 Patriots had come together and their leader wasn't sure what to do. As the British marched forward, a shot was fired; no one could say with certainty which side fired it. In response, the Americans fired into the redcoat mass, and the British commander gave the order to fire a volley. Most of the shots went high, but eight Americans and two redcoats were killed in the fray. The American militia dispersed, and the British marched confidently on toward Concord.

By the time they arrived it was dawn and they were met with an entirely different situation from the one at Lexington. Gathered on a hill above Concord were 400 to 500 colonials from every town militia in the area. The British crossed one of the two bridges over the Concord River in order to search the farmhouse and outbuildings where the cannons and other military stores were said to be hidden. Very little was found, except a few wooden gun carriages, which the redcoats burned. Other British soldiers in the town found a few more gun carriages and set them afire. To the militia watching on the hill, it appeared the British were burning the town.

An order was given for the militia to cross the second wooden bridge over the Concord River, also being held by the British. Then came what would be called through history the "shot heard round the world." To the astonishment of the British, the Americans attacked and left half a dozen dead at the bridge. Some militiamen had gone into the cover of woods or behind stone walls and had gotten on the flanks of the redcoat formations, where they did "serious execution." Early that morning General Gage had sent a thousand reinforcements toward Concord, and that column arrived in early afternoon, only to share the fate of the two original British regiments.

The British officers began marching their weary men back to Boston, but the Patriot minutemen and militiamen shadowed them. As more American bullets found their mark, the British withdrawal turned into a retreat and finally, by day's end, a rout. Once back in Charlestown, across the harbor from Boston, the redcoats took up defensive positions.

For the entire day the Americans had harassed and sniped at the British regulars. Many other town militias were drawn to the scene, so that by nightfall about 3,900 armed colonists were on the scene. The butcher's bill for the day was 73 (and as many as 120) British killed, a shocking number of them officers, and 174 wounded. Forty-nine Americans had lost their lives and 39 were wounded. It was clearly an American victory, and Hugh Percy, the British general who had led the reinforcements to Concord, remarked of the American soldiers, "Whoever looks upon them as an irregular mob will find himself much mistaken. They have men amongst them who know very well what they are about, having been employed as rangers against the Indians. And this country, being much covered with wood and hills, is very advantageous for their method of fighting."[55]

The next morning the most pressing subject of discussion among the Patriots "was nothing less than what to do next." The committee of safety voted to raise an army of 8,000, who would serve until the end of the year. In the days that followed, militiamen from all over the region poured into Cambridge, across the Charles from Boston, which had suddenly become the Patriots' military headquarters. The provincial congress voted to raise an army of 30,000 to be led by Artemas Ward, a veteran of the French and Indian War. There was discussion of attacking the British in Boston, but this was abandoned when someone raised the point that the British war fleet would "knock the city to pieces."

Within a week all routes into Boston had been sealed off by the colonial militia, and Gage had hunkered down for a siege. He might not get food and stores by land anymore, but he always had the warships and British merchantmen in the harbor to supply him.[56] The city soon became an economic ghost town, and high anxiety reigned among Loyalists and Patriots alike. Dr. Joseph Warren, who was fighting with the Americans, arranged with General Gage for the redcoats to allow Patriot sympathizers to leave Boston unmolested, but the general broke his promise. After further consideration, it was decided they could go, but they had to leave their muskets behind.

Within a week of the Lexington and Concord battles John Adams set off on horseback for Philadelphia to participate in the

Second Continental Congress. Only a servant accompanied him. By then Adams knew most of the congressional delegates from the year before. They were divided in their opinions, and often bitterly so. Some, including John and Samuel Adams, wanted independence and a complete break with Great Britain; others wanted repeal of parliamentary tax measures and the Coercive Acts but wished to remain within the British Empire.[57] The placating Joseph Galloway was no longer in Congress; he had become a full-fledged Tory. Later he joined the British army occupying Philadelphia and ended in exile in England.

The moderates were now led by John Dickinson of Pennsylvania, a man of great wealth and ability. His faction proposed that "An Humble and Dutiful Petition" be composed to George III, stating that Congress would like an immediate "negotiation of the unhappy disputes" and that the colonists were ready "to enter into measures to achieve it." This became the so-called Olive Branch Petition.

John Adams could not contain himself and branded the petition an act of "imbecility." He pointed out there were fifty dead colonists, Boston was under military rule, and more reinforcements from England were coming for both army and navy. Adams accused the "accommodators" of wasting precious time. An American national army and navy needed to be formed, and men designated to command them. Alliances with European powers—France, Holland, Spain—needed to be made. "Defense of the continent needed to be tended to before there was any 'negotiation,'" Adams spat out the word as though it were a vile and profane thing.[58]

Dickinson buttonholed Adams later and threatened to "break off from [New England and] . . . carry on the opposition by ourselves in our own way." "You are wasting your time, Mr. Dickinson," Adams told him. "I am not to be threatened. Let the Congress judge between us," and he spun away on his heels.[59]

Building an army was then addressed, but who was to lead it? Adams was all for George Washington, but there was competition—Artemas Ward, for one, and, surprisingly, John Hancock. The most serious rival was Gen. Charles Lee, who was fighting with the militiamen in Boston. A wealthy British officer on half-pay, he kept a manor in the Shenandoah Valley and liked to declare that he was more American than the Americans. But he was also an Englishman by birth, and Adams was certain an American army would not follow anyone with that pedigree.

Washington, on the other hand, had been a colonel in the British army during the French and Indian War and had valuable military experience. He was a majestic, thoughtful figure. Abigail at first had reservations about Washington as a slaveholder and member of the Virginia gentry, but soon she came to know him as "Dignity with ease . . . the Gentleman and Soldier are agreeably blended in him." With John Adams championing him, Washington got the job. When the issue of compensation was brought to the floor, Washington stated he could not accept any pay. He would, however, keep a careful account of his expenses and, after his services had ended, Congress could reimburse him, if it wished.

Setting up a colonies-wide army and navy from scratch was a daunting challenge. Men from each of the colonies would have to be enlisted, so it was decided that a man who could raise a platoon of fifty men would be made a lieutenant, a man who could raise a hundred became a captain, and so on. They would have to be supplied with uniforms, weapons, gunpowder, artillery, horses, wagons, and myriad other military implements. And food. Like Massachusetts, each village and town in the colonies had a militia going back to the days when fending off Indian attacks was a frequent occurrence. That provided at least an incipient military framework and a barebones of men and matériel. But a continental army would have to be heavily and skillfully trained if it was going to win battles against the highly disciplined redcoats.

A navy was an entirely different matter. The British navy was a match for any two or three navies in the world combined, and the Americans had not one warship. As a start, with John Adams as the chairman, the naval committee commissioned the construction of thirteen frigates. These relatively small, fast warships, akin to today's destroyer, were armed with twenty-four to thirty-two guns each. Though they could not compete with ships of the line, with their two and three decks of guns, frigates were useful in defense, during blockades, or in seizing enemy ships.

But even these smaller ships would take time to build—so what to do in the meantime to break the British blockade of the American coast? It was decided that merchant ships would be put to navy use and issued "letters of marque," commissioning them as privateers to roam the seas and prey on British ships—especially those carrying war material bound for the British army in the colonies. Eventually, these privateers would capture more than fifteen hundred British merchant ships.

In the midst of all this planning Adams became the center of an embarrassing episode. A private messenger he had hired to take letters to Boston was captured by Tories. Among the letters was one to Abigail in which Adams vented his spleen about Congress, lambasting among other things the "Fidgets, the Whims, the

Caprice, the Vanity, the Superstition, the Irritability, of some of us." In another letter, to Dr. Warren, Adams referenced a fellow congressman—obviously John Dickinson—saying that "great Fortune and piddling genius whose fame has been trumpeted so loudly, has given a silly cast to our whole doings." Within days, these and other private writings of Adams appeared in Loyalist newspapers, to the delight of his enemies and the disgust of some of his fellow congressmen, who saw no humor in portraying that body in such a fashion. For a time, John Adams was shunned.[60]

ON JULY 3, 1775, George Washington left Philadelphia to command the Patriot militia surrounding Boston. He had scarcely ridden two hours when a fast dispatch rider from Massachusetts revealed details of the battle on Bunker and Breed's Hills in Charlestown. The Americans had established themselves on Breed's Hill the night of June 16, working until dawn to build strong defensive redoubts and breastworks. When the sun rose and the British beheld the host of soldiers in the entrenchments on the hills, they were shocked.

Gage, in a conference with three newly arrived generals—William Howe, John Burgoyne, and Henry Clinton (each of whom would bear a major role in the fighting to come)—determined to attack immediately. Soon the British fleet in the harbor began firing toward the American positions. By mid-afternoon 2,000 British regulars were boarding ships for Charlestown and an assault on the Patriot militia—which, they had been taught, would never stand up to a full-fledged attack by British infantry. They soon found otherwise.

The first British attack on Breed's Hill, led by General Howe, was a disaster that ended in a downhill retreat. Some of the redcoats even got back into the boats that had brought them and had to be rousted by officers using the flat of their sword blades. Breed's Hill was strewn with the bodies of dead and dying redcoats, "thick as a flock of sheep in a fold." When the second British charge unfolded, colonial grapeshot mowed down the regulars like stalks of corn; that assault also failed.

Horrified British officers began organizing the survivors for a third assault. Howe was determined to try again, this time marching in two columns instead of in broad lines. "As fast as the front man was shot down," said an American Patriot of the third British charge, "the next stepped forward into his place, but our men dropped them so fast they were a long time coming up. It was surprising how they would step over their dead bodies as though they were logs of wood."[61]

But the Americans were beginning to run out of gunpowder. Some militiamen broke open artillery cartridges, dispensing their contents to men desperate to load their weapons. "We fired till our ammunition began to fail," said one of the militiamen in the redoubt, "then our firing began to slacken—and then it went out like an old candle."[62]

The British began to enter the redoubts and bayonet the packed-in Americans. Desperate hand-to-hand fighting ensued. When it was over, the British held the hills, but at a terrific cost. More than 500 of their men were dead and 500 more were wounded or dying. The loss in officers was stunning; 80 had been shot, 20 of them fatally. The American casualties numbered 115 dead and 305 wounded. A British victory, perhaps, but certainly a pyrrhic one for the Crown.

Outside Philadelphia, Washington and his party digested the news and headed north. The newly appointed commander had no idea what he would find when he reached Massachusetts, but what he had just learned impressed him. Those Americans outside Boston would stand and fight.

But when Washington reached Cambridge on July 2, 1775, he was soon distressed at what he found. The various militias that had come to assist in the siege of Boston were among the most unmilitary people he had ever commanded. The soldiers "came and went as they pleased, did not bother to salute officers, gambled, drank, and cursed openly, and took every opportunity to swim naked in the Boston area rivers that flowed past homes that contained women and children." There was an unfortunate rivalry among colonies as well; as an example, Massachusetts militiamen objected to having Rhode Island men join their regiments, while men from South Carolina protested the presence of free black troops anywhere in the army. There was trading, drunkenness, and fighting among all units, and encounters with female camp followers resulted in "the itch."[63]

While he was trying to instill some discipline, Washington faced a far greater danger: an epidemic of the severe intestinal ailment dysentery swept through the army in August. Ten thousand soldiers were affected, and thousands died. John Adams's brother Elihu was one of them, and John took his body back to Braintree for burial. Abigail's mother was felled. Whole families perished. The pestilence lasted into the fall.

The one bright feature of those summer months was the arrival of at least 1,400 Pennsylvania troops. They brought with them what came to be known as the Kentucky long rifle. Made in fact by Pennsylvania blacksmiths for western backwoodsmen, it was accurate at up to four times the effective firing range of the British Brown Bess. The long rifle wreaked havoc on British troops and damaged their morale.

In October a British naval force spitefully burned the town of Falmouth (now Portland, Maine), turning 150 houses and businesses into ashes. The British threatened that Portsmouth was next, and that if the American army attacked the British in Boston, the city would get the same treatment from warships in the harbor. War was a rough game, and Britain had been at it for a long, long time.

By then John Adams was back in Philadelphia with the Continental Congress and faced with an overwhelming agenda. Washington sent a lengthy packet of requests by messenger weekly, and sometimes more often. He needed everything, he said, from weapons to uniforms, shoes, food, tents, and other military paraphernalia. Congress would have to appropriate and acquire it all; there was no quartermaster nor any ordnance departments.

Artillery for the army was desperately needed. The militia had acquired a few smaller cannons, but nothing that could command Boston Harbor or the town itself. Then a minor miracle occurred. At the outbreak of hostilities a hundred Vermont Green Mountain Boys (who had organized to protect property rights) proposed a raid on Fort Ticonderoga, a British installation at the north end of Lake Champlain that guarded the approaches to the St. Lawrence River. On May 10 the group, led by Ethan Allen, rowed across the lake, scaled the unguarded ramparts at dawn, and with the help of another Patriot fighter, Benedict Arnold (who also had plans to take the fort), captured the entire British garrison without a shot being fired. It was a terrific feat of arms—not least because the fort contained fifty-six cannon and fourteen heavy mortars (a few weighing 5,000 pounds) along with an immense store of shot and gunpowder.

When Washington learned of the cache, he deputized twenty-five-year-old Henry Knox, a Boston bookseller who had left his business behind to join the Patriot cause, to go to Ticonderoga, retrieve the artillery, and bring it back to Boston. Knox left on November 17, 1775. Over the course of the next two and a half months, in sometimes thawing and sometimes freezing New England weather, Knox and his small company of men hauled the 60 tons of ordnance across frozen lakes and a partially frozen Hudson, up and down mountains, on miserable trails and roads, through swamps and heaths. At last on January 25, 1776, Knox presented Washington with the "noble train of artillery."

Washington wasted little time. When all of Knox's ordnance had arrived and trained men sought out to man it, he laid his plan. On the night of March 4 he ordered 3,000 soldiers, armed with pickaxes and shovels, to move silently up Dorchester Heights, a commanding position overlooking Boston Harbor. By the light of the moon, they constructed fortifications and embrasures for the cannons, despite the fact that the ground was frozen 18 inches deep. By dawn they were done and trudged back downhill. They were replaced by a fresh 3,000 infantrymen and cannoneers.

General Gage had been ordered back to England, and General William Howe, who now commanded the British forces, studied the new American fortifications with his spyglass. "My God, these fellows have done more work in one night than I could make my army do in three months," he said sourly. After due consultation, Howe decided to attack this new insult to his military prowess. All day Royal Navy ships were loaded at Boston's wharfs with men and arms for a dawn assault on Dorchester Heights. But right at dusk the wind picked up precipitously, and by dawn a full northeast gale was howling through the ships' riggings. It blew all day and the next, making any attempt to land troops below the heights a practical impossibility.

While the gale blew itself out, Howe had the opportunity for some sober thinking. He had led the charge and seen the slaughter at Bunker and Breed's Hills. Now there were all these black cannon muzzles staring him in the face across the crest of the heights. Could he send men into that? The answer became clear—but at the same time he realized he could no longer remain where he was. His troops were down to eating weevily biscuits and rancid bacon, thanks to the siege and the depredations on British transports by American privateers. Howe was embroiled in a stalemate; the Americans couldn't get at him, nor he at them. It was maddening. He made a decision he knew would be vastly unpopular at home: he decided to evacuate Boston.

Word of this was sent to Washington, with the warning that if the Americans contested the redcoat evacuation, the entire city would be burned to the ground. For Washington it was a pure Hobson's choice: he could kill or capture a lot of British soldiers but at what price? The total destruction of Boston? Washington let Howe and his army go in peace, along with more than a thousand Boston Tories. On March 17 a hundred British ships sailed out of Boston Harbor, headed ignominiously for Halifax, Nova Scotia, to reprovision.

WHILE WASHINGTON was dealing with the British army, John Adams had thrown himself into the work of the Congress, trying to divine by trial and error the best ways to invent a system of government for a democratic republic. Philadelphia was alive with the rites of spring, and the streets were decorated with Maypoles, gaily adorned with dogwood blossoms, tulips, cherry blossoms, hyacinths. Maypole celebrations were ancient, dating possibly from the time of the Druids; they had long been banned in New England for their pagan origins, but Adams felt uplifted by their cheery exuberance. "My mind is overborne with Burdens," he wrote a friend in Boston. There were "cares" from everywhere, he complained—from New England, from all the colonies to the north and south, from Canada, from "all parts of Europe," from "innumerable Indian tribes," from colleagues. "It would be of some comfort to be pitied," he wailed, "but Avaunt ye Demons!"[64]

The colonies were more bound together now, Adams concluded, more ready to fight. With the British blockade extending all along the East Coast as far south as Savannah, Georgia, many Americans had become united by a shared fury at the actions of King George. Within Congress and among the people, the notion of independence had begun to gain traction, though it still unnerved moderates, or "accommodationists," and continued to perfectly horrify the Tories. Adams believed there were so many Tories in the mid-Atlantic that if Pennsylvania, New Jersey, and New York—and even Maryland and Delaware—were given a choice, they would side with Britain. They were prevented from this by their proximity to New England in the North and Virginia in the South. "I have seen all along my life such Selfishness, and Littleness," Adams wrote piously, "even in New England, and I tremble to think, although we are engaged in the best cause ever to be employed by the Human Heart, yet the prospect of success is doubtful, not for want of Power or of Wisdom, but of Virtue."

Adams was so convinced that complete independence from Great Britain was going to be the end result of the present conflict that he wanted to advertise the fact with a "declaration." For what purpose, demanded the moderates. A declaration would foreclose any chance for reconciliation with Britain. It would antagonize every monarch in Europe. It might produce anarchy within the colonies and lead to mob rule. They claimed that, at that very moment, a new British fleet was sailing for America bearing "peace commissioners" who would parley with the colonists over their grievances.

"Nonsense," answered John Adams. The die was cast, he said. The colonies must immediately construct their own government independent of the Crown and vote for independence by sending Liberty Party members to Congress. Many of the colonies asked Adams for advice on how to set up a colonial government. He gave it freely.

Congress, however, was unprepared for a Declaration of Independence at that time. Instead it issued a resolve, which set out aims and goals for how Congress should approach the Crown. Adams himself wrote the preamble: "Whereas his Britannic Majesty in common with the lords and commons of Great Britain [Parliament], has . . . excluded the inhabitants of these United Colonies from the protection of his Crown," and refused to answer their "humble petitions" for redress, and "the whole force of that kingdom . . . is to be exerted for the destruction of the good people of these colonies," all British government in America was rendered null and void, and the colonists would henceforth exert their own authority for "the defense of their lives, liberty, and properties against the hostile invasions and cruel depredations of their enemies."

Upon hearing this, the moderates went into a frenzy of disputation on the floor of the Continental Congress. By the time each had spoken his piece, it was late afternoon on May 15, 1776. A vote was taken. It was seven colonies to five in favor of the preamble and resolve, with Maryland abstaining. Adams had won. The path to independence had been set.

Three weeks later it arrived like a bolt from the blue, when Virginia's Richard Henry Lee rose on the statehouse floor and read from a piece of paper: "Resolved, that these United Colonies are, and of right ought to be, free and Independent States: that they are absolved of all allegiance to the British Crown; and that all political connection between them and the State of Great Britain is, and ought to be, totally dissolved."

That was about as plain as it could be put. Before any of the moderates could object, Adams seconded the resolution, and a horrendous debate began to rage. Three days later, when it was apparent the sides were hopelessly deadlocked, they agreed to postpone a vote until July. It was also agreed to draw up a Declaration of Independence, so that it wouldn't have to be "huddled up in a hurry by a few chiefs," if the independence faction prevailed.

A committee of five, led by John Adams, was selected to write the document. The other members were Thomas Jefferson, Benjamin Franklin, Roger Sherman, and Robert Livingston—the last two being moderates.

Adams and the liberty men believed they could carry a vote along the lines of the Resolves, but they understood at the same time that it wouldn't be enough. Any act of congress so monumental needed to be unanimous, or very close to it. They knew that any colony voting against independence could simply be excluded from the confederation—but that wouldn't do either. It would hamper military operations if it became necessary to cross one colony to aid another, and the British would obviously exploit such a fissure. Not only that, but the term "United Colonies" or "Independent States," as Lee had written, would become moot.

Adams offered the following colloquy to describe how Thomas Jefferson came to write the Declaration of Independence.

Jefferson: "You should do it."

Adams: "Oh, no!"

Jefferson: "Why will you not? You ought to do it."

Adams: "I will not."

Jefferson: "Why?"

Adams: "Reasons enough."

Jefferson: "What can be your reasons?"

Adams: "Reason first—You are a Virginian, and a Virginian ought to appear at the head of this business. Reason second—I am obnoxious, suspected, and unpopular. You are very much otherwise. Reason third—You can write ten times better than I can."

Jefferson: "Well, if you are decided, I will do as well as I can."

Adams: "Very well. When you have drawn it up, we will have a meeting."[65]

Jefferson produced the declaration in seventeen days. Adams and Franklin made minor changes, and the document was presented to Congress for debate. After more editing and trimming, the declaration was submitted to a vote. On the fourth day of July, 1776, Pennsylvania delegate John Dickinson and his moderate cohorts were absent by design. Each colony voted in favor of the Declaration of Independence except New York; its delegates had not received instructions on how to vote, but within days the New York Provincial Congress voted to support independence. Americans, by their own proclamation, were officially free of British rule. John wrote to Abigail that the date would be commemorated "as the Day of Deliverance," and that it would be "solemnized in Pomp and Parade with . . . Bonfires and Illuminations from one end of the Continent to the other from this time forward forever more."[66]

Even as Adams and other Patriots had pushed for independence in Philadelphia, Washington and his army had moved on to New York, anticipating an attack by the British fleet there. Another American army was assembling in upstate New York under Gen. Philip Schuyler and Gen. Horatio Gates. A third army under Gen. Charles Lee was organizing in Virginia and the Carolinas.

Howe's army, meanwhile, was sailing south for the attack Washington anticipated. The British commanding general hoped to destroy or capture the American army—or at the very least to drive it out of New York—so that the British could use the city as their base of operations. In fact, a fleet of seventy ships, including ships of the line, had recently been sighted from Sandy Hook, New Jersey. The fleet's commander, Adm. Richard Howe, was the brother of Gen. William Howe.

On August 27 Howe's army successfully attacked George Washington's army on Long Island, then moved up the island to Brooklyn. Washington had managed to save his army three days later by ferrying it across the East River in a foggy night operation. By November 16 the British had chased Washington and his army from New York City. The redcoats would occupy the city for the remainder of the war. "The situation is chilling on every side,"

Adams wrote. "Gloomy, dark, melancholy and dispiriting. Where and when will the light spring up."

Adams was furious at the poor showing of the American army, and the reports of cowardice, of desperate running away in the face of the enemy. "I am ashamed of the age I live in," he lamented.

As chairman of the Board of War, Adams instituted better incentives for the soldiers—cash bonuses, higher pay, and eventually free land—when (and if) the conflict were won. He also instituted a series of capital offenses for which a soldier could be punished, with cowardice at the top of the list. As many as forty American soldiers were put to death for these offenses during the war.

Adams then took a long leave of absence from the Continental Congress and vowed not to run again as a representative. He had been in Philadelphia for ten months, and his farm was going to seed. Abigail, with four children to raise, was frantic for his return. In his absence, she had not only to tend the children, but to oversee the hired man and his helper in running the farm.

John spent some time in Braintree, but he could not tear himself away from the momentous events in Congress, and in January 1777 he did go back as a delegate. Congress was then sitting in Baltimore, because following the American defeat at Brandywine the British had also occupied Philadelphia.

While in Congress in the fall of 1777, Adams heard the news of the American victory at Saratoga, and his spirits immediately soared. He saw it as the turning point of the war. He took another break from his congressional duties to return to his family in Braintree.

In late 1777 letters from Congress arrived in Braintree naming John Adams as the new emissary to France. He was instructed to persuade the French to come full force to the American cause against Great Britain. Abigail, needless to say, was distraught.

February was a daunting time to be on the North Atlantic in any year, but in 1778 it was particularly dangerous for Adams. British warships prowled the high seas, and if he was taken prisoner he faced the prospect of a noose around his neck. Nonetheless, he and his ten-year-old son John Quincy boarded the American frigate *Boston*, one of America's few warships. Constructed in a Massachusetts shipyard, it was 114 feet long, carried twenty-four guns, and was captained by Samuel Tucker of Marblehead, a no-nonsense skipper. His poorly trained crew, however, were undisciplined, not skilled at the guns, and, according to Adams, "some hardly [knew] the ropes"[67]—referring to the ship's rigging. Adams's presence aboard the *Boston* was cloaked in a veil of secrecy.

A driving snowstorm forced the *Boston* to wait for several days in Marblehead, but at last on February 17 it weighed anchor and set out for the open sea. Not only was this the Adamses' first time abroad, it was the first time father and son had been aboard a ship. Adams immediately set about to learn French, which he knew not a word of, from a lesson book. But on the first night at sea, the constant rolling of the ship caused nearly everyone to become seasick. For Adams, the onset of *mal de mer* made him aware of the unpleasant aromas aboard ship. "The Smoke and Smell of seacoal, the Smell of stagnant, putrid water, the Smell of the ship where the Sailors lay, or any other offensive Smell will increase the Qualminess," he wrote.[68]

The next morning three enemy ships were sighted ahead. One, the HMS *Apollo,* peeled off and chased the *Boston* for two days before giving up. During this time, Captain Tucker ordered the guns to be run out in case of an encounter with the enemy; that dramatically threw off the balance of the frigate. She was overgunned for her tonnage anyway, causing leaks to spring in the seams. The pumps had to be manned constantly night and day to keep her from sinking.

Later that evening the ship entered the Gulf Stream (Adams called it the Gulph Stream), and the captain rode it for three days, adding its five-knot current to the speed of the ship. "It would be fruitless for me to describe what I saw, heard, and felt," Adams moaned, "the waves, the wind, the ship, her motions, Rollings, Wringings, and Agonies—the Sailors, their countenances, language, and behavior. No man could keep upon his legs and nothing could be kept in its place . . . Wreck of every thing in all parts of the ship, Chests, Casks, Bottles &tc. No place or person was dry." They faced another full month at sea.[69]

In the midst of this initial torment a violent thunderstorm struck the ship. Lightning hit the ship's mainmast, electrocuting three sailors, one of whom "died three days later, raving mad." Shortly afterward another storm carried away the ship's main topmast. Adams was aware from others aboard, as well as the captain himself, that they had been, and were still, in danger, but he proudly told his diary that he found himself "perfectly calm," throughout it all. He was concerned, however, that he had brought John Quincy along, but he noted that his son bore the danger and discomfort "with a Manly Patience."[70]

Once out of the Gulf Stream, Adams began to wander around the ship making himself obnoxious. He found fault with practically everything and expressed his disappointments to Captain Tucker, who also bore Adams's onslaught with "Manly Patience." The ship, Adams noted, was not furnished with pistols, nor good spyglasses, and there was a general "inattention" and "relaxation of order and discipline" to everything. Neither the ship nor its crew were clean, Adams complained, and "The practice of profane cursing and swearing . . . prevails in the most abominable degree," by officers as well as sailors. To placate him, Captain Tucker gave Adams a present—a history of Paraguay—which he thought his officious passenger might find interesting (enough, possibly, to keep Adams occupied).[71]

This may have worked to some degree, but Adams persisted in his hectoring. Meals, he complained, were not served on a regular basis but were dependent upon the duties of the crew and also, apparently, the mood of the chief cook. Adams found this to be both disorderly and unhealthy. To serve victuals punctually, he said, "would be for the health, comfort, and spirit of the Men, and would greatly promote the business of the ship."[72]

Friday, February 27, turned up "calm," and "soft and warm as Summer." Captain Tucker ordered everyone below to bring up bedding, clothes, and other soggy things, including the sick, to dry out on the decks topside. The captain went down into the "Cock Pit . . . that Sink of Devastation and Putrefaction," Adams wrote, "in pursuance of the advice I gave him in the morning," and ordered all the hammocks brought up and aired out.

Meantime, the becalmed ship had become surrounded with schools of large black fish that the officers called "beneaters" — possibly bonitas—and the crew caught some for their dinner. Next day the captain showed Adams a maritime curiosity the crew identified as a Portuguese "Manowar," which were in large swarms about the ship. Adams stabbed one of them with his penknife and "it shrunk up almost to nothing."

Two weeks into the voyage a gentle breeze struck up, and the *Boston*'s sails billowed once more. Adams said he slept as "quietly and soundly as on my own bed at home." Captain Tucker used the occasion to make repairs to the masts caused by the storm.

Soon the wind picked up and blew steadily stronger. Seasickness took hold again. Adams complained to his diary that there was nothing to do, no conversation, no reading, only "Sky, Clouds, and Sea, then Seas, Clouds, and Sky." Captain Tucker ordered gunnery practice, followed by a "frolic" that included a dance on deck by the sailors and some kind of ceremony in which a number of them were powdered down with flour then soaked with buckets of cold seawater.[73]

On March 10, just when it seemed the boredom would last forever, a sail was sighted ahead. The *Boston* soon caught up with the ship, which turned out to be a fourteen-gun enemy privateer named the *Martha*. Her lookouts had seen the *Boston* only bows-on, not broadside, so they didn't yet realize she was a frigate.

Her gun ports open, *Martha* began firing at the *Boston*. Adams was watching from the quarterdeck when a shot tore right over his head and went through the mizzen yard. He found himself more surprised than alarmed. Captain Tucker ordered the frigate brought around broadside to send and receive fire. But as soon as the enemy skipper realized he was fighting a fully armed frigate, he immediately struck his colors and surrendered.

This was a great prize for Tucker and his crew. The captain looked up the *Martha* in his Lloyd's of London registry and found that she was worth £80,000 (roughly $10 million in today's dollars). Prize money for captured ships at the time was generally split proportionally among the captain, his admiral, the ship's officers, and the remaining crew. Different nations had different rules and portions.

Tucker dispatched *Martha* back to Boston under command of some of his officers. The *Boston* was nearing the French coast now, and Tucker ran down several other vessels in hopes of making another prize, but the ships turned out to be French. When the Americans entered the Bay of Biscay, the French and Spanish coasts loomed on the horizon at last. They turned up the Bordeaux River, where navigation was difficult, and by the evening of March 28 they were becalmed. Dozens of small shorebirds—and larks among them—took up residence in the *Boston*'s rigging. One of the men produced a fiddle and started playing cheery tunes. The sailors began to dance, and Adams recorded that this "seemed to have a very happy Effect on their Spirits and good Humour."[74]

The next day they took on a French bar pilot, who helped navigate upriver to Bordeaux. The pilot announced that France had declared war on England the previous Wednesday. Adams was four days too late to accomplish his mission, but he didn't care. He was overjoyed to be near land again "after so long, so tedious and so dangerous a voyage." He marveled at the sights along the French shore; "The cattle, the Brattle Squares, &c. . . . It gives me a pleasing melancholy to see this Country, an Honor which a few months ago I never expected to arrive at—Europe, thou great Theater of Arts, Sciences, Commerce, War—am I at last permitted to visit thy territories—may the design of my Voyage be answered."

Adams was now an American minister to the Court of Louis XVI. What his duties would be remained to be seen, but he vowed to become less obnoxious.[75]

CHAPTER THREE

Thomas Jefferson was a true Renaissance man. He was a student of philosophy and law, a scientist, inventor, architect, musician, and lover of fine things—a man of vision. He was a planter, a Virginia gentleman, expert horseman, and owner of slaves. He was a brilliant writer and, as the new nation formed, he became an important politician. In that capacity, he was secretive, sly, and cunning. Then he became president and in many ways changed the course of the country.

When Thomas Jefferson was born on April 13, 1743, his birthplace, a plain wooden house in the shadow of the Southwest Mountains, sat near the edge of the western wilderness. Despite that, the boy was hardly a product of the raw frontier. He was the first son of Peter Jefferson, a tobacco planter and third-generation Virginian. Family lore had it that the first American Jeffersons were descended from a clan that lived at the base of Snowdon Mountain, the highest peak in Wales. But by the time Thomas was born, the Jeffersons were suitably English, living as they did under the benign rule of King George II.[76] Thomas's mother, Jane Randolph Jefferson, was a daughter of Virginia's entrenched colonial aristocracy and deeply proud of her English pedigree.

The Jefferson plantation, Shadwell, was a thousand-acre tract carved out of a vast wilderness where deer and bears roamed freely in the plentiful forests. The small town of Charlottesville was close by, yet Indian settlements were also not far off. In the distance to the west rose the Blue Ridge Mountains, which "shone in a summer sun like the rich hue of the ripe wild blue grape." The Rivanna River, a clear, fast-moving tributary of the James, cut through the Shadwell lands and provided a watery highway to transport hogsheads of tobacco downriver to the Chesapeake.

When Thomas was two or three, the family left Shadwell and moved south to the plantation of Jane's cousin William Randolph. He had died an untimely death, and his will stipulated that his "dear and loving friend Mr. Peter Jefferson do move down with his family to my Tuckahoe house and remain there till my son comes of age." Overlooking the James River, the elegant Tuckahoe was situated in the older, more refined Virginia Tidewater. Thomas's earliest recollection, he later said, was of a slave on horseback carrying him on a pillow from Shadwell to Tuckahoe.

Jane Jefferson and her children spent five years at Tuckahoe, but Peter returned often to the wilder lands he loved. A tall, well-muscled man in his mid-thirties, he impressed his friends and neighbors with prodigious feats of strength. Energetic and enterprising, he was, aside from a planter, a land surveyor of some repute and had established the western border between Virginia and North Carolina. This stupendously hard work required traveling across timber-strewn ridges and deep snake-infested ravines with streams so dreadful that Jefferson gave them names such as Purgatory and Styx; the last he described as so awful as "to strike terror in any human creature." He was celebrated for producing, along with his fellow surveyor Joshua Fry, the first accurate map of Virginia: the Fry-Jefferson map. As a sign of the respect he garnered, Jefferson was elected to the rank of colonel in the Virginia militia.

Like other Virginia planters, Peter Jefferson owned slaves to work his fields and tend his estate. Slavery had been a mainstay of colonial life for more than two hundred years and was practiced in varying degrees in all of the colonies. Over time, as Peter grew more prosperous, he acquired more land—and of course more slaves to work the land.[77]

THE SOCIETY INTO WHICH YOUNG THOMAS had been born was more established than that of the rest of the thirteen colonies. Virginia had been named in the late sixteenth century for Elizabeth, the Virgin Queen. But the first permanent European settlement in Virginia had not taken hold until 1607, when a small band of colonists had built a palisaded fort they called Jamestown after their king; they named the river it sat by the James as well. The early colonists had a rough time merely staying alive. By the mid-1600s the settlement had begun to thrive, thanks to the cultivation of a mild Caribbean tobacco that had led to a pipe-smoking craze all across Europe.

In 1619 a Dutch ship debarked the first African slaves at Jamestown, and the demand for more soon became voracious. In an age before machinery, cultivating large tobacco farms was labor intensive, and slavery became the solution to the need for manpower. By the end of the century Virginia was producing tons of the addictive weed for shipment to European pipe smokers and snuff addicts.

After the English Civil War placed Oliver Cromwell in power, many of the loyalists who had supported the beheaded King Charles I sailed for Virginia and the New World. These Cavaliers had fought and lost against Cromwell's Roundheads, and they brought with them their Cavalier identity—"children of Honor, well-borne and bred, with a clearer countenance and bolder look than other men." They blended easily into the colony's established church, the Church of England. They took advantage of the riches tobacco cultivation promised, and were given to good food, drink, and conversation. They saw themselves in direct contrast to the Puritans of New England, whom they disparaged as humorless, dour, Calvinist yeomen who worked small farms and were not loyal to the king.

The tobacco-planting culture spread north and west from Virginia's Tidewater and soon reached the rich-soiled Piedmont, where the Jeffersons' Shadwell was located. By the early eighteenth century some of the early colonial families—the so-called First Families of Virginia—had become astonishingly wealthy. In addition to their elegant plantation homes along the Tidewater's abundant rivers they built had fine town houses in Williamsburg, which had become the colonial capital. There was much socializing and frequent dinners and dances. Soon a kind of colonial aristocracy took root.

According to Jefferson's first biographer, Henry Randall:

> *The . . . aristocracy of Virginia resembled . . . [that] of the mother country. Numbers of them were highly educated and accomplished, by foreign study and travel; and nearly all . . . obtained an excellent education at William and Mary College . . . As a class they were intelligent, polished in manners, high*

> *toned and hospitable . . . Their winters were often spent with gaieties and festivities of the provincial capital; their summers, when not connected to the public service, principally in supervising their immense estates, in visiting each other, and in such amusements as country life afforded. Among the latter, the chase [fox hunting] held a prominent place. Born almost to the saddle and to the use of firearms, they were keen hunters; and when the chase was over they sat round groaning boards [British slang for dining tables or feasts] and drank confusion [bad luck] to Frenchmen and Spaniards abroad, and Roundhead and Prelatist [government by Catholic officials] at home.*[78]

Thomas Jefferson's paternal grandfather hadn't been part of this aristocracy, but neither was he poor. With hard work and a good marriage he had gained the status of gentry, which gave his son Peter a better than average chance to become a Virginian of note.

As the eldest son of a successful planter, Thomas did not want for anything nor have to do physical work, though he was expected, as his father before him, to do his civic duty. While Peter's education had been, in his own words, "much neglected," he was determined to rectify that with Thomas. By age five the boy was enrolled at the local English school and at nine he was learning French and the rudiments of Latin and Greek from a Scottish clergyman. Around this time Peter moved the family back to Shadwell, which he had enlarged and refined, adding numerous outbuildings, including barns, a dairy, and a smokehouse.

About five years later, when Thomas was fourteen, Peter Jefferson was struck down by an unspecified illness, leaving his eldest son, for all intents and purposes, the man of the house.

The death was of course a devastating blow, and Thomas had few besides his teachers he could turn to for advice. By then the family had grown to two sons and six daughters. (We know little of Thomas's relations with his mother, because in 1770 Shadwell was mostly destroyed by fire, and all the correspondence along with it.[79])

Despite his father's death, Thomas continued his studies under the instruction of a Reverend Maury, who taught him advanced Latin, Greek, and the classics, which had a profound effect on the young, scholarly boy. At seventeen Jefferson entered the College of William and Mary in Williamsburg.[80] At nearly six feet two inches—very tall for his day—he had strawberry blond hair, blue eyes, and light skin that freckled. He had learned to dance the minuet and Virginia reel, though clumsily, but he was accomplished at the violin.

Thomas stayed in college two years under the tutelage of Dr. William Small, a Scottish mathematician who, Jefferson ruminated, "probably fixed the destines of my life." He consumed with pleasure Homer, Horace, Virgil, Demosthenes, Cicero, Epictetus, Tacitus, Plutarch, and others. Of the moderns, he read Fielding, Smollett, Sterne, Shakespeare, Dryden, Pope, Moliere, and the philosophers Locke, Hobbes, Descartes, and Hume.

Jefferson and Dr. Small became closely attached, with the older man enthusiastically sharing his expertise in philosophy, metaphysics, mathematics, ethics, rhetoric, and belles lettres. Dr. Small also introduced the young scholar to Virginia's popular royal governor Francis Fauquier, and to a law professor, George Wythe, who would loom large in Jefferson's life until his remaining days.[81]

Jefferson spent the then typical two years at William and Mary, after which he stayed on in the colonial capital to "read the law" under Wythe's supervision. In 1767 Wythe sponsored the twenty-four-year-old Jefferson as a member of the Virginia bar. He still had to be examined by a three-man panel to be admitted, but in the meantime he continued his social relationships with Wythe and Governor Fauquier, including regular attendance at balls given in the Governor's Palace.

Around that same time Jefferson also plunged headlong into the leading element of a young man's fancy: he fell in love. Sixteen-year-old Rebecca Burwell was an orphan under the care of her uncle by marriage; her aristocratic father had once been Virginia's acting governor. Jefferson had apparently met her at one of the dances at the Apollo Room in the Raleigh Tavern, which, along with the Governor's Palace, was a Williamsburg center of socializing for Virginia's gentry. How often Thomas and Rebecca encountered one another isn't known, but Jefferson told friends he was determined to "have a word with her." What exactly that meant is also not known, but one might presume it was more than casual conversation.

Jefferson was shy around women—inept, in fact—and instead of approaching his beloved in writing—his strongest suit—he apparently fumbled for words and in a stammering voice said he needed to go to England but would speak to her "at some later time." These apparently were not the things Miss Burwell wished to hear, because within a few months she became engaged to and married a wealthy, slightly older man.[82]

Jefferson was heartbroken for a while, but the study of law for the bar exam gave him solace. He plunged into legal commentaries by the English jurists Coke and Blackstone—he preferred the plain language of Coke to Blackstone's "honeyed" phrases. Though he complained at times of being thrown into the company of "card-players, horse-racers, fox hunters, and rum drinkers," Jefferson occasionally indulged in the activities himself.[83] At other times he extolled the virtues of the town. He regularly attended sessions of the House of Burgesses to hear speakers such as Peyton Randolph and the captivating Patrick Henry; Jefferson heard him speak out forcibly against the Stamp Act on May 30, 1765.

This might have been Jefferson's first acquaintance with the notion of disobedience of, or at least resistance to, the Crown and Parliament. The Stamp Act was so all-encompassing that the colonists' outrage was palpable. Every document was to be taxed—birth certificates, school graduation certificates, mortgages, deeds, insurance policies, bills of lading, newspapers, pamphlets, books, bonds, liquor licenses, legal contracts, advertisements, playing cards, dice, and death certificates. From the cradle to the grave nothing was spared.

The hated stamps arrived in Williamsburg in the custody of the new stamp agent, Colonel Mercer, who was—or at least had been—a well-liked and respected member of the gentry. Carrying the stamps in a large box, Mercer brought them to Governor Fauquier, who was sitting on the porch of Charlton's, Williamsburg's coffeehouse, entertaining several high-ranking politicians. An angry group of prominent citizens followed behind the embarrassed Colonel Mercer, grumbling and occasionally shouting threateningly.

The governor had concluded that the Stamp Act was unenforceable and now realized the scene could turn ugly. He told Mercer to follow him, and they set off for the Governor's Palace through the crowd, which parted amid murmurs and mutters. But there was no violence as there had been in Boston, where the lieutenant governor's house was destroyed and his papers scattered to the winds. Mercer quickly resigned as stamp agent. No one else wanted the job.

Whether Jefferson was in town to observe this is unknown. But he surely learned of it quickly enough—for these were the first stirrings of outright defiance among Virginians, who had once been unquestioning and loyal subjects of the Crown.

By then, Jefferson was enjoying the life of a country squire. He and Dabney Carr—his close friend, college classmate, and cousin—frequently rode together in the Piedmont and sometimes climbed to the top of a small mountain on Jefferson's inherited land. Here, Jefferson would describe his plans for making a home with the finest gardens in Virginia. They often rested under a magnificent oak tree and once swore a promise that when either died, the other would see him buried beneath it. In 1765 Carr married Jefferson's sister Martha, which pleased Jefferson immensely.

In 1767 Jefferson successfully passed his Virginia bar examination and was admitted to practice law. His specialty was what today would be called real estate law but was then known as land cases. He also found time to take several cases in which slaves sought their freedom, but he found resistance to this by the courts. In one case a slave was seeking his freedom on grounds that his grandmother was a mulatto and under the law he was required to give servitude only until the age of thrity-one. "Everyone comes into this world with a right to his own person," Jefferson argued to the court. "This is what is called personal liberty, and is given [to] him by the author of nature . . . Under that law, we are all born free," he told the startled judge, who refused to hear any more such talk and ruled against Jefferson's client.

As the Jefferson biographer Dumas Malone points out, "That he [Jefferson] had come to such a philosophical position by the time this case was adjudged in 1770 is a significant item in the history of his thought."

The year before, Jefferson had been elected by his citizens in Albemarle County to represent them in the Virginia House of Burgesses. He introduced an act that would allow masters to govern the emancipation of their slaves rather than having to ask permission from the courts and royal officers, but this was met with strong opposition and the legislation went nowhere.

In 1768 Jefferson began work on his Italianate home atop the mountain he and Carr often visited. He called it Monticello—in Italian, "Little Mountain." He designed the residence himself, using plain geometry, along the lines of the sixteenth-century architect Palladio. The home would eventually be the crowning feature of his 5,000-acre estate, built by the labor of local masons, carpenters, and Jefferson's own slaves. To facilitate construction, and probably just to be closer to the breathtaking views, Jefferson had the workmen build a small bachelor's quarters on the property, where he intended to spend most of his free time.

Along with guiding work on the Monticello home and gardens, Jefferson immersed himself in the books he had begun collecting. Aside from the philosophers, scientists, novelists, and other thinkers who had always appealed to him, he gravitated to the cluster of ideas known as the Enlightenment. This great intellectual revolution had begun as a pattern of novel thoughts and notions dating to the previous century and to Sir Isaac Newton. The Enlightenment thinkers sought to throw off the superstitions, delusions, misconceptions, and blind faith to popes and kings that had ruled Western thought since the Middle Ages and replace them with a world governed by science, logic, and humanity. Among the leading Enlightenment practitioners in the American colonies was Dr. Benjamin Franklin of Philadelphia. Jefferson became infatuated with the movement and remained an earnest adherent for the rest of his life.

In the parlance of later generations, Jefferson was a Renaissance man. He was roundly read in the humanities and sciences of his day. He was a profound thinker and lover of fine music. He thrived on intellectual conversation with convivial friends, and his tastes gravitated to excellent, expensive things. He collected fossils, including the jawbone of a great woolly mammoth found in Kentucky. He designed his own furniture. He was an amateur botanist and astronomer. He was respected enough by his peers to be reelected to the Virginia House of Burgesses and was known to be a first-rate lawyer and highly competent planter. He was kind and generous to his slaves. If that sounds like an incongruity, it must be remembered that Jefferson was still a man of his times.

While Jefferson was constantly curious, socially charming, and comfortably wealthy, he was also lonely. There had been no more attempts at romance after the disastrous business with Rebecca Burwell—until sometime in the early months of 1770, when Thomas Jefferson once more fell in love.

Martha Wayles Skelton—Patty—was the daughter of John Wayles, a lawyer who, like many lawyers at the time, had actually made his fortune as a planter, slave trader, and debt collector. His wife had died giving birth to Patty, and he twice remarried, only to lose those wives as well. Patty had herself been married briefly before, but both her husband and her four-year-old son had died. She was again living on her father's Tidewater plantation, the Forest, when Jefferson met her. He was immediately enthralled, extolling her as "distinguished for her beauty, her accomplishments, and her solid merit . . . Her complexion was brilliant—her large expressive eyes of the richest shade of hazel—her luxuriant hair of the finest tinge of auburn. She walked, rode, and danced with admirable grace and spirit—sung and played the spinet and harpsichord . . . with uncommon skill . . . She also was well read and intelligent; conversed agreeably, possessed excellent sense and a lively play of fancy; and had a frank, warm-hearted, and somewhat impulsive disposition." Jefferson had found his perfect match.[84]

As a gift for Patty, he ordered a fine piano built, "with plenty of extra strings." The two talked, danced, drank wine, and Jefferson played his violin. He was twenty-eight and Patty twenty-three; they married on New Year's Day 1772 in her father's home.

After the wedding, Jefferson hurried Patty off in a carriage for Monticello. It had begun to snow lightly as they left the Wayles estate, and by the time they reached Charlottesville they were battling a blizzard. Jefferson recorded that the snow was three feet deep as they tried to climb the mountain. They abandoned the carriage and rode its horses up mountain trails, where the treetops had mitigated the amount of snowfall.

They arrived at Monticello right after sundown. It was "horribly dreary," as the only habitable building was Jefferson's bachelor's quarters, which he called the South Pavilion. The fires were out, the servants had gone, but they found part of a bottle of wine and for the young newlyweds the night was lit "in song, and merriment, and laughter." Nine months later Patty bore a daughter, Martha (called Patsy).

The year after their marriage, Patty's father died, bequeathing her 135 slaves and from 3,000 to 11,000 acres of land, depending on various accounting. A considerable inheritance, it doubled Jefferson's worth and holdings since in those times husbands mostly controlled their wives' inheritance. But along with the wealth, Jefferson also inherited Wayles's debts, which came to an unsettling £3,749.12—more than half a million dollars in today's value. This debt would nag Jefferson to the end of his life.

Despite the debt, the early years of his marriage were by far the happiest period of Jefferson's life. Work on Monticello continued apace, and Jefferson continued to acquire the fine things he enjoyed—exquisite silver settings, magnificent European furniture, carpets from Paris and Persia. Patty supervised the entertaining and the cuisine, reading out recipes for particular dishes to the kitchen cooks and help.

An excellent horseman, Jefferson always kept a stable of fine-blooded animals, many of them named out of antiquity or after celestial bodies: Cucullin, the General, Caractacus, Wildair, Tarquin, Diomede, Arcturus, Jacobin, Castor, Eagle. Riding was a solitary tonic to Jefferson, and he nearly always went out alone, without the company of the servant that usually accompanied most Virginia gentlemen.

The gardens at Monticello were coming together nicely, as Jefferson noted in his Garden Book, a lifelong record of his agriculture. He planted cherry, peach, almond, apple, and plum trees in the orchards. He tried numerous varieties of peas, beans, and greens. There were cabbages, radishes, and parsley. He plucked apricots. There was lettuce, carrots, Siberian wheat, corn, potatoes, and rice in the meadow. Celery, asparagus, lentils, broccoli, spinach, and beets pushed up the soil in the gardens.

He planted several varieties of raspberries and strawberries, as well as turnips, peppers, squash and pumpkins, and a profusion of melons. There were also elaborate grape vineyards that produced a respectable wine.

Inevitably, there were insects and other pests to contend with, as well as funguses and blights—and the unexpected. For example, this from his Garden Book on May 4, 1774: "The blue ridge of mountains covered with snow," followed by this frustrated entry the next day: "A frost which destroyed almost everything. It killed the wheat, rye, corn, many tobacco plants, and even large saplings. The leaves of the trees were entirely killed. All the shoots of vines. At Monticello nearly half the fruit of every kind was killed; and before this no instance had ever occurred of any fruit killed here by frost. In all other places in the neighborhood the destruction of fruit was total. This frost was . . . equally destructive . . . [in] the neighboring colonies."

THE STORM THAT BROUGHT THE KILLING FROST was a temporary distraction from the greater storm that had been building over the colonies since the 1765 Stamp Act. There had been a splendid, almost grateful, sense of relief and satisfaction when Parliament repealed that detested act—but it was short-lived. The colonists had concluded that their protests, both formal and informal, had gained an ear across the Atlantic, and that England was complaisant to their grievances. They soon found otherwise. The subsequent Townshend Duties—British taxes on sugar, paper, tea, and other commodities—led to the Boston Tea Party. Instead of backing off, this time England doubled down. A

British fleet soon blockaded Boston Harbor and the town was garrisoned by redcoats.

These events were watched in Virginia with growing consternation and alarm. The notion festered that if Great Britain could strong-arm *one* of its colonies, it could do the same to all of them. Virginians—Thomas Jefferson included—considered themselves Loyalists. The idea of separating from the mother country was anathema to them. But protests, peaceful or otherwise, were being met by force. In Boston Paul Revere, Samuel Adams, and other Sons of Liberty talked revolution and separation. But Virginians as a group were not yet ready to cross that vast, dark chasm.

That said, Thomas Jefferson, like some of his fellow lawmakers, had begun to contemplate the nature of tyranny, which he declared "wrong in theory and generally stupid in practice." King George III, Jefferson concluded, had become a tyrant.[85]

When Virginia's governing body, the House of Burgesses, met to discuss the dreadful situation in Massachusetts, they were thwarted by the new British governor. The much-admired Governor Fauquier had died, as had his successor, the courtly and pleasant Baron de Botetourt. His replacement was the dour, tone-deaf Lord Dunmore, a fatuous Scotsman and stooge of the English king. At the first sign of dissension Dunmore dissolved the burgesses—which, under English law, he had the right to do. This merely gave Virginians pause to consider how the Crown was violating their rights. And the more pause they took, the more they realized that they had no rights other than what the king was willing to grant.

When Dunmore dissolved them, the burgesses left the Capitol and reconvened in nearby Williamsburg's Raleigh Tavern, where an altogether different association was born: the committee of correspondence. Its aim was to communicate by letters and other means with its counterparts in the other colonies. This was the first formal manifestation of a united front against British tyranny in the American colonies.

Jefferson then called for a further action, which may seem mild by contemporary standards but which was received throughout Virginia, according to him, "like a shock of electricity, arousing every man and placing him erect and solidly on his centre." He called for divine intervention against the tyranny being visited upon the Americans, putting forward the idea of a day of prayer and fasting; this was adopted by the other burgesses, with the effect of "translating the local grievance of Boston into a common cause."

More and more, Jefferson became convinced that self-government in the colonies was far better than tyranny from abroad. His chief concern in the fateful year 1774 was to preserve self-government as it presently existed—and was currently being threatened by representatives of the British Crown.[86]

In July Jefferson produced a heated paper, *A Summary View of the Rights of British America,* which soon circulated as a widely read pamphlet both in the colonies and in England. Though Jefferson was not listed as author, it became known that he had written the elegant repudiation of Parliament's authority over British Americans. Before long it "gained wider currency than any other writing of his that was published during the Revolution except the Declaration [of Independence], and it clearly anticipated that more famous and polished document."[87] George Washington bought a copy, as did John Adams, who called it "a very handsome public paper." In short *A Summary View* put Thomas Jefferson on the map.[88]

Jefferson quickly became a champion of the Patriots in Virginia and throughout the colonies. The colonists should remain loyal to the king, Jefferson asserted. But unlike the relationship between England and Scotland, Parliament had denied representatives from the American colonies to join them, while at the same time taxing, bullying, and subjugating them, most recently with the Intolerable Acts (the Townshend Duties). "The true ground on which we declare these acts void," Jefferson wrote, "is that the British Parliament has no right to exercise its authority over us." But the heart of the paper was this gem: "The God who gave us life gave us liberty at the same time, the hand of force may destroy [the colonies], but cannot disjoin them." Philosophical in nature, it was also breathtaking in concept to Americans, who had had drummed into them from childhood that they were the subjects of an all-powerful British monarch.[89]

From September 5 to October 26, 1774, the First Continental Congress met in Philadelphia to consider what measures to take against the actions of Great Britain. Though Jefferson was not a delegate, the congress did vote for a nonimportation, nonconsumption resolution, meaning a total boycott of British goods. The mechanism for the congress to pass actionable bills was severely limited, Jefferson thought, and it was his conviction that a stronger body of deliberation should have been formed.

THROUGHOUT 1774 AND INTO THE SPRING OF 1775, matters festered in Boston and elsewhere as the British government applied pressure to bring the colonies back in line. In Virginia and elsewhere, militias were strengthened and drilled in case war came.

Military stores were hoarded. Assemblies and committees met frequently throughout the colonies to keep tabs on the increasingly tense situation. More and more citizens were convinced that Great Britain would have to be dealt with by force.

In March 1775 the Continental Congress called on each colony to supply troops to form a Continental Army. King George forbade the congress from meeting but the order was ignored. A convention was formed in Virginia, to which Jefferson was named a member. Its one hundred delegates met at St. John's Anglican Church, perched on a hillside in Richmond. This port upriver on the James was little more than a settlement at the time, but beyond the reach of Lord Dunmore, who continued seizing arms and powder from the citizens and breaking up their assemblies.

The delegates sat through various preliminaries. Then Patrick Henry rose and called on the colony to prepare for war. In what became the most celebrated speech in American history, Henry thundered, "Gentlemen may cry Peace, Peace—but there is no peace. The war is actually begun! I know not what course others may take, but as for me, give me liberty, or give me death!"

A hush came over the delegates, then cheering erupted and continued at length. Jefferson called the speech "sublime beyond imagination." A man named Carrington, listening outside the church window, requested that he be buried on the spot where he was standing when Henry gave his oration, and his wish was honored. The delegates voted to supply soldiers and arms, and Jefferson was named to the committee to work out the details.

When word spread in the spring of 1775 of the encounter in the Massachusetts countryside that produced the "shot heard round the world," there was consternation among those Americans appalled at the idea of an all-out war with Britain. To meet the emergency, the Second Continental Congress was convened in May in Philadelphia. This time, Thomas Jefferson attended as a Virginia delegate. History was now fast in the making.

The "olive branch" was duly composed, sent, received, and ignored by George III. That left little room for further negotiations, but some members thought otherwise. The thirty-six-year-old king had been on the throne for fifteen years and seemed weary of his ungrateful subjects across the Atlantic. Besides, he had been felled for several months with an incapacitating skin disease that at times rendered him insensible. His doctors frequently bled him as a cure, which likely made him even more insensible.

In August 1775 Jefferson departed Philadelphia and returned to Monticello, where he intended to spend a blissful period with his wife, enjoying his new home, uplifting music, and fine wine. He looked forward to it as a great restorative for his soul. Instead, he returned to his beloved Martha, who had been in ill health, and to the extraordinary and alarming news that Governor Dunmore had decreed that any slave who left his master and joined the British in the fight against the Patriots would thereafter be free. To the colonists, this sounded as if the governor was authorizing a slave uprising that would bring terror and massacres to the state.

Then on March 31, 1776, Jefferson's mother died of a stroke at age fifty-six. Jefferson had her buried at Monticello. Jane Jefferson's death caused him such grief that for a period of weeks he was unable to write, read, or do much of anything else, but he ultimately pulled himself out of his depression. In June he returned to Philadelphia, where the Second Continental Congress was once more in session with the same burning issue: should the colonies break off with England for good or try again to negotiate a solution?

Weeks of debate ensued, with no conclusion except that a final vote would be put off until the beginning of July 1776. In the meantime, some kind of declaration of independence would be drawn up, in case the vote went for independence. Jefferson was appointed to a five-man committee to draft this declaration.

In his autobiography Jefferson observed that in the case of independence being declared, an American ambassador should at once sail for France and other European nations to solicit alliances against England; a strong, properly expressed declaration of America's intentions would go a long way in persuading other nations. "A declaration of independence alone," he wrote, "could render it consistent with European delicacy for European powers to treat with us, or even to receive an Ambassador from us."[90]

Jefferson's fellow committee members had no interest in drafting the declaration, and initially neither did Jefferson, in part because he was focused on a convention taking place in Virginia that summer. Like all of the colonies, Virginia was rushing to replace its old colonial charter with a new state constitution; Jefferson took it upon himself to write one and sent it forth. And then, reluctantly, he turned to drafting a declaration for all the colonies.

He had roughly three weeks to compose the document that would become so famous. He had taken rooms in a handsome building owned and constructed by a Philadelphia bricklayer. Across the hall from his bedroom was a small drawing room where he kept his writing desk, which he had designed himself. There, Jefferson set about composing the famous words. From his intensive study of Enlightenment thinking and his own legal and historical mind, he worked to create a statement of what *liberty* really meant. Jefferson explained later in his autobiography that the job was "not to find out new principles or new arguments . . . but to place before mankind the common sense of the subject." The Declaration, he said, was "intended to be an expression of the human mind."[91]

From time to time throughout history various peoples had agreed to form some sort of democracy or republic. Yet too often humans were governed instead by monarchs and despots. Now, many among Jefferson's own fellow colonists were contemplating the need to leave the grip of the British monarch and develop a new and separate country governed as a democratic republic. Just how that would work no one could say—but the leaving part first had to be accomplished. Jefferson chose his words carefully.

"When in the course of human events, it becomes necessary for one people to dissolve the political bands which have connected them with another, and to assume, among the powers of the earth, the separate and equal station to which the Laws of Nature and of Nature's God entitle them, a decent respect to the opinions of mankind requires that they should declare the causes which impel them to the separation.

"We hold these truths to be self-evident, that all men are created equal, that they are endowed by their creator with certain unalienable Rights, that among these are Life, Liberty, and the pursuit of Happiness. That to secure these rights, governments are instituted among men, deriving their just powers from the consent of the governed. That whenever any form of Government becomes destructive of these ends, it is the Right of the People to alter or to abolish it, and to institute a new Government, laying its foundation on such principles and organizing its powers in such form as to them shall seem most likely to effect their Safety and Happiness."

Jefferson went on to note that such changes or separations from long-established governments should not be taken lightly. He included a lengthy indictment of the king, citing such abuses as closing colonial courts and legislative offices and sending an army to suppress the citizens of Boston. "He has plundered our seas, ravaged our coasts, burnt our towns, and destroyed the lives of our people," Jefferson wrote. In addition, the king was guilty of cutting off American trade, imposing taxes without consent, and a host of other transgressions, which, Jefferson wrote, absolved the United States "from All Allegiances to the British Crown." He concluded that, "for the support of this Declaration, with a firm reliance on the protection of Divine Providence, we mutually pledge to each other our Lives, our Fortunes, and our Sacred Honor."[92]

After some debate and some changes, the Declaration of Independence was adopted and on July 4 announced to the public. In August it was signed by fifty-two delegates, most conspicuously by John Hancock, president of the Continental Congress at the time. His outsized signature stands as the ultimate symbol of rebellion.

Jefferson in his autobiography was droll in the momentous events of that summer, writing simply that "The declaration was signed . . ." John Adams was more enthusiastic. In Philadelphia, he wrote, "The bells pealed all day long and most of the night."

WHILE JEFFERSON WAS IN PHILADELPHIA that historic summer, Patty apparently had suffered a miscarriage. Jefferson was initially beside himself with the desire to go to her at once—but he knew that if he did, it would leave Virginia without the requisite number of delegates in the Continental Congress. He implored his friend Richard Henry Lee to come to Philadelphia and take his place. But until that happened, Jefferson was stuck in Pennsylvania.

On September 9 the Continental Congress officially adopted the name United States of America, to replace the former United Colonies. Jefferson had left Philadelphia the previous week, finally able to return to his family. Once back in Virginia, he found Patty on the mend and his daughter Patsy about to celebrate her fourth birthday. Knowing that he needed to confer with a great many people about the new state constitution, Jefferson moved his family to Williamsburg, where the politicians and great minds congregated. The British-conceived House of Burgesses had been abolished; Virginia's laws were now made in the General Assembly, of which Jefferson was a member.

Jefferson approached the new government with a blizzard of bills, some of which departed radically from existing British law. In particular, he attacked the law of primogeniture. A leftover from England's baronial past, it mandated that large landowners leave all of their inheritance to a single heir—for the most part, to the eldest son. The English had employed this law in order to maintain an aristocracy of great wealth, power, and continuity, and Jefferson—even though he, himself, was the heir to his father's estates—felt that a British-style aristocracy had no place in the newly minted American democracy.

He likewise sent up bills to reform the criminal justice codes and establish a public education system in Virginia. He also petitioned to have the state capital moved from Williamsburg to Richmond, because it would be more central to the growing population beyond the Tidewater. And he engaged in a long-standing effort to abolish the British Anglican Church as the sole legal religion in the state, so that "the Jew and the Gentile, the Christian and the Mohametan, the Hindoo, and the infidel of every denomination" would be free to practice their religion as they saw fit. The tax that Virginians paid to support the Anglican clergy would likewise be abolished.[93]

Jefferson also tackled the thorniest issue of the day head-on: the question of slavery. Despite Lord Dunmore's edict that any slave fighting for the king would be declared free, few slaves had (or had been able) to take him up on the offer; Dunmore had sailed back to England in any case in August 1776. Jefferson now proposed that all slaves "born after a certain date" be declared free and emancipated. Moreover, former slaves, "at a proper age," would be deported to Africa.

The notion that both races could coexist peacefully was beyond Jefferson's comprehension. "Nothing is more certain in the book of fate than that these people are to be free," he wrote, but added, "Nor is it less certain that the two races, equally free, cannot live in the same government.[94] Nature, habit, opinion," he went on, "has drawn indelible lines of distinction between them."

Jefferson explained that his proposal of emancipation and deportation would take place "peaceably, and in such a slow degree" that for white Virginians "the evil will wear off insensibly," and the places filled by former slaves would be "filled up by free white laborers."[95] But he warned that if his emancipation project was not accepted, "human nature must shudder at the prospect held up," referencing Spain's brutal deportation of the Moors (actually Christianized Moors by the early 1600s), which sparked violent rebellion.[96] But Jefferson's conception of ending slavery was an idea whose time had not yet arrived; this was still the case even at the end of his long, full life.

While Jefferson continued with his lawmaking bills, he and Patty lost another child in May 1777: an infant son who lived just seventeen days. Fifteen months later, another daughter, Mary, was born, and would be called Polly.

It was during this period that James Madison came to Jefferson's attention. Madison was twenty-five, Jefferson thirty-three; they made a somewhat curious pair, given that Madison came up only to Jefferson's chin and weighed less than 100 pounds. The scion of a wealthy Virginia tobacco planter, Madison had graduated from the College of New Jersey (now Princeton) and was also a member of the General Assembly. Gentle-spoken but firm, he became an indefatigable ally of Jefferson in a mutual friendship and political relationship that lasted a lifetime.

BY THE SUMMER OF 1780, it seemed inevitable that America would lose its war with Britain. The fighting had moved to the South, and the British had taken Savannah and Charleston. For all intents and purposes, they controlled Georgia and South Carolina, and the fighting was fierce in North Carolina. It was fairly obvious that Virginia was next, and in that grim atmosphere Thomas Jefferson began his second term as the state's governor. (He had been elected governor for a one-year term beginning in June 1779 then went on reluctantly to serve again.)

By the spring of 1781 Jefferson's official and personal troubles had become so great, according to his biographer Dumas Malone, that "even reading about them is painful." On April 15 Jefferson's daughter Lucy Elizabeth died at the age of five months. A month after her birth a British invasion force led by the American arch-traitor Benedict Arnold had sailed up the James to Richmond, capturing the city and burning many buildings.

Washington dispatched Lafayette, with his regulars and some Virginia militia, to help defend his home state, but the danger was far from over. Arnold and his forces hoped to join with Cornwallis's army, marching up through North Carolina. When the two forces combined, the British would have a 7,000-man army in Virginia. And the threat of another amphibious invasion along the many rivers that flowed between Virginia and the lower Chesapeake Bay always loomed.

To the west beyond the Blue Ridge the British had allied with Indian tribes and were attacking American settlements along the Ohio River in what was then western Virginia. Reports of their brutality reached Richmond, describing white babies "torn from their mother's arms and their brains beat out against trees."

With the specter of war hovering over his state, Jefferson did not know where to turn. Lafayette and his force of about 1,200 regulars and militia were no match for a large British force. The Virginia militia were not mustering in the face of the threat, and nothing seemed to move them.

Then, in May 1781, word reached the government that Cornwallis's army had entered Virginia, burning, pillaging, and plundering. In May Jefferson called a session of the General Assembly, directing that they meet not in Richmond but in the safer environs of Charlottesville. Jefferson himself took up residence at Monticello. On June 2, the last day of Jefferson's second term, the assembly was scheduled to vote on a new governor, but it was decided to delay the vote until June 4.

June 3, 1781, was a terrible day for the thirty-eight-year-old Jefferson. British soldiers were running rampant against the outnumbered Continentals, now commanded by both Lafayette and General von Steuben. Virginia's militia had all but disappeared, having either deserted their units or refused to respond to repeated call-ups. The state coffers were completely empty. Virginians throughout the state, many seeing the enemy in force close-up for the first time, were fearstruck and despondent.

With the political situation in collapse, Jefferson had declined to run for a third term. He was exhausted, wrung out by the crisis. He had pleaded with George Washington, who remained with the main Continental Army in New York, to come to Virginia and take charge, "to restore full confidence of the people."[97] But Washington would not leave New York, which he still hoped to take back from the British.

Cornwallis had moved his headquarters to Elk Hill, about 40 miles west of the new capital of Richmond. Jefferson had large holdings at Elk Hill, and Cornwallis approached them "in the spirit of total extermination," according to Jefferson. The Englishman, Jefferson said, "destroyed all my crops of corn and tobacco. He burned all my barns," which, in addition to last year's corn and tobacco, contained "great quantities of wheat, hemp, flax, cotton, barley, and 1,000 barrels of flour." The British carried off hundreds of head of cattle, sheep, and hogs and stole all of Jefferson's horses "capable of service; of those colts too young for service he cut their throats, and he burned all the fences on the plantation so as to leave it an absolute waste." The British also absconded with thirty of Jefferson's slaves. "Had this been done to give them their freedom he would have been right," Jefferson fumed, "but it was to consign them to inevitable death from small pox then raging in his camp. This I knew afterwards to have been the fate of 27 of them. I never had any news of the remaining three, but presume they shared the same fate." Jefferson recorded the name of each slave in his Farm Book.[98]

In early June Cornwallis had called for his favorite cavalry leader, Lt. Col. Banastre Tarleton, and about 250 of his dragoons to ride to Richmond or to wherever the Virginia legislature was meeting, disrupt the government, and arrest its leaders. Six months earlier, in January, Tarleton had suffered one of the worst British defeats of the war when the American general Daniel Morgan utterly outfoxed him at the Battle of Cowpens in South Carolina. "Butcher" Tarleton had lost nearly 80 percent of his command and was spoiling for revenge. He was known to be a severe if not brutal leader, accused by the Americans of slaughtering Continental soldiers when they tried to surrender during another battle, at Waxhaws. A thirteen-year-old courier at that battle was taken prisoner and viciously slashed about the head and wrist by one of Tarleton's raiders when he refused to shine the officer's boots. The boy's name was Andrew Jackson.

On Saturday, June 2, Tarleton's raiders, now scouring the Virginia countryside for Jefferson and other Virginia lawmakers, stopped for refreshments at a crossroads establishment with the outstanding name Tavern Cuckoo. They talked openly of capturing Thomas Jefferson at his famous aerie Monticello, which occupied a mountaintop not far away. Jack Jouett, a captain in the Virginia militia, happened to be near the tavern, and when the dragoons left on the road toward Charlottesville he followed them on a fast Thoroughbred. He knew the area well and took back roads and trails as he shadowed the British at a distance, believing they must be headed to capture the governor. When he saw a dozen soldiers break off from the main group and head toward the road up to Monticello, Jouett was once more able to outride them through the woods and mountain trails. Tree branches "cruelly lashed" his face, and the scars of his ride would remain with him for the rest of his life.

Just after dawn Jouett arrived at Jefferson's door to warn of the danger. Jefferson heard him out with no apparent sense of alarm and invited Jouett in for a glass of Madeira. The governor was entertaining two guests that morning at breakfast, the speakers of both houses of state government.

By all accounts Jefferson seemed unperturbed but sent these gentlemen off across the Blue Ridge to Staunton. Then he gathered his wife and their two daughters. He put them in a carriage with two of his servants and sent them to stay with friends at Blenheim Plantation. Next he went to his library and secured a number of important papers from a hiding place while he waited for his favorite horse, Caractacus, to be shod by a blacksmith on the property. Once that was done, he rode to a spot with a good vantage of Charlottesville and looked down at the town through his spyglass. The streets seemed quiet, and Jefferson wondered, as he rode away, if Jouett's warning hadn't been a false alarm.

He had not gone far when he discovered that, while kneeling to adjust his spyglass, his small walking sword (sword cane) had slipped from its sheath. He went back to the spot to retrieve it and as an afterthought took another look at the town. It was swarming with enemy cavalry.[99] Jefferson rode on toward Blenheim.

British dragoons had arrived at Monticello only five minutes after Jefferson left. Encountering Martin Hemings, Jefferson's personal servant, the dragoon captain pointed a pistol at him and demanded to know Jefferson's whereabouts, threatening to shoot if Hemings would not tell him. "Fire away, then," Hemings coolly replied, but the redcoat didn't shoot. Instead, the dragoons began searching the house. A second servant, Caesar, was huddled under the planks of the portico with hidden silver and other valuables. He stayed in that dark pit for eighteen hours, with neither food nor drink, while the British waited for the governor, thinking he might return.[100]

Jefferson did not return. He and his family took refuge at Poplar Forest, a large and isolated plantation he owned in rural Bedford County, about 70 miles south of Monticello. Much later his enemies would accuse him of cowardice for eluding the British and ridicule him for "fleeing in terror." It was untrue, of course, by any contemporary account. But even if he had fled who could blame him? Tarleton was not known for leniency toward rebellious American Patriots, especially not leaders such as Thomas Jefferson. If captured, Jefferson could have been shipped to a dungeon in the Tower of London, where other Patriot leaders languished—or even hanged.

Jefferson remained at Poplar Forest throughout the summer of 1781, until the danger passed. That occurred when George Washington finally marched his army down from New York to Virginia to take on Cornwallis in Yorktown. The Americans then drove Cornwallis and his redcoats toward oblivion there.

Thomas Jefferson should have been overjoyed with the victory at Yorktown, but he was not. The death of his young daughter still clouded his spirit, and the British rout of the legislature and invasion of Virginia clouded his reputation. One dissatisfied state delegate called for an investigation of the last months of Jefferson's administration; the main complaint was how the British had overrun Virginia with such ease. Jefferson had no forces, however; what militia he had he'd sent south, units refused to muster, and Washington had sent him little or no help.

Jefferson always believed the instigator of the inquiry was the previous governor Patrick Henry, now his political opponent. While he had admired Henry's patriotic speeches in the years before the war, and they had become friends, Jefferson had come to see Henry as lazy, slothful, and hate-filled.

During the inquiry, Jefferson responded in writing to a series of questions and also appeared before the General Assembly. The matter was debated, and in the end he was completely exonerated by the legislature. Yet for a man so sensitive to criticism, it was the low point in a long and generally successful political career.[101] He suffered a crisis of confidence, "mortified" that he hadn't been able to give the people what they had wanted: protection from a British invasion. He speculated that he should have called up the militia two days before he actually did, even if they couldn't withstand the onslaught of the British. With his wisdom, his ethics, and his honor challenged, he could, he said, "only be cured by the all-healing grave."

Still, Jefferson was not so overcome with remorse and anger that he was unable to function. In late 1781 he took his sister Martha Carr and her six children into his home for a time. Martha was the widow of his great friend Dabney Carr, who had died in 1773.

Jefferson had had him buried under the promised oak at Monticello, and he effectively adopted two of Carr's sons, Peter and Samuel, who frequently lived at Monticello.

In April 1782 Jefferson received a visit from the the Marquis de Chastellux, a major general in the army of America's French ally General Rochambeau. A fellow of the Royal Academy, Chastellux was recording his American experiences and heard of the famous Jefferson, author of the Declaration of Independence, and of his fabulous mountain home. Monticello, said Chastellux, was "elegant, and in the Italian taste, though not without fault."[102] During his weeklong stay, the scholarly general at first found Jefferson "cold." But as conversation between the two men progressed, "we were as intimate as if we had passed our whole lives together." He later produced this description of his host: "Let me describe to you a man, not yet forty, tall, and with a mild and pleasing countenance, but whose mind and understanding are ample substitutes for every exterior grace. An American who, without ever quitting his own country, is at once a musician, skilled in drawing, a geometrician, an astronomer, a natural philosopher, legislator, and statesman."

A man of glaring contradictions, Jefferson's warmth with his new French friend was doubtless sincere. But beneath the surface, he seethed at other goings-on. That the Virginia legislature had produced a resolution of thanks for his "Ability, Rectitude, and Integrity" while serving as governor did not assuage Jefferson's rage at former Virginia governor Patrick Henry. It was a rage, "slow-burning and inextinguishable," that remained for the rest of his long life.[103]

On May 8, 1782, the Jeffersons' sixth child was born: another daughter named Lucy Elizabeth, after the daughter who had lived so briefly. Patty had taken seriously ill after giving birth and was soon confined to her bed, where Jefferson watched over her night and day. If he took time off, it was to note the first blossoms of his jonquils, iris, hyacinth, nasturtiums, tulips, peonies, lilies, and the like. In midsummer, when he recorded the opening of the first Crimson Dark Rose, Patty herself was fast beginning to fade.

She lingered until September 6, 1782, when a grim tableau gathered around her deathbed. Jefferson sat by her side, while half a dozen of the house slaves, including nine-year-old Sally Hemings and her mother, forty-seven-year-old Betty Hemings (both inherited from Patty's father), clustered around her bed. Right before Patty died, she was said to have raised her hand and put it in Jefferson's, telling him that "she could not die happy if she thought her three children would ever have a stepmother brought in over them." When she was growing up, Patty had had two stepmothers after her mother died, and apparently the experiences were not good. "Mr. Jefferson promised her that he would never marry again. And he never did," according to the account given by one of the slaves present.[104]

Jefferson was inconsolable. He took to his room for three weeks and paced incessantly night and day between "violent bursts of grief." After that he spent long hours on horseback in the woods, alternately galloping for stretches then stopping to cry. His love, his best friend of a decade, was gone, and there was nothing to be done about it.

The previous year Jefferson had been appointed an American minister to France to serve alongside Benjamin Franklin and John Adams. He had turned the post down, because of Patty's declining health. In the autumn of 1782, two months after her death, word came from the Continental Congress, renewing the offer for Jefferson to go to France. Despite his grief, he was enthralled with the prospect of spending time in Europe, land of the Enlightenment and seat of all things fine, from architecture and art, to clothing and furniture, to music and wine. It was a restorative tonic that he badly needed, and Jefferson accepted it with magnanimity. He would go abroad for the first time, to France.

CHAPTER FOUR

The decisive American victory at Yorktown was barely over when twenty-six-year-old Alexander Hamilton departed the army and sped north toward Albany, where Eliza was pregnant with their first child. He rode so furiously that his horse gave out and had to be traded for another.

Hamilton had left the army with the agreement that he could keep his active commission as a colonel but would receive no remuneration. Now he was faced with supporting a family. He could have joined his father-in-law in running the vast Schuyler estates, but he was out for larger game.

Convinced that somehow he could be of further service to the young nation, Hamilton took advantage of a ruling that allowed a veteran of the Revolution to be excused from serving a three-year legal apprenticeship before taking the bar exam—but only if the applicant had studied law prior to his service. He had not, but he managed to get around the rule by cramming three years' worth of legal study into six months. Hamilton passed the bar, was admitted to practice, and from the beginning proved himself brilliant; in one biographer's estimation, he became "the leader of his profession in the state." Yet the woes of the young nation remained uppermost in his mind.

As much as anyone in the United States, Hamilton knew of the shortcomings of the Articles of Confederation under which Washington's army and all federal functions were controlled. As constituted, the current national government simply wasn't able to summon from the individual states the resources it needed to govern or to protect the vulnerable young country. America was despised by Britain, which reigned as Europe's trading giant and also maintained the world's most powerful navy; ignored by France, which was in the throes of official corruption and on the verge of its own tumultuous revolution; and colonized by Spain, which claimed territory from Florida to Texas. Adding to its problems, the United States was burdened by enormous debt from the war and from other borrowing; its economy was not yet geared to trade on the world stage. Overall, the new country was floundering in a limbo of confusion and consternation. With no leader and only an unruly and divided Congress at the helm, the world's only democracy faced serious problems that needed to be solved. It was as though Americans had suddenly awakened to find the monster (Britain) gone—but what they thought would be a garden of Eden was instead a tower of Babel.

In June 1783 soldiers who had not been paid in months, or even years, marched on Congress in Philadelphia with bayonets fixed; some officers even threatened a military coup. George Washington was obliged to call out cavalry troops from West Point to put down the protest. In the immediate years following, Congress met in Annapolis, Trenton, and New York City rather than return to Philadelphia, because the Pennsylvania governor had refused to call up the militia to protect the delegates.

In the final years of the war the federal finances became so debased that Congress appointed Robert Morris, a wealthy Philadelphia patriot, as superintendent of finance. U.S. paper money, known as "continentals," was becoming worthless. Monetary inflation was so rampant that a pair of boots costing five dollars in prewar America cost nearly fifty dollars in 1781. Instead of paper money, merchants traded in British pounds sterling, Spanish doubloons, "pieces of eight," gold sovereigns, and other hard currency—including tobacco and whiskey. This created a hardship on most citizens, but particularly on soldiers who were due back pay (six dollars per month) and bonuses; when the pay was finally handed out it would be agonizingly devalued.

As the fighting wound down, payments to the federal government that had been made sporadically and reluctantly by the states during the conflict began to dry up altogether. In an attempt to restart the collection process, Robert Morris went to New York in the spring of 1782 and offered Alexander Hamilton the job of receiver of taxes for that state. All through the long war, in between his military duties, Hamilton had made a study of finance. In an attempt to understand the mutual relationship among money, governments, and the people of a country, he had read Adam Smith's increasingly popular book *The Wealth of Nations,* as well as many other, more obscure works. Yet at first Hamilton, intent on building his law practice, balked at Morris's offer. But when Morris offered him a percentage of everything that was owed he accepted.

Hamilton and Morris discussed ways to alleviate the problems posed by inflation and in collecting taxes, as well as the looming issue of the huge U.S. war debt. Owed mostly to foreign nations, it had to be paid or the new country's credit would be ruined.

Hamilton expressed the notion that the states' debts should be assumed by the federal government and paid off, so long as the government was given the right to tax the states' inhabitants, which it currently did not possess. This would soon become a crystalizing issue around how the new nation should be governed, and Hamilton would be in the vanguard of shaping the nation's financial future—whenever that nationhood became a full reality.

Terms that would officially end the war were still being negotiated in Paris when, in the late autumn of 1782, Alexander Hamilton arrived in Philadelphia as a delegate to the Confederation Congress. He had made an all-too-brief visit to the city during the war, before the redcoats had driven Washington's army away. Now, he had time to explore the nation's largest city and marvel at its wide, clean, well-lit streets and its many elegant homes. Those that were not elegant were at least neat, which could not always be said for New York City. Located at the confluence of two rivers near the head of the Chesapeake Bay, Philadelphia was a bustling seaport for tall, oceangoing ships, as well as for smaller sloops and workboats trading on the bay and its tributaries.

If Hamilton was impressed with the city, he was not impressed with Congress. A few months before, immediately after he had been appointed a delegate, he had written to Congress calling for a constitutional convention, the first member to do so. The states continued to act like separate countries, charging duties and imposing various levies and taxes. They did not seem to understand that they were now a part of a single entity: the United States of America. Petty jealousies played out often, and under the existing rules a small group of delegates could frustrate or defeat desperately needed measures. As the Hamilton biographer Ron Chernow put it, the government's structure under the Articles of Confederation "guaranteed paralysis."[105]

With the officers and men of the American army still unpaid in their camps at Newburgh, New York, the odor of mutiny again hovered in the air. Hamilton proposed that Congress vote to assume the debts of the states, then levy taxes on them to raise the money necessary to pay the army and the country's creditors. Delegates from various states, however, balked at this, fearing it would concentrate power in the hands of the federal government. Though Hamilton's motion went nowhere, he was appointed to sit on a committee of three to see what could be done to mollify the American soldiers.

In the meantime Hamilton wrote a private letter to Washington—the only person Hamilton felt was capable of mediating between a desperate and angry military and a hopelessly deadlocked Congress. Hamilton suggested that Washington, still commander in chief, threaten Congress that if the army did not receive its pay it might take over the government. It was the first communication between the two in more than a year. Washington of course declined the outlandish suggestion and responded to Hamilton politely but firmly that "the army . . . is a dangerous instrument to play with."

Hamilton and others in Philadelphia did manage to pass a congressional resolution imposing more import duties. These were inadequate for fully funding the pay of the men and officers of the army but were at least a step in the right direction. He also introduced a resolution that would have amended the Articles of Confederation to permit Congress to tax the states directly. It got nowhere in the disunited Congress, whose sole major accomplishment was the ratification of the provisional peace treaty with England.

For his part, Washington was working to hold the army together, at least until the peace treaty was signed. Benjamin Franklin, John Adams, John Jay, and Henry Laurens were in Paris negotiating the terms of peace—but until that happened, British troops remained in New York, Charleston, and along the nation's western frontier.[106]

The eight long years of conflict had already cost the lives of some 25,000 American combatants. (Among them was the closest friend Hamilton probably ever had—John Laurens, brother of the Paris negotiator Henry Laurens.) Before Hamilton had left for Philadelphia, he had received a letter from John, suggesting that whatever kind of leadership the country should elect, he hoped Hamilton "would fill only the first offices of the republic." Hamilton answered him in August, imploring Laurens to "Quit the sword, my friend, put on the toga. Come to Congress. We know each other's sentiments, our views are the same; we have fought side by side to make America free, let us hand in hand struggle to make her happy."[107]

Whether or not Laurens received the letter is unknown. That same month he was killed by a British bullet when the cavalry patrol he was leading tried to ambush a foraging party of redcoats outside Charleston. Hamilton was heartbroken, writing Lafayette, who had also been close to the South Carolinian, "Poor Laurens, he has fallen as sacrifice to his ardor in a trifling skirmish . . . You know how truly I loved him and will judge how much I regret him."

ON JANUARY 14, 1784, the Confederation Congress ratified the Treaty of Paris, formally ending the war. The United States of America was a sovereign nation, and British troops would at last leave its environs. Many of the Tories still in New York also left, on British ships bound for England, Canada, or the West Indies. Even before the Paris treaty was signed, some 29,000 Tories had sailed from New York. The enormous sums of money they kept in England and elsewhere but had in the past often spent in America would never again benefit the U.S. economy.

Hamilton was appalled by the anti-Tory statutes being passed by the state legislature, where many of the delegates were Sons of Liberty adherents. The laws were chasing the remaining wealthy Tory merchants away, and Hamilton wrote indignantly, "Our state will feel for twenty-years, at least, the effects of this popular phrenzy."[108] He began representing Tories against what he considered tyrannical laws and soon acquired more such clients, of varying degrees of wealth. This, unfortunately, also led to Hamilton's pro-British reputation, which his political enemies would later use against him.

As a member by marriage of the New York aristocracy, Alexander Hamilton had no shortage of cases and legal work to do for other wealthy and influential clients as well. By the mid-1780s he cut a debonair figure in New York society. He was just turning thirty years old, with blue eyes, a level Grecian nose, and a slight smile at the corners of his mouth. His features conveyed an impression of strength, determination, and inquisitiveness, and his dress was stylish but not overdone. Every day his dresser came to his office to make sure he presented a proper appearance. He wore his hair in a long pigtail, which he tied up in a bun with a black ribbon. On the days he appeared before a judge, the dresser made sure his wig was correctly fitted and powdered.

The Hamilton family settled into a comfortable house on Wall Street not far from his legal offices, the courthouse, and city hall. Like Jefferson's, Hamilton's reading habits were insatiable. In the evenings he pored over the works of Sterne, Fielding, Swift, Walpole, Gibbons, Hobbes, Hume, and Voltaire. Nor did he neglect his lifelong love affair with the classics. In addition to English and French, with his upbringing on Danish St. Croix he got by enough to converse in German with his old military compatriot Baron von Steuben, who had settled in America after the war and was eventually given a congressional grant of 16,000 acres in upstate New York, in gratitude for his service during the Revolution.

New York continued to prosper as a maritime and financial center, and Hamilton's legal practice prospered with it. A generous benefactor of many New York institutions and charities, he also frequently lent money to friends and acquaintances who were down on their luck, and he served as a trustee of his alma mater—no longer Kings College but now Columbia.

In the late winter of 1784, Hamilton's brother-in-law John Barker Church, a rich Englishman who was married to Eliza's sister Angelica, asked him to form a bank. At that point banks in America were extremely rare and often looked upon with suspicion—but Hamilton believed in them. In the years to come, he struggled mightily to obtain an official charter for the Bank of New York but was thwarted by the powerful New York governor George Clinton, who thought such an institution was detrimental to the farmers in his constituency.

Eventually, in 1784, Hamilton simply founded the bank without a charter. Among the bank's initial shareholders was

Aaron Burr, another of the city's rising young lawyers. There were only a handful of lawyers in New York at the time, and Burr and Hamilton were frequently thrown together on cases or in social situations. Together, they assisted in financing Erasmus Hall Academy in Brooklyn, which became the oldest high school in the state. They were also neighbors on Wall Street, and sometimes dined at each other's homes; Eliza and Burr's wife, Theodosia, became close. Hamilton had known Theodosia during the war, when she was married to a British officer. Despite that, she had opened her elegant New Jersey home to such patriotic luminaries as George Washington and James Madison, as well as to Hamilton himself. Burr, too, was sometimes among the guests. In 1781 Theodosia's husband James died in Jamaica while dealing with political disturbances there. Nine months later she married Burr, ten years her junior.

From the start, Hamilton and Burr were "opposed in politics," Hamilton said, "but always on good terms. We set out in the practice of law at the same time and took different political directions." Burr was a steadfast and ambitious member of the New York aristocracy. His grandfather had been a distinguished theologian and his father a classical scholar who became the president of Princeton. But a smallpox epidemic in 1758, when Aaron was two, took not only his mother and father but his grandmother, grandfather, and great-grandfather. The orphaned boy was taken in by a wealthy uncle but became a withdrawn child. At thirteen, when he entered Princeton and it was apparent that he was a brilliant scholar, he lost much of his shyness. After graduating, he studied law and then fought in the revolution as a colonel commanding a regiment and a general's aide.

The handsome Burr employed his well-honed wit and sophistication skillfully, but his personality was draped in a deep-rooted secrecy, run through with currents of concealment and intrigue. He once described himself as "a grave, silent, strange sort of animal, inasmuch as we know not what to make of him." He stored up grudges and bore them poorly, but his looks and charm nonetheless "had a mesmerizing effect on men and women alike."

For his part Hamilton had what his biographer Chernow called "an incorrigible weakness for women in need." In one instance in December 1786, he was representing pro bono a spinster named Barbara Ransumer, charged with stealing fans, lace, and other items. When Hamilton inquired as to her defense, she admitted guilt and said she had none. Later, in court, Hamilton put on an act for the jury. On the verge of tears, he cried out, "Woman is weak! She requires the protection of a man!" When the all-male jury acquitted Ms. Ransumer, Hamilton was suddenly consumed by guilt and declared, "I then determined that I would never again take up a cause in which I was convinced I ought not to prevail."[109]

Time had not abated Hamilton's long-standing antipathy toward slavery. Nevertheless, his father-in-law kept no fewer than twenty-seven enslaved black people employed at the family home in Albany and in his planting fields farther north in Saratoga. Hamilton had apparently grown accustomed to that at the Schuyler estate, as Eliza had been raised with slaves doing the cooking, cleaning, and other household chores. And in New York City, even at the turn of the next century, about 20 percent of the households owned slaves.

After the Revolution some states—notably Pennsylvania, New Hampshire, Vermont, and Massachusetts—enacted various plans for freeing their slaves, generally through gradual emancipation. Most of the better-known abolition groups did not organize until well into the next century. But in 1785 a group of New Yorkers, including Alexander Hamilton, formed the New York Society for Promoting the Manumission of Slaves. It sponsored lectures and distributed printed material averse to slavery. It also operated the African Free School in lower Manhattan to educate black students.

The society was not a militant abolitionist group, and some of its members themselves owned slaves—possibly even Hamilton and/or Eliza. Hamilton chaired a committee formed to rectify this embarrassing situation and came up with a plan for the members to free their slaves through gradual emancipation. The plan, however, was too radical for many members to accept, and after some technical maneuvering by opponents Hamilton's committee was disbanded. Instead, the society members approved a motion that they would *consider* freeing their slaves but would not be compelled to do so.

Several months later Hamilton was a signatory to a petition produced by "an illustrious cavalcade of dignitaries" that included his longtime friend John Jay. The petition demanded that the New York legislature put an end to the slave trade in the state. It would be another three decades before New York's slave markets were closed and the slaves of New York declared free.

THE POSTWAR AMERICA THAT DEVELOPED in the wake of the peace was never the placid, pastoral place that many had envisioned. In New York, Tories who did not flee to England were often beaten, spat upon, or tarred and feathered. The state legislature passed draconian laws denying them the vote and all manner of civil and property rights. Hamilton thought this was wrong and said so in long published essays under the name Phocion. This figure of classical myth had come to Athens from a foreign land and a questionable background but became a general who pleaded forgiveness of one's enemies when war ended. Unfortunately, tempers in New York ran so high that Hamilton's advocacy for the Loyalists was resented, and he lost some of the luster that had illuminated him as a trusted aide to George Washington.

Throughout the nation citizens seethed under the dreadful financial conditions that existed. The country was virtually bankrupt, still drifting rudderless under the paltry Articles of Confederation. Prosperity was not around the corner. Working people labored under low wages, with little spare cash to pay for merchandise. Merchants were left creditless and many went bankrupt. Hit particularly hard were Massachusetts farmers who staggered under high property taxes, foreclosures, and little or no available credit. One man in particular decided to do something about it.

Daniel Shays had been a captain in the army and a veteran of the Breed's and Bunker Hill battle. Shays and other soldiers were still owed money by the government, and what little money they did have was mostly worthless paper, while their creditors demanded coin.

In the summer of 1786 Shays and hundreds of his fellows—mainly farmers and veterans of the Continental Army, armed with pitchforks, clubs, and guns—marched against various county courthouses in western Massachusetts, where judges frequently ruled against them in debt proceedings and ordered foreclosures on their land. Shaysites, as they became known, forcibly closed courthouses or intimidated jurors from entering. Shays's Rebellion lasted on and off for nearly a year before it was finally broken up by a private army of troops employed by the Massachusetts governor. As rebellions go, it wasn't particularly violent, but it was covered by newspapers and called acute attention to the need for some sort of effective national government.

Both Hamilton and George Washington were appalled by the disturbance, which they considered a threat to the new nation. When Jefferson, then in Paris as a minister to the court of Louis XVI, learned of the uprising, he wrote James Madison, "I hold that a little rebellion now and then is a good thing." Jefferson was more sanguinary when writing to another friend. "The tree of liberty," he said somewhat chillingly, "must be refreshed from time to time with the blood of patriots and tyrants."[110]

During that same period a movement emerged that would lead to the vital changes Alexander Hamilton had espoused since the war ended. Commercial and trade relations among the states had become so muddled that in 1786 a conference was called in Annapolis to iron out the differences. The conference was poorly attended, but Hamilton was among the two representatives from New York. It became apparent to the delegates that there was no easy way to smooth out the disputes among the states, because various legislatures kept passing laws selfishly beneficial to their states or their cronies or themselves. The upshot was a public resolution by the delegates to hold a convention in Philadelphia the following year to amend the Articles of Confederation. The Annapolis resolution would lead directly to what John Adams described as "the most intricate, the most important, the most dangerous business"—the Constitutional Convention of 1787 and the creation of a strong federal government.[111]

Hamilton arrived in Philadelphia for the convention on May 18, 1787. He was filled with trepidation that the delegates would be unable to come to solid conclusions as to how to set up a national government. (In fact, he himself was in a minority in his belief that the Articles of Confederation needed to be discarded, rather than amended.) Hamilton found Madison even less optimistic but was heartened when George Washington was elected presiding officer of the convention by unanimous vote. Washington remained a towering, almost mythic figure on the American scene, and his very presence and wise counsel would go far in subduing overripe passions that might otherwise lead to rancor and dissension.

Washington forthwith appointed Hamilton to a three-man committee to formulate the rules and procedures for the convention. It was agreed that each state would have one vote on any matters to be decided, and that the proceedings and deliberations would be carried on in utmost secrecy. The meetings were held in a room of the state capitol building whose windows were often closed so there could be no eavesdropping from outsiders. Journalists and visitors were barred from the premises, and the delegates were themselves sworn to secrecy. Hamilton explained this utter lack of transparency thusly: "Had the deliberations been open while going on, the clamours of faction would have prevented any satisfactory result." Hamilton biographer Chernow observed, "The closed door proceedings yielded inspired, uninhibited debate and brought forth one of the most luminous documents in history."[112]

The factions to which Hamilton alluded were based mostly on ideological beliefs and state and regional interests. Over the coming years, those interests would solidify into political parties, which is something that horrified George Washington, as he believed they would eventually spell the doom of the republic.

The Constitutional Convention had ostensibly been called to amend the Articles of Confederation. But right at the beginning Virginia's delegation submitted an entirely new proposal: a document largely composed by delegate James Madison that became known as the Virginia Plan. It basically scrapped the Articles entirely and called for a national government that would be superior to state law and consist of coequal executive, legislative, and judicial branches. The question the delegates must answer, as Hamilton framed it, was "whether the United States were susceptible to one government," or whether every state would insist on "a separate existence." This set the stage for sharp arguments.[113]

The delegates were mostly in their forties; Hamilton and Madison were even younger, in their thirties. They were all white men, many of them lawyers, mostly affluent, educated, and bright. With a few exceptions, they approached their task with earnest solemnity for the national good. They were forced to deal with all sorts of snags in setting up an entirely new type of government. Smaller states, for example, worried that they would be underrepresented if representation was determined by population proportion. And skepticism ran high about the federal sovereignty championed in the Virginia Plan. A second proposal, the New Jersey Plan, was introduced, in which states would have more authority. "The states will never sacrifice their essential rights to a national government," one New York delegate snarled.[114]

Hamilton sat through these brisk discussions for two weeks with silent, sphinx-like perseverance. Then on June 18 he rose to speak and did not stop for six hours. He rejected both plans, he said, and made clear that while his plan would probably not be popular, he was bound to introduce it in the secret session if for no other reason than it offered food for thought.

It was his opinion, Hamilton told the audience in the hot, stuffy, fly-buzzing room, that the country needed a chief executive assured of enough power to prevent him from seeking more—in fact, a kind of *monarch,* who would be elected for life, "unless he misbehaves," in which case he could be recalled. The same lifetime election went for U.S. senators, to ensure continuity in government. He went on record alluding to the British government as "the best in the world," a notion somewhat impolitic in the wake of an eight-year war with Great Britain. A delegate from Connecticut recorded that Hamilton's speech "has been praised by everybody [but] supported by none."[115]

The reasons behind his line of thinking were many. Hamilton likely envisioned this ruler-for-life as George Washington, who was as competent and benign a leader as would ever be found. He had served with him throughout the war and saw him in action as the sole commander in chief of the army, winning the war despite the ineptitude of Congress.

Additionally, likely influenced by his own difficult childhood, Hamilton had come to America with an abiding mistrust of human behavior. Many people in his own family had let him down terribly, as had the politicians in the Continental Congress years later. These things must have weighed on his mind and made the idea of a pure democracy terrifying to him; he saw it as little better than mob rule. In fact, he told the delegates, if they wanted to see what would happen in a pure democracy, they should look no further than the history of ancient Greece, which in its last days had degenerated into a "mobocracy . . . Their very character was tyranny," Hamilton said. "Demagogues whipped the poor into a frenzy against the rich" and the mob "ostracized leaders to whom a short time before they had raised statues."[116] Since tiny Rhode Island was the only state that did not send delegates to the convention, Hamilton could not resist the temptation to declare that its legislature was "the very picture of a mob . . . engaged in the art of cheating creditors."[117]

Hamilton's message, he said later, was to put before the delegates the notion that if a fine, honest, competent man was elected to become the country's chief executive and continued to do a good job, there was need to keep him. And he also worried about how to keep a bad man from becoming president—New York governor George Clinton, Hamilton's political enemy, likely came to his mind.

Hamilton believed that if frequent elections were held, the odds were that sooner or later one of these bad or incompetent people would be elected and could do harm to the country. The fact that he had been a subject of the British king until the Revolution may have influenced his thinking—but so was the fact that he had spent most of his adult life at the very pinnacle of the military. Over time, he had come to believe that the sprawling, brawling, grumbling, unsettled American populace needed a monarch-like figure to run it efficiently (*efficiency* being Hamilton's constant watchword). Yet *monarch-for-life* became what he was known for. That expression would stick with him and bedevil him for the remainder of his days.

For nearly two weeks the debates went on. Should there be a three-man executive branch, an executive committee, a one-house legislature, a two-house legislature, executive veto power, no veto power, states alone empowered to impeach an executive, a standing army and navy, no standing army or navy, king or no king? Eventually, the crux of the debate came down to how to ensure fair representation for the big states and the little states. And there the delegates stalled in anxious deadlock. Hamilton, who had remained silent since his June 18 tirade, arose again on June 29, 1787. "It is a miracle that we [are] now here exercising our tranquil and free deliberations on the subject. It would be madness to trust to future miracles," he declared.

Thus far, the convention had avoided the subject of foreign policy, but Hamilton faced it head-on. "No government could give us . . . happiness at home, which did not possess sufficient stability to make us respectable abroad," he told the members, warning them that the country must remain strong enough to defend itself against foreign attack.[118]

New York's other two delegates to the convention were stooges of Governor Clinton and had left the proceedings, stating that, "There was a plot afoot to establish a consolidated government." Their absence nullified Hamilton's right to vote, for the rules specified that at least two delegates from each state must be present. Hamilton asked them to return, but they not only ignored him but went straight to Governor Clinton and—in direct violation of their oaths of secrecy—spilled everything they knew of the proposals being debated in Philadelphia. [119]

With his vote nullified, Hamilton left the convention in disgust, expressing in a letter to Washington his fear that the convention would either vote for a weakened national government or dissolve in disunity. Washington wrote back, echoing Hamilton's disgust with the proceedings thus far. "I am sorry you went away," he told Hamilton. "I wish you were back."[120] And he soon was. He spent the next months going back and forth between New York and Philadelphia.

Meanwhile, Governor Clinton began making wild accusations and predictions in the press about the possible outcome of the convention. Hamilton responded by excoriating Clinton in a newspaper essay of his own, accusing the governor of trying to sabotage the attempt to form a national constitution. In doing this, Hamilton made a mortal enemy of the most powerful man in New York State—but that bothered him not at all. Clinton simply did not want to give up any of his power to a federal government.

Back in Philadelphia, the delegates to the convention had finally arrived at an agreement to break the stalemate. Known as the Connecticut Compromise after its author, Connecticut's Roger Sherman, it gave the small states greater powers by allowing them each two Senate members, just as the larger states had. The House of Representatives, however, would be elected by population proportion, which gave the big states more power.

With the stalemate unlocked and the convention drifting into September, the delegates began debating other thorny political issues. How would the chief executive, or president, be elected? At first, according to the compromise, the Senate would elect the president. But this was unsatisfactory to many, including Hamilton. There was always the popular vote option—but once more the small states, or those with smaller populations, objected that election results would always be dictated by the larger states. So the delegates arrived at the Electoral College solution, which gave the smaller states a greater measure of influence. Additional powers—which heretofore had been felt to be the purview of the Senate—were given the president: he could make treaties and appoint cabinet members and federal judges, including Supreme Court justices, but only with the tempering "advice and consent" of the Senate.

Slavery presented a major impediment to adopting a constitution. First was the issue of whether slaves should be counted in a state's population for voting purposes. Slavery had been, or was gradually being, abolished in five of the thirteen states. In the North slaves were not nearly so plentiful as in the South, where they reached as much as 40 percent of the population of some states. After much hashing out, it was agreed that three out of every five slaves—though they could not actually vote—would be counted toward a state's total population, thus giving southern states more representation in Congress and the Electoral College.

Next, the question of the international slave trade arose. Many delegates wanted it abolished immediately, but southern states threatened to boycott the convention if that happened. A committee debated the issue and arrived at a compromise, and the future date of 1808 would be set in the Constitution to take up the issue. Southerners agreed, and another stumbling block to the constitution was removed.

Many northerners and not a few southerners—including George Washington and Thomas Jefferson—despised the institution of slavery but relied on it for their economic well-being. They had inherited slaves as capital in the way a northerner might inherit land, cash, or stocks. Land in the South was cheap and sometimes even free, but to work it was difficult and expensive. Over the years slave labor became the answer.

During post-Revolution times, a great many people in both North and South believed that slavery was basically uneconomical and was dying out—and they were initially right. But in less than a decade that would change with Eli Whitney's invention of the cotton gin and the spread of the industrial revolution. The mills of England and France skyrocketed the demand for cotton to make clothing for the world—and the American South provided that cotton, with the labor from a growing population of slaves.

But those were unforeseeable events as the delegates met in September 1787, where the haggling and horse trading continued. As it drew near the time for the delegates to vote on the Constitution, Hamilton raised another obstacle. He believed the Constitution was an imperfect, overly compromised document, but that it was certainly better than the despised Articles of Confederation. The problem now was that under that document, Congress was not allowed to amend the Articles and thus adopt the Constitution without the unanimous vote of all thirteen states—and two, New York and Rhode Island, were not in favor and did not have the necessary delegates in attendance to vote.

A proposal was made and passed that would allow the Constitution to be adopted if just nine of the states voted in favor—but the lawyer in Hamilton took exception. If there were a shred of illegality associated with the formation of the new government, he felt, a stain would rest upon it forever. Many of Hamilton's friends were aghast that at such a time he would raise such an issue, but he proposed yet another compromise. The delegates would return to their state legislatures with a copy of the Constitution and a proposal that they vote to ratify it. The Constitution "would not take effect until nine states had ratified it." That, Hamilton said, "would remove the onus of illegality."

Hamilton's proposal was agreed to, and the glimmer of a new sun began to shine on the United States of America.[121]

WHEN THE CONSTITUTION WAS SENT TO THE STATES for ratification all hell broke loose. And as usual Hamilton was in the middle of things. The Constitution had satisfied few if any of the convention delegates, but most considered it better than nothing—and certainly better than the Articles of Confederation. Hamilton saw it as too weak. He had argued that "We must establish a general and national government completely sovereign, and annihilate the state distinctions."[122]

As the Constitution was distributed to the various state legislators, other people began to see flaws in its design; for some, the flaws were serious, and for others they were fatal. Most of the objections centered on the rights of citizens and of states. The way the Constitution was written, few rights were specifically enumerated. On the other hand, the document stated that whatever rights were not named in the Constitution became the rights of the states.

Some prominent Patriots—including Patrick Henry and Samuel Adams—felt this wasn't good enough and might even engender tyranny. These people demanded a list of changes to the Constitution—changes that would later be reflected in a series of amendments known collectively as the Bill of Rights.

All of these issues were debated in newspapers of the day and argued in statehouses, taverns, and households throughout the land. Some of the arguments turned violent, as in the Massachusetts legislature, where debates became so heated that fistfights broke out. Hamilton opposed the addition of a bill of rights, on grounds that there were so many rights to identify (perhaps a right to eat soup with a spoon, for example) that making such a formal declaration would be impossibly messy. "The people [should] just take it as it is and be thankful," Hamilton said, implying that they might get something worse instead. He felt certain that almost anything was better than the old Articles of Confederation.[123]

While each state was deliberating on whether to ratify the Constitution, essays began appearing in newspapers opposing its adoption under any circumstances. The tenor of most of these arguments centered on the powers of states versus a federal government. Many Americans were born into families that had lived in a particular colony for generations and had developed an attachment to it similar to an allegiance to a country. Instead of saying, "I'm a Dutchman or an Englishman," they would say, "I'm a New Yorker, or a Virginian." Their allegiance, except to the British monarch, had been to their colony, and old habits died hard; the idea of a United States as an actual governing entity was foreign to them.

Hamilton, of course, was free of such prejudices. He'd been born in the West Indies, and having gone through six years of war in the Continental Army, his sole focus was on building a strong government that would never again have the dire financial problems and other difficulties that the fledgling country had had during the war.

To combat the negative newspaper articles, Hamilton began writing positive essays of his own that appeared in New York papers and were often reprinted elsewhere. He was joined in the project by James Madison of Virginia and John Jay, who was again practicing law in New York. Each man's essays appeared in print under the pseudonym Publius, the name of the founder of the Roman republic. The essays were lucid explanations and defenses of the various clauses in the Constitution, written in a way that most literate Americans could understand and appreciate. In less than six months, eighty-four of these essays appeared and are now collectively known as *The Federalist Papers*. Hamilton wrote two-thirds of them himself. The essays had a persuasive effect, especially in New York, where ratification was undergoing a severe trial thanks to Governor Clinton's opposition.

Hamilton and his followers became known as Federalists, and the Federalist political party began to take shape. Their opponents became known as Anti-Federalists—and eventually, seeking a more positive definition, as Democratic-Republicans.

Each state had organized its own constitutional convention to debate and vote on ratification. Hamilton and John Jay were delegates to the New York convention, but the majority of delegates were Clinton men and against ratification. Hamilton kept in close communication with James Madison to see how Virginia was leaning. Madison thought the odds looked good, except for a troublemaker who had recently appeared in Richmond to stir up opposition. His name was Eleazer Oswald, a former newspaper publisher and, like Hamilton, a former colonel in the Continental Army.

And the similarities did not end there. Oswald had been born in England, the son of a ship's captain, but had immigrated to America after his father was lost at sea. He arrived in Richmond and was apprenticed to a printer, whose daughter he married. In 1787 he was publishing a newspaper in Philadelphia while the Constitutional Convention was in progress. His journal was generally favorable to the Constitution, even after it was published. But strangely and suddenly, he turned venomously against ratification.

Oswald next showed up in New York City in early 1788, where he quickly opened a newspaper and began attacking ratification of the Constitution, Federalists in general, and Alexander Hamilton in particular. When Hamilton answered him in print, Oswald challenged Hamilton to a duel; it nearly came off but mutual friends managed to arrange a satisfactory "settlement."

Hamilton had utterly lost confidence that the New York convention would vote in favor of the Constitution. "The more I dread the non-adoption of the Constitution by any of the other states, the more I fear eventual disunion and civil war," he told Madison. "God grant that Virginia accede. Her example will have a vast influence on our politics."[124]

Opposition to the Constitution boiled down to three things: fear of authority, "the proprietary interests of local politicians," and slow and imperfect communication among the states. Although it would take only nine states to form a union, if New York were to vote no it would sever New England from the mid-Atlantic states; if Virginia also balked, it would sever the nation again, cutting off the rest of the South.

The issue of taxes was a constant bugaboo. Some New York delegates favoring the old Articles of Confederation feared that a Congress under the proposed Constitution would "devour all the revenue sources and annihilate the states." Hamilton answered them by pointing to a letter to Congress from Governor Clinton during the Revolution, in which he complained bitterly that New York was stuck with excess requisitions for funds, because Congress could not then compel other states to meet their quotas. The war requisitions, Hamilton told the convention, "have been the cause of a principal part of our calamities."[125]

On July 2 an express rider arrived at New York convention headquarters and handed Hamilton a letter from Madison: Virginia had ratified the Constitution. (New Hampshire had ratified earlier, becoming the requisite ninth state, but word of that had not yet reached New York.)

As the news from Virginia spread, it brought down the house. The Federalists celebrated by marching around the courthouse with a fife and drum. This, however, did not sway the Anti-Federalists, who continued to delay, condemn, demand amendments, and threaten rejection. For his part, Governor Clinton publicly stated, "If convulsions and a civil war are the consequence, I will go with my party."[126]

After three more weeks of arguments, however, and word arriving that other states had approved ratification, the Clintonites began to falter. It became apparent that if they continued to balk, New York would wind up as "odd man out." So they pressed their case for amendments; one stipulated that if New York didn't get its way with the proposed amendments, it would have a right to secede. Word came back that New York could either ratify the Constitution or go its own way.

New York approved the new Constitution on July 26, 1788—in no small measure due to the tireless, earnest, and effectual efforts of Alexander Hamilton.

TO SET THE NEW GOVERNMENT IN MOTION, the first order of business was to elect a president. George Washington was almost everyone's favorite. The presidential ballots were cast strictly by sixty-nine electors, representing various states; the states in turn each had their own system for choosing electors, some by appointment by the legislature, others by some form of popular vote. On February 4, 1789, the electors met and overwhelmingly elected Washington president; John Adams, with the second highest number of electoral votes, was elected vice president. Governor Clinton, bitter to the end, ran for the presidency but was defeated. (Still, New York was to be the new capital, and Congress would sit in old Federal Hall.) Hamilton's father-in-law, Philip Schuyler, was elected a senator and James Madison became speaker of the house. Henry Knox would head the War Department, and Thomas Jefferson, recently returned from France, would serve as secretary of state.

Two weeks after his swearing in, Washington invited Alexander Hamilton to become secretary of the treasury. Hamilton, in his early thirties, was the youngest cabinet member appointed. It was certainly the most challenging position in the government, mainly because of the nation's $79 million debt, but Hamilton felt he was up to the task. Some $12 million was foreign debt incurred during the war. Domestic debt was $54 million, and the total debt of the states was $25 million.[127]

President Washington was uncertain of the social protocols of the infant republic, but at Hamilton's suggestion he asked prominent New Yorkers to organize a variety of social events—dinners, parties, balls—to acquaint the people with their new leader. In time the inner workings of the American government began to hum into gear. Questions arose and answers were sought. What sort of military would the country need? What would entail the American foreign policy? And, most pressingly, how would the debt be retired and the nation's credit restored?

In the meantime, there was the matter of Hamilton's sister-in-law Angelica Church. She was the beautiful, witty wife of the wealthy Englishman John Barker Church, who had invested Hamilton with the funds to start the Bank of New York. Angelica, in contrast to her younger sister Eliza, was extremely vivacious, clever, and politically astute. She enjoyed bantering with the equally clever Hamilton to the extent that some began to gossip there might be more to their relationship than met the eye. Some of Hamilton's biographers have read much into a postscript in one of his letters to Angelica in which he closed with, "Yours as much as you desire."

Church had taken Angelica with him to England during the latter part of the war, and they had become the toast of London society. But she quickly became homesick and wrote to Eliza, "Ah, you were a lucky girl to get so good and clever a companion," and again, later, "I am really so proud of [Hamilton's] merit and abilities than even you [Eliza] might envy my feelings. Embrace your master for me, and tell him that I envy you the fame of so clever a husband, one who writes so well."

Angelica and Hamilton had corresponded as well, he explaining his political problems and she answering with sage advice. But occasionally it went beyond that. Upon her departure for England in 1786, Hamilton wrote her: "You have, I fear, taken a final leave of America, and of those that love you . . . I confess for my part I see one great source of happiness snatched away." And again: "Some of us are, and must continue to be inconsolable for your absence." And once more: "How do you manage to charm all who see you?"[128]

In 1789, after three years in England, Angelica had returned to America without her husband or her children. At balls in the city

Hamilton was seen dancing with his sister-in-law, which might have raised eyebrows in some quarters, although Eliza never seemed to have trouble with their association. With the lack of any positive evidence to the contrary, it is most likely the relationship was a harmless one between two witty, often tantalizing, personalities who genuinely enjoyed each other's company.

Even as the rumors swirled, Hamilton had been focused on the problem of the nation's credit, and he thought he'd found the solution. His notions were modern, complex, and powerful, but to many of his contemporaries, including Thomas Jefferson and his compatriot James Madison, they were frightening and dangerous—perhaps even treasonous.

Hamilton's plan was presented to Congress in three parts, beginning in December 1790 and continuing into January. First the federal government was to assume the debt owed by the states and retire it by borrowing the money to do so from Europeans at lower rates. Revenue to repay the loan would be raised by tariffs on foreign goods. Congress debated the issue with great rancor for six months before Jefferson and Madison arranged a transactional deal that gave them something they wanted in return for their support: as a regional compromise, the new capital of the country would be located midway between North and South. With Washington's encouragement, a site on the Potomac River, which formed the border between Virginia from Maryland, was chosen. Hamilton promised to support the compromise deal.

Next Hamilton proposed the formation of a national bank modeled on the Bank of England; it would hold government funds, collect taxes, and make loans to the government and to qualified borrowers. Jefferson and Madison, who were now firmly in the Anti-Federalist camp, argued that such a bank was unconstitutional because it wasn't mentioned in the Constitution. Hamilton produced a lengthy response, countering that Congress had authority to create a bank because the Constitution granted Congress authority to do anything "necessary and proper" to carry out its fiscal duties. In the winter of 1791 Congress voted for the bank, giving it a twenty-year charter, and President Washington signed the bill into law in February.

Last of all, Hamilton wanted to enact legislation to foster the country's new and struggling industries; he had seen how the industrial revolution was transforming Great Britain and envisioned a similar manufacturing boom in the United States. The government would provide loans and subsidies to manufacturers and industries, improve roads to speed transportation, and make other capital improvements.

Predictably, there was another hullabaloo over this suggestion—particularly from Jefferson, who dreamed of an America dominated by egalitarian farmers tilling prosperous fields that stretched into the sunset. "Those who labor in the earth are the chosen people of God," Jefferson wrote. Moral corruption in farmers was unknown in human history, Jefferson said, adding that, "When we get piled upon one another in large cities, we shall become corrupt, as in Europe, and go to eating one another, as they do there."

While Hamilton's vision of a nation of commerce clashed with that of the Virginian, his ideas would allow America to become self-sufficient. And he believed that an industrial America would also, of itself, bring an end to slavery—a notion Jefferson was unwilling to concede.

Those things, however, were in the future. In the early days of 1791 Congress approved some aspects of Hamilton's program, including assuming the war debts of the states, and rejected other parts. It did approve raising tariffs on certain foreign-made products that were in competition with U.S. goods, and of raising taxes on others including a tax on domestic whiskey. This last was to cause trouble later.

In general Hamilton's plan to restore the national credit and get the nation's financial house in order was astonishingly successful. In a few years the United States would be known as one of the safest nations in which to invest and its bonds and securities on European exchanges would trade far above par. His countrymen had Alexander Hamilton to thank for that.

THE PERSONAL ENMITY between Hamilton and Jefferson had begun with the defection of James Madison, Hamilton's friend in Congress and co-author of *The Federalist Papers.* Hamilton was surprised, hurt, and enraged at Madison's sudden switching of sides. Without any warning whatever, Madison suddenly stood in complete opposition to Hamilton's financial plans to save the nation's credit; Hamilton ultimately blamed Jefferson for Madison's defection (though he had at first viewed Jefferson favorably upon his return from France).

Historian Noemie Emery's explanation for Madison's switch is probably as accurate as any: "He was a southerner, attached to his region and its agrarian culture." Madison's vision of Federalism, Emery believes, "did not anticipate the practical consequences" of Hamilton's view of the power of the federal government. For his part, Hamilton told a friend, "The opinion I had entertained of the simplicity and fairness of Mr. Madison's character has given way to a decided opinion that it is one of a peculiarly artificial and complicated kind."[129]

If Hamilton was distrustful of Jefferson's influence on Madison, Jefferson blamed Hamilton for "seducing" George Washington, and was envious of the treasury secretary's access to the president. Hamilton and Jefferson shared a vision of a free, happy, peaceful, and prosperous country, but their definitions of these ideals diverged widely—as did their ideas for achieving them. The ferocity with which each man defended his position went beyond the philosophical to the personal; ultimately, the Hamilton-Jefferson relationship devolved into one of sheer venom and hatred.

Other politicians were not immune to this disease; John Adams could harbor an abiding hate for enemies. But Jefferson and Hamilton attributed the basest motives to the other, which left no room for compromise or even civil disagreement. The arguments were reduced to innuendo, ridicule, slander, smearing, and dirty tricks.

Their enmity might be attributed to the fact that no one really knew very much about how to create a solid democracy, or republic, or constitution, let alone how to ensure freedom and ward off tyranny. Having recently fought a bitter war, these early founders were terrified of doing something—anything—that might blow up the experiment in a democratic republic. Each man and each political faction looked into the future and were alarmed by what they saw. A nation ruled by a great aristocratic slave power or a nation of mechanics tinkering at menial work in water mills? A benign national government nurturing a prosperous economy that would one day become a giant of the world or an octopus of federal authority eternally reaching into every household to strangle its occupants? These sorts of emotional dichotomies created a brand of paranoia in the factions that seemed all too frequently to border on madness.

Jefferson, for example, hired an out-of-work poet named Philip Freneau as a translator in the nascent State Department for the sole purpose of establishing a press to write slanderous articles about Alexander Hamilton and the Federalists. Hamilton's people, for their part, persuaded a young printer, John Fenno, to establish a newspaper lauding Hamilton's policies and bashing the Jefferson faction. Hamilton wrote many of the articles himself under his Publius pseudonym and other pen names.

Charges flew back and forth of sedition, corruption, treason, and attempts to turn the country toward either despotism or anarchy. When Washington pleaded with the factions to cease, they only attacked each other more vehemently.

In 1793 Jefferson found a Virginia congressman named William Giles and persuaded him to introduce to Congress a series of resolutions accusing Hamilton of engaging in speculation and mismanagement of government funds and demanding his dismissal from office. Jefferson secretly had Giles submit the accusations near the end of the session, hoping the charges would linger and rankle throughout the long congressional recess—but Hamilton burned the midnight oil and successfully answered them on the floor, winning a full acquittal. He remained furious long afterward. What enraged Hamilton was that Jefferson always claimed his innocence in these and other public attacks, presenting himself as a philosopher, intellectual, and bon vivant and, at other times, as just a farmer trying to do the right thing.

In Hamilton's case he knew that he was not guilty of the charges against him. He, personally, had always acted with the utmost rectitude while in office and did not speculate, embezzle government money, nor use treasury secrets to profit (although there was probably ample opportunity for him to do so). Even so, there was one blot on his otherwise pristine escutcheon: the presence in the Treasury Department of his friend and cousin by marriage William Duer.

Duer was a charming, Eton-educated Englishman several years older than Hamilton, and for a time Hamilton looked to him as a role model. Duer had inherited his family's plantations on the island of Antigua, from which he derived an income; his marriage into the fashionable Stirling family cemented his station in New York society. He became a member of the state legislature and later a delegate to the Continental Congress and the Constitutional Convention. He had supported Hamilton by writing in favor of New York's adoption of the Constitution. When Hamilton was named treasury secretary, he brought in Duer as assistant secretary.

As time wore on, it was whispered that Duer was becoming an unstable, unprincipled speculator. He lost his properties in the Caribbean and fell deeply into debt. He became desperate as creditors closed in on him and formed a company to buy up the war bonds that American soldiers of the Revolution were given in lieu of pay (though they were then practically worthless because of currency depreciation). But Duer had secret knowledge that Hamilton intended for the U.S. Treasury to redeem the soldiers' paper promises at par; therefore, his actions were a gross violation of fiscal propriety and had the effect as well of cheating the soldiers out of their rightful compensation for their years fighting the war. For a brief time this activity gave Duer a windfall profit. But he lost that as well, and then embezzled some $200,000 from the treasury, a fact that was not uncovered for several years.

Hamilton had already dismissed Duer upon learning from Philip Schuyler of Duer's machinations, duplicity, indebtedness, and speculations. Through it all, Hamilton had sought to help Duer as a once faithful friend and relative by marriage, but the damage had been done. The Duer affair gave Jefferson and his followers an opportunity to excoriate Hamilton in the Giles resolutions before Congress. The accusations didn't stick, because Hamilton had no knowledge of Duer's conduct. But it rankled, because Hamilton had always gone out of his way to be a man of scruples and honor. He took his reputation very seriously.

At length, Duer somehow organized a huge stock speculation that burst spectacularly, resulting in the Panic of 1792. Fortunes great and small were lost across all classes of investors, and Duer was thrown into jail in lower Manhattan, where a mob gathered to demand he be released to them for punishment. Up until he died, in 1799, he was still writing to Hamilton proclaiming his innocence.

The Duer scandal was intimately linked with another that threatened to ruin Hamilton. It began on a summer morning in 1791 in Philadelphia, just after the federal government had moved there. Eliza and the children were staying in Albany with her father, when a beautiful woman in her early twenties appeared on Hamilton's doorstep. She told Hamilton that she was from a reputable New York family (her sister had married a Livingston, she said), but that her husband had abandoned her and their young daughter for another woman and she needed money to get home. She couldn't think of any place to get it, so she came to the person she figured knew where money was—the U.S. treasury secretary. Her name was Maria Reynolds.

Hamilton later said he found "something odd" about her tale but was emotionally stirred by her palpable distress, as well as her great beauty. He told her he would bring her funds after the Treasury's offices closed. That evening he arrived at her boardinghouse with "a bank bill" from his own funds and was taken to her bedroom by the landlady. After handing her the money and after further conversation, it was soon established, Hamilton said, that in repayment of the loan "other than pecuniary compensation would be acceptable."[130]

Hamilton thereupon commenced an affair with Mrs. Reynolds that lasted on and off for nearly a year. Sometimes it was conducted at her lodgings and sometimes in his own bedroom. The woman seemed genuinely attached to Hamilton and over time laid out her sad situation. She had, she said, been married as a young teenager into a family where the father was in debtors' prison. She said almost from the beginning that her husband, whom she soon learned was a part-time con man and extortionist, was in and out of jail; he was also a serial adulterer, had treated her "very cruelly," and then left her without funds.

After some months Mrs. Reynolds informed Hamilton that her husband had reappeared seeking a reconciliation. She asked Hamilton what he thought, and he advised her to do it, divorce rarely being a viable option in those days. Not long afterward she told Hamilton that the reconciliation had taken place. Then she said that her husband had been speculating financially and "could give information respecting the conduct of some persons in his [Treasury] department which would be useful." If at this point Hamilton did not appreciate that Mrs. Reynolds's husband was fully aware of their affair—if not behind it—he should have.

Hamilton met with Reynolds, who told him that in the course of his speculations he had obtained from someone in the Treasury

Department a confidential list of the names of former soldiers who held the government certificates issued to them in lieu of pay. Reynolds indicated that he had been able to purchase many of these at deeply discounted prices before it became known that the United States was going to pay off the full amount at par.

Who was this person, Hamilton asked?

William Duer was the reply. Duer had been long gone from Treasury by then, forced out by Hamilton. But Hamilton, "in the interest of [the perception of] friendship," told Reynolds he appreciated the information. Reynolds's revelation indicated the grossest kind of malfeasance— but by then Duer was in much deeper trouble. Soon Reynolds reappeared, asking for a job as clerk in the Treasury Department. Hamilton, having long assessed his character, rejected the request but continued stringing him along. Meanwhile, Hamilton's affair with Mrs. Reynolds resumed apace, and it soon became apparent that Reynolds was prostituting his wife. This was testified to later by a boarder at one of the houses where the Reynoldses had lived.

On December 15 Hamilton received a threatening letter from Reynolds in which he professed to have been unaware of his wife's adultery until that very day. He claimed that Maria "fell on her knees and asked forgiveness . . . I am robbed of all the happiness in the world," adding that, "There is no person that knows any thing as yet." Reynolds said he wanted a meeting with Hamilton. That same day a letter also arrived from Maria, who seemed to back up her husband's story. "He ses [*sic*] if you do not come . . . he will write to Mrs. Hamilton." A few days later a note from Reynolds requested a meeting at the George Tavern, as "your house or office is no place to converse about these matters."

Hamilton stated afterward, "I could no longer be at a loss that he wanted money." He gave Reynolds a thousand dollars for his silence—and, so it seems, to be allowed to continue the affair with Maria. She frequently sent Hamilton passionate, lurid notes, claiming all manner of distress in her life and a need to see Hamilton for his advice and consolation. Reynolds continued to dun Hamilton for "forced loans," confirming his role as a pimp and extortionist.

Things quickly got crazier when Maria sent a note saying she was dying and wanted to see Hamilton as a last request. Hamilton found he was having trouble distinguishing between reality and deception. He seemed to have a genuine attachment to Maria Reynolds and was moved by her anguish, while at the same time feeling that the entire thing might be a setup. When he did not go to see her, she threatened suicide and claimed that Reynolds planned to have Hamilton murdered. "I could not be absolutely certain if it was artifice or reality," Hamilton later wrote.

A month later Hamilton received a letter from Reynolds, saying Hamilton could "renew" his visits to Maria, whom Reynolds described as "cheerful and kind when you have been with her," adding, "but when you have not, she is [the] reverse, and wishes to be alone by herself." Hamilton by now was dancing on the edge of a very sharp knife. He continued seeing Maria and making "forced loans" to Reynolds, but eased off on his affair when Maria began acting even stranger than usual, again using suicide as a threat and saying other bizarre things.

By July 1792 Reynolds had been incarcerated again, this time for attempting to seize in court the estate of a deceased Revolutionary War soldier. He insisted that Hamilton use his influence to have him released. Hamilton ignored the correspondence and before long learned to his horror that Reynolds and an associate, one Jacob Clingman, had bargained with Hamilton's political enemies to accuse him of speculation

Clingman was even more duplicitous than Reynolds. He had for some reason often been present at the Reynolds residence while the affair with Maria was taking place. According to Clingman's story, Hamilton had made $30,000 by illegal speculation and had told William Duer that if he, Duer, had hung on for three days longer, before the financial bubble burst, he would have made $15,000.

Clingman had once been a clerk to Anti-Federalist congressman Frederick Muhlenberg of Pennsylvania and took the story to him. According to Muhlenberg, Clingman told him that Reynolds had said he "had the power to hang the secretary [Hamilton]." The congressman later testified that those charges had "created considerable uneasiness in my mind, and I conceived it as my duty to consult with my friends."[131]

The friends turned out to be Thomas Jefferson's fellow Virginians and political supporters the senators James Monroe and Abraham Venable. Smelling political blood, Monroe and Venable decided to conduct an ad hoc investigation. The next day they went to visit Reynolds in prison and Maria at her residence. Reynolds informed them that he had "a person in high office [Hamilton]" under his thumb, and that because Hamilton had not helped him out of jail, he intended to "persecute him."[132]

When they interviewed Maria the mystery only deepened. She failed to mention the amorous affair between herself and Hamilton but said she had burned a number of letters from Hamilton to her husband at Hamilton's request. She claimed that Hamilton had attempted to bribe her husband to leave town, but he had refused and was then arrested.

Armed with this inconclusive information, Monroe, Venable, and Muhlenberg went to see Hamilton at his office. When he learned what their concerns were, he told them to come to his home that evening. Hamilton showed them to his study, where his friend from the army the former major general Oliver Wolcott, of Connecticut, was present as a witness.

Hamilton proceeded to tell the story, from the beginning. He described his affection for and affair with Maria Reynolds, her husband's transition from pimp to blackmailer, the misdeeds of William Duer, Hamilton's complete innocence of speculation or any other dishonesty of financial transactions, and his utter humiliation at the entire situation. He spoke unsparingly of "his own vanity, his confusion, his fears," to such an extent that Muhlenberg and Venable begged him to stop, but it seemed that for Hamilton it was an exercise to free himself from what had become a recurring nightmare.

At length he finished the tale, and there was an embarrassed silence in the room. Then the men, chastened by these sordid revelations, agreed to take an oath not to disclose anything of what they had heard. Among gentlemen in those times, it was considered unseemly to reveal news of a person's private affairs. Notes of the conversation had been taken and given to James Monroe, who in turn gave them over for confidential safekeeping to the clerk of the House of Representatives, John Beckley, who was a former indentured servant and friend and political ally of Jefferson.

Hamilton had received some hopeful news from his brother-in-law John Church, who informed him by letter that Eliza had learned of the accusations, but they made "not the least impression upon her, only that she considers the whole Knot of those opposed to you to be scoundrels."

After Hamilton's break with Maria Reynolds, her husband vanished for an extended period and she at last sought a divorce; her lawyer was, of all people, Aaron Burr. Immediately after her divorce was final, she married none other than Jacob Clingman. After a while Hamilton began to breathe easier.

Thus Hamilton's "Reynolds affair" seemed to end with a whimper. He remained in his position as treasury secretary and the newspapers moved on to other things. If Hamilton's wife and family were upset over the affair, there is no evidence of it.

CHAPTER FIVE

After their harrowing transatlantic voyage, American emissary John Adams and his son John Quincy arrived in Bordeaux on March 31, 1778. Just that week, after news of the Continental Army's victory at Saratoga had reached France, Louis XVI had agreed to support America in her war with Britain; he would soon sign a formal declaration of assistance. Adams's own first duties had now changed from convincing the French to enter the war to negotiating and adjusting the terms of the Franco-American pact. News of alliance had of course infuriated Great Britain, and British ships had already begun to attack French ships at sea.

Adams spent his first weeks in Bordeaux being feted by local dignitaries and Americans in residence there. On a morning soon after they arrived, the Adamses were delighted to encounter William McCreery of Baltimore. The next day Adams had supper with McCreery and was seated next to a very beautiful young Frenchwoman. Leaning over, she said through an interpreter, "Mr. Adams, by your name I conclude you are descended from the first man and woman, and probably in your family may be preserved a tradition . . . I could never explain." He told her pray go on. "I never could understand," she continued, "how the first couple found out about the Art of lying together."

"Having been confined to America," he wrote later, "this question was surprising and shocking. I believe at first I blushed." Then he considered his situation. "I thought that it would be as well for once to set a brazen face against a brazen face and to answer a fool according to her folly." And so he answered, "Madam, my family resembles the First Couple both in their name and in their frailties so much that I have no doubt we are descended from that in Paradise. By tradition the answer to your question is, by Instinct, for there is a physical quality within in us resembling the Power of Electricity or the magnet, by which when a pair approached within striking distance they flew together like the needle to the pole or two objects in electrical experiments." Adams then sat back, somewhat self-satisfied, while the interpreter explained his answer. The woman looked at him, surprise in her eyes, and said: "Well, I knew not how it was, but this I know—it is a very happy Shock!"

On another evening, an American commercial agent, a Mr. Bondfield, took Adams to dinner, a play, and the opera. Of this last, Adams wrote in his journal: "The scenery, the dancing, the music afforded to me a very cheerful, sprightly amusement—having never seen anything of its kind before."[133] During the years abroad that would constitute his diplomatic posting Adams would frequently describe in detail in his journal the splendid, near-nightly feasts that the aristocratic and upper-class French threw in his honor; he also listed the other guests and the castles, chateaux, and town houses where the fetes were held. He was both awed and aghast at the quantity and quality of French cuisine and the superb wines served at these events. Overall, Adams was impressed by the prosperous beauty and hospitality of provincial France[134]—an impression confirmed when, on April 4, the Adamses boarded a carriage for the 500-mile journey north to Paris.

Road travel was never comfortable in those times, and this experience was no exception. Still, the roads in France were better than those in America, and Adams was consistently astounded by the sights he passed. Of the countryside he wrote, "Every part of it, is cultivated. Fields of Grain, the Vineyards, the Castles, the Cities, the Parks, the Gardens, everything is Beautiful—yet every place swarms with beggars."[135] He described Tours as "the most elegant place we have yet seen." The next evening his carriage crossed the Seine and arrived in Paris, where "the streets were crowded with carriages, with livery servants." All the best Parisian hotels were full, but Adams finally found respectable lodgings at the Hotel de Valois on the rue de Richelieu, though due to the general demand for lodgings and lack of less spacious accommodations he was required to rent an entire floor.[136]

ONCE IN PARIS, John Adams turned his attention to the business at hand: diplomacy. He knew he must urge even more support from America's new and powerful European partner, but he was one of several other U.S. emissaries (or commissioners, as they were called). Paramount among them was seventy-two-year-old Benjamin Franklin, the internationally celebrated American philosopher, scientist, inventor, polymath, author-printer-publisher, and renowned wit. Adams would later assess other qualities—not so distinguished—about Franklin. But for now the old Philadelphia philosopher was the toast of France.

The morning after he arrived in Paris, Adams went by coach to pay his respects to Benjamin Franklin in Passy, the fashionable neighborhood in which he was living. About three miles south of central Paris on the right bank of the Seine, the area offered extravagant views of the river from its long, high bluffs.

That first afternoon Franklin took Adams to dine in a Paris mansion where "it would be vain to attempt a description of the magnificence of the House, gardens, Library, Furniture or [food] on the table," according to Adams's diary. In attendance at the midday feast were the French comptroller of finances and the Duchess D'Anville, mother of the powerful Duc de La Rochefoucauld, along with "twenty of the great People of France."

That evening Adams "came [back to Passy] and supped with Dr. Franklin on cheese and beer."[137] Franklin immediately insisted that Adams move into his Passy quarters. It was a generous offer, as Franklin was living in one of the buildings on the estate of the wealthy M. le Ray de Chaumont; Chaumont let Franklin use it rent-free in hopes that if the Americans won the war Chaumont's hospitality might be reciprocated by a large land grant from the U.S. government. Adams accepted Franklin's offer and enrolled John Quincy in a private Parisian academy, where he would learn French, Latin, and the classics. Adams himself continued his study of French, but he never got much beyond the *parlez-vous* level.

Besides Franklin and Adams, the other American commissioner was Arthur Lee. The dour Lee, brilliant in his own way, was a member of a large and prominent Virginia family. Educated at Eton College and the University of Edinburgh, he was both a doctor and a lawyer. In the early days of the Revolution, he had stayed on in England and served as an agent for the colonies, as well as an American spy, and thus had spent his entire adult life in Europe. Never married, he vehemently disapproved of Franklin's carousing and philandering, and soon the two commissioners refused to speak. None of this boded well for the American mission to France.

Adams had heard of these animosities among the commissioners but decided to wait and see for himself how the situation would unfold.

As soon as Adams was settled, Lee and Franklin went with him to Versailles to introduce him to the twenty-four-year-old Louis XVI—and to the influential French foreign minister, the Comte de Vergennes, upon whom the fortunes of America's success would so often rest in the future. Nothing of consequence in those times could be done without the direct approval of the king, as he was an absolute monarch. But all foreign diplomats to the court understood that it was essential to gain the ears of the king's advisers in order to sway his opinion. Vergennes was the most influential among them in the area of foreign affairs.

After the proper introductions Vergennes escorted Adams up to the king's lavish bedchamber, where he was being dressed by other ministers—an old French tradition. Adams was wearing fine new French clothes, a powdered wig, and carrying his dress sword—another custom. Vergennes told the king that Adams spoke no French, and the young majesty immediately departed the room. Yet Adams was impressed with the king and saw "goodness and innocence" in his face and strength in his physical carriage.

Adams quickly set out to understand the operation of the American commission. He was soon appalled to realize that neither Lee nor Franklin comprehended the desperation and deprivation of the soldiers and citizens back in America. In general, he did not approve of his fellow commissioners' work habits. Usually up before sunrise, Adams was at his desk for hours before either of the other two arrived. Franklin often played chess in the mornings with his neighbor Madame Anne Louise Brillon de Jouy, a famous harpsichordist, who liked to tackle the game while taking her bath. Franklin rarely came into the office (which was actually in Adams's drawing room, right across from Franklin's plush quarters) until late in the day—and many days he did not come in at all.

"It was late when he breakfasted and soon as breakfast was over, a Crowd of carriages came to his [door] with all sorts of people, Philosophers, Academicians, Economists, literary friends . . . but by far the greater part were women and children come to have the honour to see the great Franklin," Adams recorded in his diary. "These visitors occupied all the time until it became time to dress to go to dinner . . . He was invited to dine every day . . . he always invited me to dine with him . . . till I found it necessary to send my apologies . . . that I might do the business of the mission . . . often when I had drawn the papers and had their fairly copied for signature . . . I was frequently obliged to wait several days to obtain the signature of Dr. Franklin."

The jovial Franklin, whatever his other accomplishments, was a hopeless libertine who enjoyed the company of his fashionable friends. Despite being ill-dressed, old, and bald, he was adored by the ladies, and he enjoyed that reputation. He even asked Adams to let it be known in America that Dr. Franklin was much to be envied: "The ladies not only allow him to [kiss] them and to embrace as often as he pleases, but they are perpetually embracing Him." Adams did as asked, including this line in a letter to Abigail in April 1778.[138] Whenever Adams confronted Franklin and Lee about the extent of so much commission work left undone and so many unanswered accounts, the two would begin to argue, then sulk and refuse to work in concert with the other commissioners.

Maddened by this feuding, Adams took up the work of the mission single-handedly. There were heaps of reports that remained unwritten and unfiled, piles of letters to respond to, negotiations to be opened with merchants and arms and munitions manufacturers, with ship captains to transport critical matériel, with agents of the French government, agents of other governments, and private agents. The business of the commission was "staggering," but Adams's experience on the Continental Board of War had prepared him well for such tasks.[139]

One of the thorniest was what to do about the disposition of British prisoners taken on the high seas by French ships and being held in France. Adams looked to use these sailors in exchange for American prisoners captured by the British—especially those held in the squalid British prison ships in New York Harbor. But so far the British had refused on grounds that the American soldiers were traitors and not subject to the conventions of war.

All these things and more needed tending to—and to complicate matters, the American legation had no clerks or assistants. More and more Adams assumed the workload, and more and more he tired of the luxurious society lifestyle that had so impressed him after he landed in France. At first it merely began to bore him, then it began to annoy him. Finally that whole side of Parisian culture began to disgust him as a direct contradiction of his strict, penny-wise, Calvinist New England way of life. He wrote Abigail: "Luxury, dissipation, and effeminacy, are pretty near at the same degree of excess here and in every other part of

Europe . . . Luxury has as many and as bewitching charms on [the American] side of the ocean as on this—and Luxury, wherever she goes, effaces from human nature the Image of the Divinity. If I had power I would forever banish and exclude from America all gold, silver, precious stones, alabaster, marble, silk, velvet and lace."[140]

It's a good thing that some British ship did not capture the mail schooner carrying this missive and publish it in the newspapers at home and abroad, as the British were wont to do; if it had, the reaction would not have been kind: American women would likely have been out with torches and pitchforks looking to hang Adams in effigy, and his recall might have been imminent. His sentiments about the jewelry and other luxuries might have been facetious, but one could rest assured that the British would put the worst possible spin on it.

This was rare candor in a letter. Adams and other diplomats had learned to be extremely careful about the content of missives sent abroad; the British were master propagandists and wasted no opportunity to make an American official seem foolish, evil, or incompetent in the press, and that reporting ultimately found its way across the Atlantic. Looking through mail was one of the first things British officers did when an American-bound ship was taken.

A letter Abigail wrote to John after his arrival in France was filled with frantic misinformation, apparently based on British-generated propaganda. She reported that the *Boston* had been captured and that its captain, a Mr. Welch, was being held prisoner by the British in Halifax; she also wrote that Welch had destroyed all of John's letters to her before the British seized them. (The *Boston* had not been taken by the British—though it would be two years later.) Abigail went on to relate "the horrid story of Dr. Franklin's assassination, which was received from France and sent to . . . Congress."

Adams worried about these rumors, but not much. There wasn't much one could do. But he did try, unsuccessfully, to persuade the French to have their naval frigates convoy U.S. merchant ships across the ocean; it would, he argued, result in a massive increase in trade and commerce that would benefit both countries. The French contended that they did not use their naval vessels in such a manner. Adams also tried to persuade the French to attack the British whaling fleet, the location of which was known to American intelligence, but was likewise turned down for the same reasons.

Adams had come to realize that sea power was the key to winning the war, and America's navy—a few frigates, no ships of the line—was minuscule compared to France's. He tried (without success) to persuade Foreign Minister Vergennes to place enough French ships in American waters to command the seas there, but his adjurations were met with polite refusal. What Adams didn't know was that Vergennes had bigger fish to fry. Pursuant to a secret agreement with Spain, he was planning an invasion of England itself.

It was during this period that Adams came to know the man who would emerge as one of America's greatest naval heroes: the young captain John Paul Jones. He had set up headquarters at L'Orient, a naval base in Brittany, and was operating in British waters. Jones was hoping to draw the Royal Navy away from the United States by staging a series of daring raids on British ships and coastal towns.

Using a combination of American and French ships manned mostly by French crews, Jones would arrive off the mouth of an

English or Scottish river and prey on commercial boats as they entered the sea. He would then sail up the river to the town, disembark a combination of infantry and seamen, and take over the municipality in question, pulling people from their beds, taking hostages, stealing valuables in the manner of buccaneers, and demanding ransom. Word of these exploits found their way into the British press, and towns up and down the English coast were terrorized by the notion of sudden attack by the ferocious Jones. Soon, British papers were castigating the Admiralty for not being able to protect the seas along the home front.

Adams thought Jones's plan was excellent until he asked the young captain what happened if towns didn't pay the ransom. Put them to the torch, Jones replied. Adams felt a need to constrain Jones in certain of his measures, inasmuch as the Royal Navy in American waters were perfectly capable of doing the same thing to towns along the U.S. coast.

Jones was in the process of creating a scheme with Lafayette, who had returned to France briefly to plead America's cause. The two wanted to attack the spa resort of Bath, where "all of London society would be gathered" from October to June. But the mission never came off. Lafayette was diverted to other things, while Jones continued his smaller raids.

Then, in September 1779, Jones's battered ship the *Bonhomme Richard,* engaged in a fierce battle with the powerful British man-of-war *Serapis* in a battle off Flamborough Head, in Yorkshire, England. When the *Serapis* commander demanded that Jones surrender his battered ship and men, he was reputed to have issued his famous refusal, "I have not yet begun to fight!"

IN JULY 1778 SILAS DEANE, the recalled commissioner whom Adams had replaced in France, arrived back in the United States. The son of a Groton, Connecticut, blacksmith, Deane had received a full scholarship to Yale and graduated with honors. Embittered at his recall, he began spreading false and defamatory stories about Adams and Arthur Lee, which, in the absence of their side of the story, resulted in Adams's recall, Lee's reassignment to Spain, and Franklin's elevation to sole U.S. minister to France.

Adams was boiling. "The scaffold is cut away, and I am left kicking and sprawling in the mire," he told Abigail in a letter announcing his departure. He was (once again) finished with politics, he said. When he arrived in America, he planned to move the family to Boston and resume his legal practice. "I will draw Writs and Deeds, and harangue jurys and be happy," he wrote sourly.[141]

Adams collected John Quincy and the two traveled to Nantes, where they were scheduled to return to America aboard the USS *Alliance,* a twenty-four-gun U.S. frigate. But the *Alliance* was under conflicting orders, and after nearly three months it was learned that she would not be sailing back to the States but would accompany a fleet led by John Paul Jones into British waters.

Adams was then told to take passage on the French frigate *La Sensible,* leaving for America with a French envoy. But the envoy was delayed, and it was another three months before *La Sensible* sailed. Fortunately, the passage was smooth and fast, taking about six weeks to reach Boston. There Adams was reunited with Abigail, who had been almost in a state of distraction since his departure some twenty months before. Everything had been left to her—the running of the farm, the raising of the children, all in an environment of runaway inflation and a constant state of national war.

Though he had vowed he was through with politics, Adams was almost immediately tapped to be part of a committee to draw up a constitution for the state of Massachusetts. As usual, Adams did almost all the work himself, priding himself on the final document, which was accepted by the state legislature. No sooner had he finished this arduous labor than he was informed Congress had named him as a peace commissioner. He was to return to France and, from there, test Britain's interest in opening negotiations to end the war.

After only seventy-one days with his family, Adams dutifully reboarded *La Sensible* in Boston Harbor. This time he took both John Quincy, now twelve, and his younger son Charles, not quite ten, to France with him. Their fellow passengers included John Thaxter, a cousin of Abigail's who was to serve as Adams's secretary; Francis Dana, who would serve as secretary to the peace legation; and several businessmen.

They sailed on November 15, 1779, a cold, squally New England day. *La Sensible* managed to avoid the several British warships lurking about, but after passing the Grand Banks she ran into a terrific three-day storm that threw the ship violently about, causing everyone to become sick and opening numerous seams that made it necessary to man the pumps twenty-four hours a day.

Though the ship stayed afloat, she was too damaged to defend herself. The captain determined to head for the nearest friendly port, which was in Spain, not France. On December 7, *La Sensible* made port in Ferrol, located in far northwestern Spain. When it was found that the ship needed extensive and lengthy repairs, Adams and the other Americans decided not to wait but to arrange land transport to France. During the several days it took to make those arrangements, Adams and his sons explored the town and vicinity.

Being a lawyer, Adams was interested in the Spanish legal system (especially the criminal justice aspects), and he was appalled to find that Spaniards still occasionally burned people at the stake. The punishment for parricide (the killing of a parent or near relative) was particularly ghoulish: the offender was sealed into a cask with a poisonous snake (adder) and a toad and "cast into the sea."[142] "The ancient Laws of the Visigoths is still in Use," he told his diary, along with "the Institutes, codes, Novelles, etc. of Justinian" (the sixth-century Byzantine emperor).[143]

Adams also met with the Spanish consul in Ferrol, who told him that Spain took a dim view of the American Revolution, fearing it would set "a bad example to the Spanish colonies" and that if the Americans "become ambitious and seized with the spirit of conquest [they] might take aim at Mexico and Peru." Adams corrected him, assuring him that "Americans hate war. Agriculture and commerce were their objects."[144]

Adams and his fellow travelers found that the only transportation available to them for the long journey into France were four calashes drawn by mules. The calash was a small, low carriage with low wheels and a folding canvas top; it proved so uncomfortable that most of the time the Americans preferred to ride the mules. The roads were nearly impossible to navigate, winding up and around the Pyrenees and dipping into swamps. The party, which consisted of Adams and his two sons and half a dozen diplomats and businessmen, made less than five miles a day, stopping at night in filthy hovels with flea-ridden bedding. "I see nothing but signs of poverty and misery, among the people," Adams wrote. "A fertile country, not half cultivated. People ragged and dirty and the houses universally nothing but mire, smoke, fleas and lice. Nothing appears rich but the Churches, nobody fat but the Clergy."[145]

It took a month to make the French frontier, and Adams later called the trek as the most severe trial of his life. At the frontier, the Americans hired a proper coach, but given the winter rains it took almost another month to reach Paris.

Once in Paris, the first thing Adams did after enrolling his two boys in a private academy was pay a call on Benjamin Franklin, whom he now despised. After a brief reintroduction, Adams departed and made arrangements to take a house in Paris as his home and headquarters. The next day the two men took a carriage to Versailles to see Foreign Minister Vergennes.

Adams did not inform Franklin of the purpose of his return, for fear that the wily old diplomat might somehow connive to usurp him by taking the mission away from him. Adams understood his undertaking as twofold. First, he had been sent as a peace commissioner to engage with the British, if they were interested in negotiations. By that spring of 1780 the war had been going on for five years, and had been fought to a stalemate. But the British held New York, Charleston, and Savannah, and the Royal Navy patrolled the East Coast, making transatlantic trade very difficult. The British had little reason to begin peace negotiations on any terms other than their own. Adams's second task was to persuade the French to increase their forces in the United States—especially naval forces.

After meeting with Vergennes, Adams was delighted to learn that was exactly what the French had in mind. The powerful foreign minister explained that the French navy was being significantly strengthened to drive the British from the American seas, and that an army of more than 5,000 men was being raised. It was expected to depart shortly from Brest, under the command of the Comte de Rochambeau. Adams could scarcely believe his ears.

But, Vergennes cautioned, Adams must under no circumstances reveal his mission as a peace commissioner; the British, he advised, would surely take that as a sign of American weakness. And he added that there should be no talk of an American separate peace with the British. They would have to fight it out and win a significant victory before there should be any sign that the Americans wanted to negotiate. Adams commenced filing reports of all this news to Congress; in his spare time he began sending stories to British newspapers under a pseudonym that was meant to counter the British accounts of American discontent and war weariness.

As the summer of 1780 unfolded, Adams's elation at France's apparent determination to win the war began to be tinged with pessimism. First, the new French fleet was sent not to America but to the West Indies, where the British had been preying on French merchantmen. Second, the new French army had arrived in America in July but disembarked at Newport, Rhode Island, and showed no signs of activity nor of linking up with Washington's forces. Despite reassurances by Vergennes that "the king is far from abandoning the cause of America," Adams had begun to conclude that the French lacked offensive spirit in their military.[146]

Then Adams received word from Congress that almost took him out of the picture entirely. A few months earlier Congress had sent one of its most outstanding figures, Henry Laurens of South Carolina (his son, John, was Hamilton's close friend), to the Netherlands to secure a loan of $10 million and a treaty of amity and commerce; it was known that the Dutch neither liked nor trusted the British and might be persuaded to aid the American cause. But Laurens's ship had been seized by a British man-of-war, and he had been taken to England and thrown into the Tower of London, where he would remain for the next fifteen months. And so it fell to John Adams to negotiate with the Dutch government and the bankers of Amsterdam.

Arriving in Holland in September 1780, Adams was at first heartened by hints that the Dutch were willing to help the American cause. He found that he liked the Dutch people. They were sober, frugal, and unassuming, more like his fellow New Englanders than the sybaritic, boisterous French.

As time passed, however, Adams realized that Dutch assistance was a fiction. Part of the problem was the language barrier; Adams spoke no Dutch and the Dutch spoke no English and little French. But the true problem was that the Dutch were paralyzed with fear of British retaliation against them if they were known to help the Americans. Already British spies had fingered Adams as having arrived in Amsterdam; the British government had convened a meeting and decided that certain Dutch ships should be detained and their cargoes seized in order to punish the Dutch for having even entertained the thought of aiding the Americans. So Adams sat in Amsterdam and bided his time.

Then he had an idea. The Dutch, as he saw it, seemed to view the Americans as bankrupt failures, so he set out to correct that impression. At the government's expense, he purchased very fine entertaining accouterments for his rented house: napkins, tablecloths, silverware, glassware, serving dishes and plates. He ordered new clothes. He bought a handsome carriage. He threw dinner parties. All of this made him new friends, but none of it got him very far in achieving his mission of a commercial treaty and loans.

TOP: Stylishly dressed Alexander Hamilton, New York lawyer and U.S. secretary of the treasury. BOTTOM LEFT: The Marquis de Lafayette, a highly influential figure during the American Revolution and friend of Alexander Hamilton and Thomas Jefferson. BOTTOM RIGHT: Sketch of Aaron Burr

TOP LEFT: This famous painting of Alexander Hamilton was completed by the portraitist John Trumbull in 1805, a year after Hamilton's death in the duel with Aaron Burr. TOP RIGHT: Elizabeth Schuyler Hamilton, 1787, whom Hamilton married while still serving in George Washington's army during the Revolutionary War. A daughter of Knickerbocker aristocracy, she brought him social standing in New York and elsewhere. After Hamilton's death at the dueling grounds, she lived on—until the mid-nineteenth century—to carry on his name and good works. BOTTOM: The Grange, the large country home that Hamilton built for his family above the Harlem River in New York, and where he expected to live out his old age. It was a long, uphill carriage ride from his law office in the flats of Wall Street to the Grange in Harlem Heights.

TOP: Surrender of the British army to George Washington at Yorktown, Virginia, 1781. The British commander Lord Cornwallis declined to attend the ceremony, sending instead an underling. Colonel Alexander Hamilton is seen standing at the far right, next to the horse. BOTTOM: Lithograph of the fatal duel between Alexander Hamilton and Aaron Burr. Hamilton insisted before and after the duel that he had thrown away his first shot in order to give Burr a chance to call it off.

TOP: The Adams family farm at Braintree near Quincy, Massachusetts, the birthplace of John Adams. BOTTOM: Peacefield was John and Abigail Adams's home in Quincy, Massachusetts, where they spent their latter years. It was purchased from a family of Tories who had abandoned it after they fled for England during the Revolutionary War.

Abigail Adams, 1766, by Benjamin Blyth

Paul Revere's famous engraving, produced in 1770, only weeks after the Boston Massacre, was widely disseminated, inflaming passions in pre-Revolutionary America. John Adams, despite the advice of friends, defended the British soldiers and officers, winning acquittals for most of them and light sentences for the others. Adams believed that every man was entitled to representation at trial.

John Singleton Copley's 1783 portrait of John Adams, painted shortly after the signing of the Treaty of Paris, which ended the Revolutionary War

John Adams, as the American ambassador to the Court of St. James's,
presenting his credentials to King George III, 1785

John Adams, Founding Father, first vice president and second president of the United States, first president to live in the White House, and father of the sixth president, John Quincy Adams, in an 1823 portrait by Gilbert Stuart.

Thomas Jefferson, ambassador to France, in a 1788 painting by John Trumbull. His nose seems longer and shaplier than in most artists' conceptions.

TOP: George Washington presides over the signing of the U.S. Constitution at the Constitutional Convention in 1787. RIGHT: Bust of Thomas Jefferson by the French sculptor Jean-Antoine Houdon, 1789. It resides in the parlor of Monticello. Another Jefferson bust sits at the entrance hall to Monticello, as it did in Jefferson's day. Per Jefferson's instructions, it faces a bust of Jefferson's slain political enemy Alexander Hamilton—the two at peace at last.

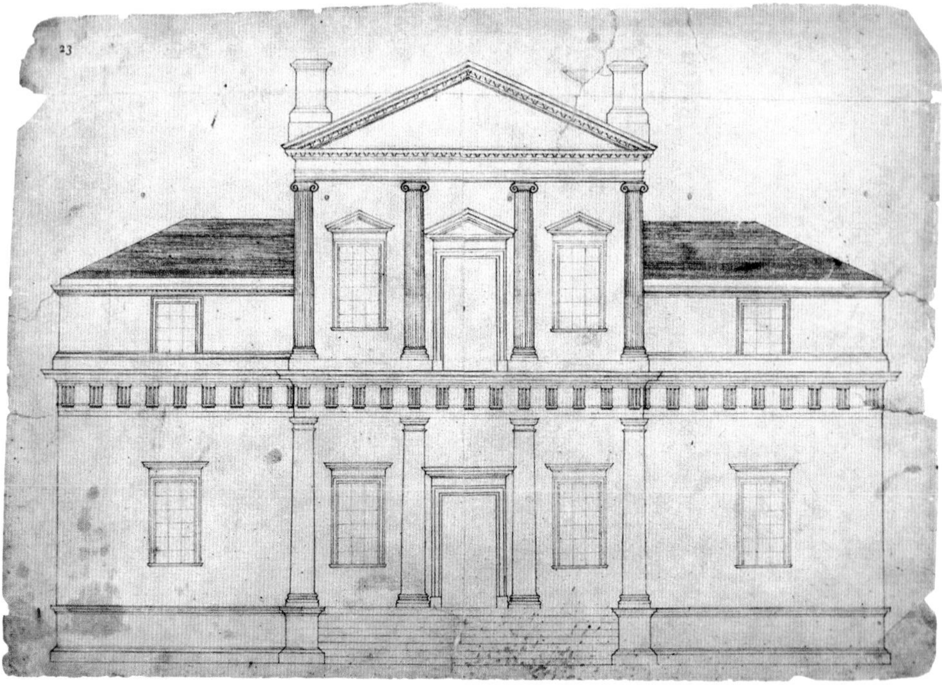

TOP: Monticello as it appeared in the early nineteenth century BOTTOM: Jefferson's original sketch of the first Monticello, before he visited Europe, with its clean Doric Greek Revival lines, 1771

Thomas Jefferson holding his Declaration of Independence,
with a bust of Benjamin Franklin at his side

Thomas Jefferson proposing to Martha Wayles,
as she plays the pianoforte, 1771

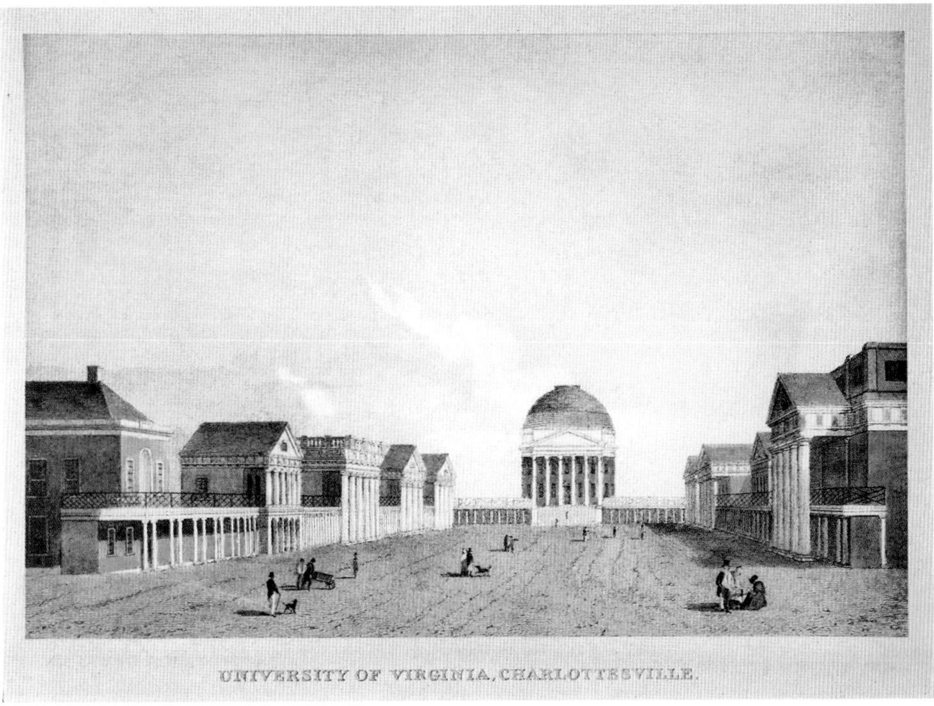

UNIVERSITY OF VIRGINIA, CHARLOTTESVILLE.

TOP: A steel engraving of the Academical Village at the University of Virginia, circa 1831, conceived and designed by Thomas Jefferson. Its famous Rotunda continues to attract visitors and sightseers today. LEFT: One of the better-known portraits of Jefferson, painted by Rembrandt Peale in 1805, at the end of Jefferson's first term as president. Painted at the White House, Jefferson chose to wear a fur-lined cape and leave his hair undressed.

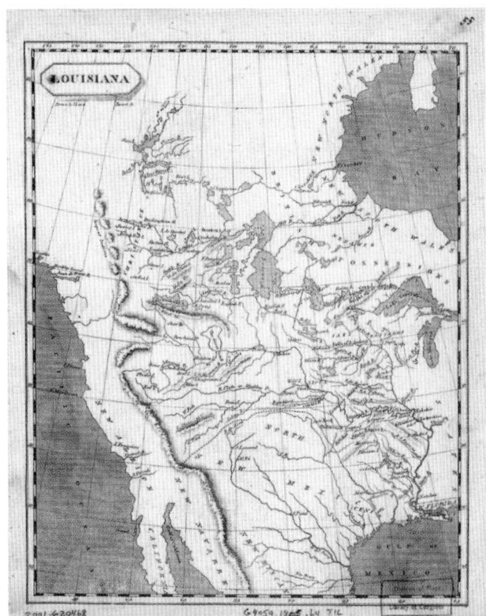

TOP LEFT: Map of the Louisiana Purchase, Jefferson's crowning achievement as president of the United States. TOP RIGHT: Portrait of Jefferson as an old man, circa 1821, by Thomas Sully. In this year Spain gratified one of Jefferson's dreams by giving up Florida and its other possessions in the American South, rounding out President Jefferson's Louisiana Purchase. BOTTOM: The Lewis and Clark Expedition, 1804–1806, mapped and surveyed the vast territory that had nearly doubled the size of the United States.

The Dutch were waiting for some clear sign that the Americans could win the war, and thus far they had seen only defeat. Adams was convinced that sooner or later they would come around—but there were precious few signs of it as the weeks and months passed.

During this year away, Adams's correspondence with Abigail had dropped off and hers with him. For John, being in the diplomatic limelight seemed to have counterbalanced any angst of solitude. But Abigail was overburdened with domestic duties and craved communication with intelligent company. Uncharacteristically, she began carrying on a harmless flirtation with James Lovell, a congressman from Massachusetts whom the Adamses had known casually for years. Lovell had been living in Philadelphia away from his wife for several years and had a reputation as a ladies' man. He had originally contacted Abigail to offer assistance while John was on assignment to Paris. She had responded in a chatty letter with her thanks, and Lovell had taken a fancy to her and begun to write often. There is no shred of evidence that the relationship went beyond letter writing.[147] It ended without John ever having known of it.

IN EARLY 1781 the news regarding the future of the American Revolution was consistently bad. One of Washington's best generals, Benedict Arnold, had turned traitor and gone over to the British; he was presently fighting his fellow Americans in Virginia. Meanwhile, Catherine the Great, empress of Russia, as well as several smaller nations, were offering to mediate the war—but the Russian scheme horrified Adams, for it contained a recommendation of a cease-fire or truce while the negotiations were taking place. Adams knew that would likely be fatal to the American cause. He insisted that no mediation or negotiations would take place unless the British recognized the independence of America.

Then came news from Franklin that Adams was cut off from all further funding. Not only that, but word came from Philadelphia that Congress had appointed five peace commissioners, of which Adams was merely one. The others were Thomas Jefferson, John Jay, Laurens if he was ever released from the Tower, and Franklin.

Thoroughly deflated, Adams went into what can only be described as a rage. He began seeing enemies where none existed. It was during this time, in the late summer of 1781, that he collapsed completely. Doctors said it was malaria and Adams spoke of it as a "fever," but some modern scholars have concluded that it was a nervous breakdown.

Adams was nearly insensate for weeks. But during those weeks, Washington at last joined with Rochambeau's French army and the combined force began a stealthy march to Virginia to take on Cornwallis. The victory that Adams had been waiting for was starting to unfold. Then on October 19, as the American fife-and-drum corps played "Yankee Doodle" and the redcoats "The World Turned Upside Down," the British surrendered.

When word arrived in Amsterdam of the Yorktown victory, Adams felt thoroughly vindicated. His remonstrations to Foreign Minister Vergennes insisting that the French navy play a larger role in the war had been justified. Now all of the pieces began to fall into place. Dutch officials began work on a commercial treaty with the United States and on official recognition of the new nation. Adams also began negotiations with Amsterdam bankers for a loan to America. Adams was treated almost as royalty, writing that there were "Sups and Visits at Court among Princesses and Princes, Lords and Ladies of Various Nations." John Adams was suddenly the toast of Holland.

Adams moved from Amsterdam to The Hague, where he acquired an elegant house that became the first American embassy. Whatever ailed him soon went away, and he was again able to enjoy his morning horseback rides. He was, he said, no longer the "Grumbletonian Patriot" but a man "complaisant, good humored [and] contented."[148]

While the Yorktown defeat was a huge shock to the British, they still held New York City and would probably continue to do so, using it as a bargaining chip in their negotiations. Then, in March 1782, the government of British prime minister Lord North, who had prosecuted the war vigorously, fell and was replaced by a government under Lord Rockingham, a friend of America. Charles James Fox became foreign secretary and favored recognizing American independence immediately. A retired Scottish businessman, Richard Oswald, was officially dispatched to Paris to open peace negotiations with the American commissioners. John Jay, one of the other peace commissioners who had recently joined Franklin in Paris, sent a message to Adams, telling him to come to Paris "soon—very soon."

When Adams arrived, he was dismayed to learn that Congress had given instructions that the commissioners were to abide by the guidance of the French. Congress's decision was based on the belief that the French had been a full partner and ally of the Americans, and that the victory at Yorktown was largely due to them.

But to Adams and Jay it seemed outrageous that their negotiations would be conducted with the French hovering over them and giving "guidance" or instructions that would undoubtedly be weighted toward French interests. Vergennes, for example, advised that the Americans start negotiations without British recognition of U.S. independence. Adams sent a letter to Congress saying that unless that stipulation was removed he would resign as a peace commissioner.

In his mid-seventies, Franklin had been ill and of not much use in the preliminary talks with Oswald that took place over the summer. But now he, too, demanded that before any official peace negotiations could take place, Britain would first have to recognize American independence. The British were slow to respond to this ultimatum, but at last in September Oswald received permission to "treat with the ministers of the United States of America" (rather than "ministers of the American Colonies"). The peace commissioners took this to be tacit recognition of American independence. The serious negotiating could begin.

Due to his wife's illness, Thomas Jefferson was unable to fulfill his mission to France, and Henry Laurens, finally released from the Tower of London (in exchange for Lord Cornwallis), was in such poor health that he could not participate in the negotiations until the very end. That left the negotiations largely to Adams and Jay; they consulted with Franklin when his health allowed.

Initially, Oswald, was "agreeable to the point of being unsuited for politics," but he was soon joined by Henry Strachey, British undersecretary of state, sent "to stiffen Oswald's resolve."[149] Having conceded American independence, the British aims were to limit French and Spanish influence in North America; to establish a brisk trading relationship with the United States (to the exclusion of other European nations); to secure the safety and restoration of the property of the Tories; and to require that American debts to British merchants and lenders be repaid (repayments had stopped during the war).

American goals were the immediate removal of British troops from American soil; the establishment of a northern border with Canada; American fishing rights on the Grand Banks and other Atlantic fishing grounds; and the return of American property (mostly slaves) taken by the British army. Both sides were anxious to exchange prisoners, and the Americans immediately promised not to molest British soldiers as they were departing.

It was Britain's unstated goal to keep America as weak and dependent as possible so as to dominate trade with it. Adams saw through this almost immediately. He called it the "wing clipping system" and vowed "to drive out of countenance and into infamy, every narrow thought of cramping, stinting, impoverishing, or enfeebling Us. To shew that it is their only interest to shew themselves our Friends, to wear away, if possible, the memory of past unkindnesses."[150]

Oswald sensed Adams's worries. "You are afraid," he told Adams," of being made the Tools of the Powers of Europe." "Indeed I am," Adams replied. "It is obvious that all the Powers of Europe will be continually maneuvering with us, to work into their real or imagined Balances of Power. They will all wish to make of us a Make Weight Candle [something put onto a scale to make the required weight], when they are weighing out their pounds."[151]

The British were quite generous when it came to drawing the border with Canada and a southern and western border as well. The northern border that was established looked much as it does today. The western border went beyond the Appalachian Mountains to the Mississippi River, and the southern border went from the top of Florida and along a strip of land called West Florida that paralleled the Gulf Coast to New Orleans. The British conceded this strip to keep the French out and confine the Spanish to their Gulf Coast domain; the American peace commissioners were pleased with the development.

There was much haggling over the Grand Banks fisheries, but Adams was tenacious because of the fishing grounds' value to New Englanders. In the end, the American commissioners secured the right to fish the Banks—but early on, before Adams's arrival, Jay had surrendered their longtime right to dry and cure their catch on the shores of British Newfoundland. The Americans also lost the protection of the British against the pirates of the Barbary Coast. These brigands preyed on shipping from Morocco to Libya, seizing merchant ships and ransoming or enslaving their officers, passengers, and crews.

The matter of American debts to the British and the restoration of Tory possessions also proved difficult to resolve. Adams and Jay argued that the U.S. government had no authority over these issues, because the prohibition against paying British debts and the confiscation of Tory property were matters for the individual states. But the British were adamant in their stance on these points. Privately, Adams told his diary that maybe he should "recollect the prison ships, and the churches of New York, where [American soldiers] were starved to make them enlist in [the British army]. It might not be remiss to recollect the Burning of Cities, and the theft of [silver], negroes, and tobacco."[152] The British argued it was a question of their national honor to see that their Loyalists were treated properly.

After much posturing on both sides, it was agreed that the U.S. government would use all of its authority and arguments to persuade the states to compensate the Tories for confiscated property and to force debtors to pay their obligations to British merchants and lenders—but that it was beyond their legal ability to force them to do so. This on-paper agreement amounted to little in the end. Tories were treated badly after the war, and most states did not rescind their laws against repaying British debts. And British promises to return stolen property—"negroes, [silver,] tobacco"—also came to naught. Little of the latter was returned, and many of the slaves taken by the British were sold in the Caribbean to work on sugar plantations.

On September 3, 1783, the Treaty of Paris was signed by the American commissioners and their British counterparts. Though it still required ratification by Congress, the long British-American conflict was effectively over. A few weeks later France, Spain, and the Netherlands agreed to settle their differences—mostly in exchange for the return, or assignment to them, of various islands in the Caribbean and Mediterranean, as well as other rights.

Peace reigned in the world. Ships could sail six of the seven seas (though there were still the Barbary pirates to contend with) without fear of capture or battle. The European aristocracy and cognoscenti resumed their tours of European capitals and countrysides without fear of imprisonment, or worse.

For Americans, the relief was greatest. After seven arduous years of war the British were finally departing. Americans had won their independence and were a free people. Times were hard and would get harder—but for now there was peace.

Though pleased and relieved, John Adams did not believe the peace would necessarily be peaceful, or would last. He had warned as early as 1776 that there would be no return to the "Happiness and Halcyon days" with Great Britain and instead predicted an "incurable animosity that would last for generations." He now believed Britain harbored an "enduring hatred" that was "blind and vindictive" toward the United States. And because the two nations would eventually compete for the same markets, Britain was America's "natural enemy" and should be shunned at all costs. Adams believed that France would become America's truest friend and trading partner—but he could not foresee the French Revolution and the consequent rise of Napoleon Bonaparte.[153]

Despite his doubts, Adams was sanguine. America would be fine if only she could maintain her independence, he believed. "Thus drops the Curtain on this mighty Tragedy," he wrote to Abigail.[154]

"THE FIRST WISH OF MY HEART [is] to return to my wife and children," Adams told Franklin's grandson William in early January 1783. But although that was the official story, the now seasoned diplomat secretly wanted to become America's first ambassador to England. He felt he was more suited for the position than anyone else, because he had studied the British for more than a decade and had dealt with their commissioners. He wanted to make sure that relations between the new nation and its former parent country went as smoothly as possible and knew there would be grave difficulties, foreseeing that there would be "animosity and vindictiveness" on Britain's part. He also knew that the British record on diplomacy was "shifty"; the nation remained the world's most formidable military and naval power, while America had lost its taste for war. In short,

America needed a man such as himself to keep the scales balanced. But no word came from Congress appointing Adams as minister to the Court of St. James's. Instead, he, Jay, and Franklin were commissioned to negotiate a commercial treaty with Great Britain.

Adams was now very lonely for Abigail. It had been four years since he had seen her, and he was still recuperating from his earlier illness. At times he had contemplated having her come to Europe but given her horrifying fear of the sea and the dangers posed by war, he had refrained from asking. Now she was asking him; she had either conquered her fear of sailing or at last overcome it by the desire to be with John.

At first, Adams was reticent in response to his wife's request, but soon he began asking, then begging, her to come to him. He declared that their younger children—thirteen-year-old Charles and eleven-year-old Thomas—were old enough to stay with relatives. Abigail agreed and added that she was bringing seventeen-year-old Nabby, who was being courted by Royall Tyler, a suitor of dubious reputation.

In October 1783 Adams took John Quincy to England; Charles had sailed for Boston earlier with a bad case of homesickness. Father and son visited Windsor Castle, St. Paul's Cathedral, the Wedgwood pottery factory, and Parliament during its state opening, when George III delivered the traditional king's speech.

Adams exulted in the teeming streets of London, with its population of three-quarters of a million. He sat for portraits by two famous American Patriots, John Singleton Copley and Benjamin West, and read Captain James Cook's final volume of his Pacific voyage, then the rage of London. Over Christmas Adams at last arrived at the ostensible object of his visit: the hot springs at Bath, whose healing properties had been recommended to him by his doctor.

He was having an excellent time when word of a calamity reached him from Holland—the American loan had not been repaid. With American credit at stake, Adams and John Quincy rushed to heal the breach. The two boarded a small packet boat and were soon struck by one of the most violent winter storms in memory on the North Sea. For three days their boat was battered until it was hardly recognizable. By the time it made landfall on a small, barren island off the Dutch coast, they were exhausted by seasickness and the violence of the crossing.

But their ordeal wasn't over; Adams and his son had to walk five miles through snow and ice before they encountered an iceboat that carried them across the frozen sea to the mainland. There, because of the weather, the only transportation available was a peasant's cart. After bucking over frozen ruts for a full day, they reached a town near The Hague, where they obtained a handsome carriage for the remainder of the trip. Adams, with understatement, described the trip as "uncouth."[155]

Once in Amsterdam, Adams managed to defuse the loan crisis by getting a second loan from the worried lenders but at the high interest rate of 6 percent. With U.S. credit restored, he and John Quincy returned to Paris.

Meanwhile, Abigail had been preparing for her great voyage. She had leased out the farm and placed the two younger boys with relatives; she had waited for June to sail, as that was the calmest month for storms on the Atlantic. But weather can be a fickle player, and two hours after her ship, the *Active,* sailed out of Boston Harbor the captain sent word "for all the Ladies to put on their sea cloaths and prepare for sickness."

No sooner was this done, Abigail said, than "we found ourselves all sick." She and Nabby were accompanied on the voyage by a manservant and a maid, but "the maid was wholly useless and the sickest of either." The manservant remained unaffected and attended Abigail and her daughter as best he could. But the next day, he was too sick to be of assistance, and the ladies were attended by a young man named Job Field; Abigail's neighbor, he had until recently been confined in English prison as a prisoner of war.

It was almost three days before the sickness abated and the passengers could go up on deck and survey their surroundings. But soon enough the rough seas returned. "It is utterly impossible to keep nice and clean," Abigail said. Along with the seas, she complained of the "Nausias Smells" of leaking whale oil in the hold, along with the cramped quarters and miserable food. It took nearly two weeks for the sickness to pass. The ship, Abigail said, was "a prison."[156]

At last after six weeks at sea, the white cliffs of Dover hove into view. Abigail and Nabby proceeded to the arranged meeting place with John—the Adelphi Hotel in London—only to find that John was not there, but detained at The Hague; he had sent John Quincy to meet them until he could extricate himself. Finally, almost three weeks later, John joined his family in London. After four and a half years of separation, Abigail, John, and Nabby were at last together again. Their reunion was tender and loving, and the next morning they set out for Paris.

Once in the French capital, they spent four days touring the sights, taking in Notre-Dame, the Tuileries, and other famous gardens, buildings, and museums. They had endured a turbulent, often painful era of fourteen years that had begun with the Boston Massacre, then continued through the Boston Tea

Party, Lexington and Concord, and on into revolution and beyond. For most of those years, John had been separated from Abigail, either in Congress or in France. Now there was peace and reunion, and Adams vowed there would be no more separations.

When the four days in Paris were over, Adams took Abigail and Nabby to Auteuil, a peaceful glade above the Seine on the outskirts of Paris. There, they stayed in the fifty-room mansion of a friend, where the ladies could relax while Adams went into town to work.

The latest crisis involved the Barbary pirates seizing a ship that belonged to a Philadelphia man, who wanted help getting it back. And the negotiations for a commercial treaty with Britain were predictably difficult. The British had forbidden Americans from bringing their goods into its ports and trading with its possessions in the Caribbean; the Americans, for their part, refused to offer the British the same duty-free trade that they had enjoyed before the war. America had negotiated a treaty of commerce only with Prussia, but Adams suspected that many other European countries would eventually follow suit.

With Abigail now by his side, Adams maintained a busy social schedule filled with fetes attended by aristocrats, diplomats, and royalty. Benjamin Franklin went out of his way to be kind to the Adams women and dined with them several times, though he was in great discomfort from gout and kidney stones. But it was Thomas Jefferson who grew closest to John and Abigail.

Jefferson had arrived in Paris only recently to replace John Jay on the commerce commission; he had brought his eldest daughter, Patsy, with him. Despite the fact that he was a soft-spoken wealthy southern slaveholder and Adams a blunt-spoken New Englander, they forged a friendship that was remarkable in its closeness. Adams admired Jefferson for his reputation as a scientist, musician, and philosopher, and Jefferson was drawn to Adams for his wit and logic. It probably also helped that both men were lawyers.

For nine months the Adams family enjoyed the serenity of Auteuil and the gaiety of Parisian social life. Then in May 1784 Adams received his coveted appointment as minister to the Court of St. James's. His nomination had not been without difficulty; some congressmen felt Adams's total candor and quick temper were not assets for an ambassador—especially not to Great Britain, where there were difficulties enough. But they had been overruled. Adams would be the first American ambassador to the former mother country.

AFTER SEEING NOW EIGHTEEN-YEAR-OLD John Quincy off on a transatlantic voyage to attend Harvard College, John, Abigail, and Nabby packed their bags and boarded a packet boat for London. They arrived at the end of May, when the English gardens were just coming into bloom. Adams found a comfortable four-story town house on Grosvenor Square near Hyde Park, an area where aristocrats and noblemen lived.

Abigail set about hiring a staff, while John presented his credentials to the Court of St. James's and was given an invitation to visit the king. On a rainy afternoon in June, Adams was escorted to St. James's Palace by the British foreign minister Lord Carmarthen. After climbing a flight of stairs, a door was opened to what was called "the King's Bed Chamber" (which, unlike France's Louis XVI, was not where the king actually slept but where he received visitors).

Adams entered bowing, as he had been told to do. As a former subject of this fearsome presence, he was anxious. In American proclamations from the Intolerable Acts to the Declaration of Independence, this English sovereign had been accused of almost every low act and deed known to history. And now before him stood this short, rotund American commoner. The king, Adams assumed, probably believed he was good for nothing but the executioner's ax.

An assortment of ministers and diplomats, aristocracy and high miters of the Church of England filled the chamber, and they peered at Adams as if he were a peculiar insect. But he got out the words he had rehearsed: "The United States of America have appointed me their minister plenipotentiary to Your Majesty,"[157] he began. "The appointment of a minister from the United States to Your Majesty's Court will form an epocha in the history of England and of America. I think myself more fortunate than all my fellow citizens, in having the distinguished honor to be the first to stand in your Majesty's royal presence in a diplomatic character . . ."

Warming to his subject, Adams reminded the king of the "old good nature and good humor" between a people "who, though, separated by an ocean and different governments have the same language, a similar religion, and kindred blood." He said that his job was to attempt to restore the king's "esteem, confidence, and affection" for the American people.

The king was visibly moved by Adams's entreaty. "The circumstances of this audience is so extraordinary," said the king, as Adams remembered, "the language you have now held is so extremely proper, and the feelings you have discovered so justly adapted to the occasion, that I must say that I not only receive with pleasure the assurances of the friendly dispositions of the United States, but that I am very glad that the choice has fallen upon you to be their minister."[158]

The king went on to say that though he had failed to prevent American independence, now that it had occurred he also wished for friendship between the two nations. The king signaled that the interview was over, and Adams backed out of the room bowing—or making reverencies, in the vernacular of the day. He was led from the palace to his carriage. It had gone very well, Adams thought, and he believed the king was sincere.

The British press, however, was a different matter. Although the *London Chronicle* reported that "His Excellency John Adams was . . . most graciously received," other accounts were less charitable, fingering Adams as a rebel bent on "cutting [England's] throat."[159]

Despite being frequently lampooned in the British press, Adams was at first relatively happy in his ministerial post. Abigail was with him at last, and she ran a tight household with the help of numerous servants. The Adamses did a great deal of entertaining in their embassy home, hosting formal dinners almost every evening.

Adams had high hopes of coming to an agreement with the British in a commercial treaty that would allow the nations to trade with one another—but there were several other matters to address first. For one thing, the British were ignoring the Treaty of Paris. They were stopping American ships and impressing sailors to serve in the British navy; they had abrogated the return of American slaves taken during the war; and they were molesting American trade with the West Indies. These violations needed resolution if the United States was to prosper as a free and productive nation.

In less than a year Adams's hopes were dashed, as it became increasingly apparent that the British remained furious at their former colonies and did not wish them to succeed. There were simply not enough votes in Parliament to arrive at a commercial agreement. Adams wrote to John Jay, then secretary of state, that the United States should close its ports to British goods. But under the weak Articles of Confederation the federal government did not have the power to regulate foreign commerce.

Adams found that most of the Englishmen he met treated him with "a dry decency and cold civility." But despite what King George had said to him, some Britons and a part of the press were actually calling for another war with America. That was John Adams's greatest fear, as he knew America could not withstand it. He wrote to Jay that America would do well to maintain a close relationship with France, as well as with Holland and Spain. There would be no war with Britain so long as France threatened to bring its vast resources in on the American side.

Abigail, too, had come to dislike the English, whom she considered haughty and arrogant. She had now been away from home for four years and, she told John, was homesick for her garden and chickens back in Braintree. One unexpected stroke of good luck concerned Nabby, who had consented to go to Europe only with the understanding that she would marry Royall Tyler when she returned. But Tyler's behavior was increasingly peculiar. He responded to none of her letters, and reports from Nabby's aunt, with whom Tyler often boarded, described his behavior as unstable and immature. In time, Nabby began seeing Adams's secretary Col. William C. Smith, a handsome thirty-year-old bachelor who had for a time during the war served on George Washington's staff. Romance blossomed, encouraged by

John and Abigail, and in the spring of 1786 Nabby and Smith were wed.

The wedding was a bright spot amid many diplomatic stalemates for Adams. Stifled in his attempts to secure a commercial treaty, he was equally repressed in trying to aid the 7,000 Tories who had fled to England, either during or after the war; some were in pitiful financial straits and most wished to return to America. But because the question was up to the individual states and not the federal government, there was little Adams could do. Meanwhile, the North African countries of the Barbary Coast were avidly extorting the United States for protection of American ships against pirates. As repugnant as that was, Adams believed the bribes should be paid: the United States simply didn't have navy enough to police the Mediterranean Sea in order to ensure its own shipping and trade.

By the end of 1786 it had become apparent that Adams's ambassadorship was a failure. Lord North, who had so forcefully opposed American independence, was back in power, and British attitudes were now intransigent and vindictive. In early 1787 Adams asked Congress to name his successor.

BEFORE THEY LEFT ENGLAND, John and Abigail bought a new home in Quincy, only a mile away from their longtime farmhouse in Braintree. It was an elegant two-and-a-half-story Georgian-style estate described as a "very Genteel Dwelling and coach house," set on 83 acres with a garden and apple orchard. It had been built in 1731 by a sugarcane planter from Jamaica and lived in most recently by Loyalists who had fled Massachusetts during the

Revolution. The Adamses had always admired it, and when a friend wrote that it was on the market they purchased it for £600 sterling, or approximately $120,000 today.

In late April 1788 John and Abigail boarded the *Lucretia* for the voyage home. Nabby and her new husband would set sail several weeks later for New York, where Colonel Smith hoped to find work with the government. Adams hadn't seen his youngest son, Thomas, for nearly eight years, and as he crossed the Atlantic one more time he had no idea what the future had in store for him.

Nine years before, when Adams had returned to Boston on *La Sensible*, no one had been there to greet him. But this time, when *Lucretia* entered Boston Harbor on June 17, a twenty-one-gun salute was delivered by the cannon in the Castle, a fort in Boston Harbor. Boston's church bells were ringing when *Lucretia* made dock, and as Adams walked down the gangplank Governor John Hancock emerged from a large crowd to welcome the Adamses home and escort them to the governor's mansion, where they were invited to stay for the next several days. Their sons Charles and Thomas, both students at Harvard, hurried across the Charles River to the governor's mansion, and John Quincy, who was clerking at a law office, arrived soon thereafter.

Almost immediately, all manner of dignitaries approached Adams about his serving in important posts in the local, state, and federal governments. Under the terms of the newly ratified Constitution, Washington was almost certain to be elected president, and many supporters suggested to Adams that he run for vice president. Adams was overwhelmed by all the attention. He had planned to resume his practice of law and tend his farm fields.

But now the pull of politics once again engaged him. Abigail assured him of her support in whatever he decided to do. He had some time to think, as the presidential voting was not set to begin until December.

Abigail and John were disappointed when they visited their new home for the first time. Abigail had ordered some painting and carpentry done but it was not complete. On that first visit they entered a low-ceilinged room with sawhorses standing about and lumber stacked in the corner. Compared with the elegance of their London town house or the mansion at Auteuil, this reminded Abigail of a "wren's house." In time, however, the improvements were completed, the lawn and gardens put in shape, and the rooms made bright and appealing with paint and plaster. When the family moved in with all the fine furniture they had purchased in Paris and London, they quickly grew to love the house. John named it Peacefield.

After several weeks in his new home, Adams made his decision: he would run for vice president. There were other candidates in the mix, but some of these dropped out when Adams decided to enter the race. His election was not guaranteed but, being a New Englander, he was almost assured of winning the votes of that large block of electors. In fact, as the election drew near, Alexander Hamilton and others began to fear that Adams might actually take more electoral votes than Washington and become the president.

At that time, only white, male, taxpaying property owners—less than 10 percent of the population—could vote in presidential elections. And they voted for their state electors, who then cast ballots for the candidates. The candidate with the most electoral votes became president and the one with the second most became vice president. In case of a tie, the selection was made by a vote in the House of Representatives.

Against the possibility that Adams might actually win or tie with Washington, Hamilton began a secret effort to have several electors vote for someone other than John Adams. When in March 1789 the votes were all in, Washington's election as president was unanimous—all sixty-nine electors voted for him. Adams was made vice president with thirty-four votes, far ahead of ten other candidates. Though he was unaware of Hamilton's machinations, he rankled at having received fewer than half of the second-place votes and threatened to refuse the post. When Abigail and Nabby urged him against that course, Adams calmed down and accepted his role as America's first vice president.

The nation's capital was now located in New York City. When Adams departed Boston in April 1789, he was given a grand send-off and cheered in all the towns and villages that his coach passed through. By mid-month he was in New York and seated before the Senate in Federal Hall— the former city hall at Broad and Wall Streets. Washington arrived at the end of the month and was sworn in on the balcony of Federal Hall to the cheering and waving of throngs on the streets below. For the first time, the country had a constitutional organization in place.

Adams quickly found living accommodations at an estate in a rural area about a mile north of the city. The twenty-six-acre Richmond Hill had an elegant flower garden and spectacular views of the Hudson, New York Harbor, and Long Island in the distance. Washington had used it for his primary headquarters in 1776. Adams sent immediately for Abigail, who had been having trouble leasing the new farm and was short of funds. Adams advised her to sell a cow or two to raise cash but in any case to come as soon as possible. There had also been some sort of trouble with Charles at Harvard; he was one of several students who had been identified running naked through Harvard Yard. Drinking was apparently involved and reprimands handed out. When Abigail arrived on June 4, she had Charles in tow. She found Richmond Hill "delightful."

The question of pay for the new government's officeholders had not been settled. Both George Washington and Benjamin Franklin were against it on the theory that service to one's country ought to be voluntary and free. Adams opposed their position both on grounds that only the rich would then be able to hold office, which would lead to despotism, and also that he, personally, needed the money if he were to devote years of his life to being vice president. In the end Congress voted to compensate officeholders, including themselves. Adams's pay as vice president was $5,000 a year: enough to live comfortably but not enough for all the entertaining he was expected to do.

Many aspects of government still needed to be decided, and an argument immediately broke out between the House and the Senate over how to address President Washington. The House had voted that the proper address should be "George Washington, President of the United States." In the Senate, however, there were all sorts of "distinctions" suggested, including "His Highness the President of the United States of America and Protector of the Rights of the Same."

The fight went on for half the summer, and Adams got mixed up in it unnecessarily; his most pressing job was to preside over the Senate and break ties. But he felt that some kind of title was reasonable "to bring dignity and respect" to the presidency and suggested "His Excellency." Adams was immediately assailed by some of the senators and others, who labeled him a "monarchist." The label stuck, and he was personally lampooned in newspapers and elsewhere as "Your Rotundity." Finally, Congress resolved the naming argument, choosing a simple "Mr. President." But the affair left a bad taste in Adams's mouth.

Despite all the frustrations of the do-nothing job of vice president, Adams was still reasonably happy in New York. Abigail, on the other hand, found it "dull" after Paris and London; there was but one theater, and New York preachers were tedious. Then, toward the end of summer, legislation was proposed by William Maclay, a radical senator from Pennsylvania, that the Senate be given the power to remove cabinet officers. This provoked a furious outcry from the Federalists, who asserted that it was a naked attempt by Congress to weaken the power of the chief executive.

Washington's cabinet was composed entirely of men who had taken part in the Revolution in one way or another, though not all were Federalist. Thomas Jefferson, now home from France, was secretary of state; Alexander Hamilton was secretary of the treasury; Henry Knox was secretary of war, Edmund Randolph the attorney general; and John Jay would preside over the Supreme Court as its chief justice. Each of the men was in his own way exceptional, and each was wholly dedicated to the success of the new nation.

The Federalists argued that dismissal of cabinet officers should be only at the pleasure of the president. The debate raged for the rest of summer of 1789, with Adams maneuvering behind the scenes to sway votes against Maclay's bill. Some suggested that the reason Adams was against the legislation was that he hoped to take Washington's job one day himself. Adams freely admitted to this, but added that even if he didn't aspire to the presidency he still would be against the measure. The vote on the measure ended in a tie, and Adams, as president of the Senate, voted to break it in favor of the president.

AS THE FIRST COOL BREEZES OF AUTUMN swept across New York City, word of the French Revolution reached America. Two years before, when he was still in Britain, Adams had begun to be alarmed by some of the revolutionary rhetoric emanating from France. The radicals were calling for a complete upheaval of French institutions and the establishment of an all-powerful legislature of common folk to run the country. Adams saw much danger in such a scheme, feeling it would lead to despotism and to Voltaire's dark, despairing predictions of the chaos brought on by mob rule.

Although most Americans eagerly commended their French allies for seeking their own freedoms, many were shocked at the violence reported in the new accounts. The old Bastille prison in Paris had been liberated on July 14 by a mob and its commander beheaded; the head had been carried through the streets to the cheering of crowds. Mobs roamed everywhere, killing government officials, hanging them from lampposts, or chopping them to pieces.

Adams began writing essays praising the notion of the revolution in France but questioning its form. He was especially despairing of the recent establishment of an assembly that would alone govern the country, fearing it would lead to untold tragedy. Nor was Adams in agreement with the French philosophers who were behind the revolution and who advocated abolishing the church as a preeminent institution in French life. "I know not what to make of a republic of thirty million atheists," Adams wrote.[160]

As the revolution progressed, Adams became ever more pessimistic of its final result. His essays, published in the pro-Federalist *Gazette of the United States*, "stressed the perils of unbridled, unbalanced democracy."

By contrast, Thomas Jefferson, who had been in Paris for the fall of the Bastille and the chaos that followed, was convinced that "a glorious new day had dawned" in France. He was satisfied that the violence would dwindle away and that the French people would soon revel in peaceful, prosperous, liberating democracy.[161] He was appalled at Adams's negative essays in the *Gazette* and began to support the rumor that Adams had become a monarchist.

While in Philadelphia to pay his final respects to Benjamin Franklin, who was deathly ill, Jefferson also called on Dr. Benjamin Rush, a former Pennsylvania congressman and signer of the Declaration of Independence. Rush was a friend of both Jefferson and Adams, and now Jefferson broached the topic of the vice president, saying cleverly that while Adams was "a great and upright man," he, Jefferson, "deplored the change" that had come over him. This marked the beginnings of a legendary political schism between two great Patriots that would last far into the century to come.[162]

THROUGHOUT THE SPRING OF 1790, while the French Revolution raged with ever increasing mayhem, two issues consumed the U.S.

Congress in acrimonious debate: where to locate a permanent national capital and whether the federal government should assume some $25 million in debts that the states had incurred during the war.

The question regarding the new permanent capital was regional: should it be located in a northern or a southern state? Everybody took sides and a deadlock ensued. The assumption of state debts was the brainchild of Alexander Hamilton, who insisted it was necessary to maintain sound public credit, which in turn was necessary for economic growth. The Anti-Federalists, however, were adamant that such a measure would put far too much power in the hands of the federal government and was consequently anti-republican in its nature. Southerners were particularly offended by the notion.

Eventually, the disputes were ironed out and the deadlocks resolved through compromise. In June, after a friendly conversation with Hamilton, Jefferson invited him and Madison, a leading Republican voice in Congress, to dinner at the palatial New York home he had rented, where, over a bottle of good wine, a deal was struck. Jefferson promised to deliver the vote of the southern states for the assumption of state debts; Hamilton agreed to use all his powers to persuade New York and Pennsylvania congressmen to locate the new permanent capital on the Potomac River, on condition that the temporary capital be moved back to Philadelphia while the new capital was being constructed. It was important, all three agreed, that the new capital be an entity unto itself and capable of defending itself; they all well remembered the 1783 debacle in Philadelphia, when the army mutinied and for political reasons the governor refused to call out the militia to protect the city or the Confederation Congress.

In July both houses of Congress voted to move the capital to Philadelphia for ten years while the new capital city on the Potomac was built. And both houses voted in favor of the assumption bill, which Hamilton continued to maintain was vital to protect the nation's credit. Naysayers immediately charged that a corrupt bargain had been struck, and the factionalism that both Washington and Adams profoundly opposed broke out anew.

"There is nothing I dread so much as a division of the Republic into two great parties . . . each in opposition to one another," Adams wrote. "This in my apprehension is the greatest political evil of our Constitution." Factions, he said, "could tie the hands and destroy the influence of every honest man." But there seemed nothing else for it. Two conflicting strains of thought ran though the country, then as now: a strong central government versus states' rights.[163]

Adams had little influence on Washington's presidency, and though the two men were not close they enjoyed each other's company. Adams dined with Washington on occasion and had tea with him on others. Occasionally, the president consulted Adams on foreign policy, particularly regarding a possible war between Britain and Spain. Adams counseled neutrality.

In May 1790 a flu epidemic hit New York City. Dozens of congressmen were stricken (one died), as were Abigail, Jefferson, and Madison. But when the fifty-eight-year-old Washington came down with the illness, it caused a crisis; the virus struck him particularly hard, and his personal physician told the family to prepare for the worst. Other doctors examined the president and came to the same conclusion. Adams had once noted that he was "but one breath" from becoming president himself, and that breath seemed imminent.

A recovering Abigail wrote a friend that Washington's "death would, I fear, have the most disastrous consequences." She pointed out that the nation's finances remained weak and that the government was not "sufficiently cemented to promise duration." Washington alone could lead the people of the United States forward; no one else, including her husband, could do so at that time.[164] The following month Washington made a miraculous recovery, and the nation was saved. It was a close call, and Adams had many anxious moments. He knew he was not ready for the job of president.

At the end of the summer, the government packed up and began moving to Philadelphia. Abigail was distraught at having to leave Richmond Hill, but Adams was happy to be out of New York; it wasn't his kind of town. He and Abigail moved to Rush Hill, overlooking the Schuylkill River. Though it turned out to be drafty and the servants were often drunk, the family was frequently together there. Thomas had graduated from Harvard and he came to live with his parents; Charles and John Quincy visited often, as did Nabby and her three children. Nabby's husband had still not found a job and was in England on a "speculative" endeavor, which was troubling to Abigail.

The country had begun to right itself after the wreckage of the Revolutionary War. Both business and agriculture were prospering; Hamilton's national bank had been endorsed by an act of Congress. But the rift between Adams and Jefferson was growing.

Thomas Paine, the great political writer of the Revolution, now back in England, had written a fiery pamphlet in 1791 entitled *The Rights of Man,* attacking the parliamentarian and philosopher Edmund Burke for his negative view of the French Revolution.

Thus far, the revolution had seen the rise of the Jacobins, the arrest of the king and queen, murderous mobs, and riots on a vast scale.

Burke deplored the direction the revolution was taking, but Paine bitterly disputed Burke's assessment. He sent an early copy of his *Rights of Man* to Jefferson, who in turn sent it to a Philadelphia printer with an enthusiastic endorsement that included the phrase "political heresies"—an illusion to Adams's purported monarchist leanings.

The printer, without Jefferson's knowledge or permission, used the endorsement on the title page, much to Jefferson's annoyance and distress. He felt he had to explain the situation to Washington and apologize, which he did. But to Adams he said nothing.

In the meantime, a Boston newspaper began running a series of essays attacking *Rights of Man* and its endorser Thomas Jefferson. It was signed "Publicola," and most people, including Jefferson, believed the essays were written by Adams. They were, but not by John; his son John Quincy was the author.

After several months Jefferson sent a note to Adams, then in Massachusetts, apologizing for the printer's error and saying he never meant it for publication. But the damage was done. Adams had been held up to ridicule in the press by numerous partisans as a monarchist, libeler, and supporter of anti-liberty and anti-freedom views. Jefferson wrote to Adams sincerely, saying, "That you and I differ in our idea of the best form of government is well known to us both, but we have differed as friends should do, respecting the purity of each other's motives, and confining our differences of opinion to private conversation." But he added an inflammatory sentence, contending that he "never in his life . . . had he written anything for newspapers anonymously or under pseudonym, and he never intended to." It was an obvious slam at Adams, still believed to be Publicola.

Adams answered, thanking Jefferson for writing, but denying that he was Publicola. He reassured Jefferson that, "If you suppose that I have or ever had a design or desire of attempting to introduce a government of Kings, Lords, and Commons or in other words a hereditary executive, or a hereditary senate . . . you are wholly mistaken." There followed a further skimpy exchange of letters, but the incident marked the almost total break between the two former friends. Jefferson and Adams were now publicly identified as being diametric opposites in the debate to see what form of government would evolve for the United States of America.

BY MID-1792, after three years as president, Washington was beginning to consider retiring to Virginia. To his annoyance and chagrin, his two smartest, most efficient cabinet officers, Hamilton and Jefferson, remained at each other's throats, refusing Washington's plea for a truce. The only thing they could agree on, it seemed, was that for the good of the country Washington must serve a second term.

The nation was still young, her body politic riven by factions, and her finances still somewhat precarious. Deferring to duty once again, George Washington was inaugurated for a second term as president of the United States on March 4, 1793, in the Senate Chamber of the Philadelphia Congress Hall. John Adams remained vice president, having accumulated seventy-seven electoral votes.

Adams was also tapped to join the American Philosophical Society, a rare distinction. Long a member himself, Jefferson, in the spirit of friendship, accompanied Adams to the induction ceremony. Abigail, in poor health from rheumatism and other ailments, had returned to Peacefield in the spring of 1792, so Adams, in an effort to save money, had taken a room in the home of a friend, Secretary of the Senate Samuel Otis. Adams had realized during his first term as vice president that he had overextended his finances in an effort to uphold what he thought was the proper role of a vice president. He vowed not to do it again.

As the bloodshed continued in France, both England and Spain declared war on their weakened enemy. The conflict would last two full decades, always threatening to drag America into the fray. In fact, a month after Washington's second inauguration, one Edmond-Charles Genêt—a French minister who styled himself Citizen Genêt, in the spirit of revolution—arrived in Charleston, South Carolina, to represent the French government. His job was to persuade the American people to take the side of France in the war against Britain and Spain, and to unleash American ships as privateers to prey on enemy shipping.

Genêt lingered in Charleston, where he was warmly received, then made his way to Philadelphia, encouraging secret "Jacobin clubs" along the way by handing out money for these and for the enterprises of pro-French privateers. By the time he reached Philadelphia, he was a sensation, greeted by an enthralled crowd of more than a thousand, who sang "The Marseillaise." Adams was alarmed that some new kind of revolution was afoot, given the secretive Jacobin clubs and the crowds that followed Genêt. Much of America, it seemed, was enraptured by the notion of the French Revolution.

Then, in September 1793, with the Jacobins fully in power, the Reign of Terror began in France. Before it was over, more than 16,000 "unrevolutionary" men and women were murdered, most beheaded by the guillotine but some drowned en masse and or mowed down by cannons at close range. That same summer, a vicious epidemic of yellow fever struck Philadelphia, killing as many as a hundred people a day. In the end, more than 5,000 died. That tragedy, coupled with news of the French depredations, dampened the revolutionary ardor that swirled around Citizen Genêt.

Jefferson called the French minister in to say he must refrain from attempting to outfit American privateers to prey on British ships, because the United States had declared its neutrality. Hamilton wanted Genêt deported, but that issue was rendered moot when France recalled him over his failure to accomplish his mission. As it seemed likely that Genêt would be executed if he returned to France, he was allowed to remain in the States, which he did quietly for the next forty years.

The French Revolution eventually devoured its own. By 1794 its two leaders Maximilien Robespierre and Georges Danton themselves faced the guillotine; the political theorist Jean-Paul Marat was assassinated. The following year a body called the Directory replaced the Jacobins and the mob. For his part Adams admonished a friend, saying, "Mankind will in time discover that unbridled majorities are as tyrannical and cruel as unlimited despots."

To Abigail, Adams wrote more plaintively and personally. "Man is not meant to be alone." She had remained at their Quincy farm, Peacefield, since her return in early 1792. Her health now made travel difficult, but she also wanted to keep a close eye on their land and affairs, as John's time, and hers, in public service had strained their finances. Adams spent as much time with her as possible, but when the Senate was in session he dared not leave it. The members, he said, were "nearly divided" between the Federalists and the Republicans, and because he was called upon to break dozens of tie votes, without him the government would take on "an entire new complexion."[165]

Adams occasionally considered retirement; he was dreadfully lonely and missed Abigail intensely. He wrote of "tedious days and lonesome nights. I want my wife to hover over and about me," he told her.[166] Yet despite his loneliness he seemed relatively content in his official role.

John Quincy, too, was achieving his own status. In 1794 Washington named him minister to The Hague, a plum post that would start him on an impressive diplomatic and political career. He took his younger brother Thomas with him as his secretary. But Charles Adams, always the bright, genial, easygoing son, seemed "not at peace with himself," Abigail wrote. The trouble he had been in at Harvard indicated he might have a drinking problem, and time bore that out. In 1792 he had graduated from Harvard, gone on to study law, and been admitted to the New York bar. But, as his parents learned, he continued to choose bad friends. Adams lectured his son in letters but was rebuffed with denials. "Things have been told respecting me which are false," Charles rejoined.

Nor was Nabby's life turning out the way her parents had hoped. Her husband, Colonel Smith, had become entangled in speculative ventures in the American West and in England, plunging the family deeply into debt. They had been forced from respectable surroundings to a very modest cottage in central New York State, where Nabby remained alone with her children for months at a time while Charles sought his fortunes overseas or beyond the Appalachian Mountains. President Washington had appointed Smith a federal marshal for New York and then New York supervisor of revenue, but it seems the colonel had bigger dreams.

IN 1795, WHEN ADAMS RETURNED for the opening session of Congress, he learned that Washington would not seek a third presidential term. This was momentous news for Adams. He believed the Federalist Party considered him heir apparent to succeed Washington. If Adams had had doubts about his readiness for the presidency in the past, he was now convinced he could do the job. Hamilton might have been a rival in the upcoming election, but he seemed to have little following and apparently was not much interested in the job. Jefferson would no doubt be the Democratic-Republican candidate and would have much of the South behind him, while Adams would have New England.

Adams concluded that if he came in second as vice president and Jefferson won, he could never serve under Jefferson. He would retire with Abigail to Peacefield, where they would become "Farmers for Life."[167] For her part, Abigail worried that if John became president, he would immediately become the target of foul innuendo and slurs by the pro–Democratic-Republican press. She knew that, unlike Washington, Adams was thin-skinned and took personal umbrage at insults and barbs. Also, if he won, John would be sixty-one years old when he assumed the office. She wondered if they would ever become "Farmers for Life." But she swallowed her concerns and got fully behind his candidacy. That was enormously important to her husband, who had sensed her initial reluctance.

The presidential election of 1796 would be a tense and exhausting time for the politicians of both parties—except the presidential candidates themselves. They stayed out of the fray. John Adams repaired for the rest of the year to Peacefield and his farming and declared he didn't really care who won. Some people almost believed him.

CHAPTER SIX

In 1784, three years after the Battle of Yorktown, Thomas Jefferson set sail for France, a land that represented sophistication, culture, reason, and enchantment. He was elated, and a little frightened. He spoke the language; he knew the culture; he'd read the philosophers; he'd seen etchings of the architecture. Now he was going to join John Adams and Benjamin Franklin to negotiate commercial treaties with European countries. It was the fulfillment of a lifelong dream.

Earlier that year, as a Virginia congressman to the Confederation Congress, Jefferson had drafted the Ordinance of 1784, which set up an outline for new states west of the Mississippi on territory occupied primarily by Native Americans. The Ohio River formed the southern boundary, the Mississippi the western, and the Great Lakes the boundary to the north. Jefferson even named the ten states to be created: Michigania, Sylvania, Metropotamia, Illinoia, Saratoga, Polypotamia, Assenisipia, Pelisipia, Washington, and Cherronesus. He had included a provision providing that slavery would be banned from the new lands—though not in the states where it already existed—but it was struck down by a narrow vote in Congress. (The provision was later reinstated in a newer version, while he was in France.[168]) Jefferson was disappointed but did not press the matter; abolition was a politically toxic subject, and he was always personally careful to avoid highly charged issues.

On the Fourth of July, 1784—eight years after an earlier Congress had adopted Jefferson's Declaration of Independence—his congressional career ended. Early the following morning he sailed for France with his eldest daughter, Patsy, and a nineteen-year-old slave, James Hemings, who was to train as a chef in the art of French cuisine; the two younger Jefferson daughters stayed behind with relatives in Virginia.

What Jefferson sought diplomatically from France was a lasting partnership, both military and commercial, that would insulate his young country from whatever mischief and machinations Britain had to offer. Healthy American trade relations with Europe would strengthen the image of the new nation as an economic power.

Most of what America had to offer was raw resources. While the Europeans produced finished goods, America had a booming whaling fleet that processed exportable whale oil for lamps. Tobacco was grown in quantities in the upper South, and a superior species of long staple, or Sea Island, cotton was exportable from the barrier islands off Georgia and the Carolinas. There was abundant lumber, grain, flour, dried beans, and dried fish to sell, as well as rice from the Carolinas. The fur trade, principally beaver pelts, was a major business for trappers and traders beyond the Alleghenies. Hemp was an important exportable staple for making paper and ropes for sailing ships. American mines disgorged iron, lead, and salt. And even before the Revolution, New England had a brisk shipbuilding industry, manufacturing one of the few "finished" products from America.

Jefferson well knew that America needed a robust trade with as many countries as possible—not only to create individual wealth but also to raise government revenue through tariffs, which constituted the main source of federal income. This would become one of his main goals during his time in France.

AFTER A SWIFT AND UNEVENTFUL transatlantic voyage, Jefferson arrived at Le Havre on July 31. He and Patsy and James then went by coach to Paris through a seemingly endless procession of farm fields that could not be "more elegantly improved." Once in the great city, Jefferson placed Patsy in school at the fashionable convent school Abbaye Royale de Panthémont, an institution so exclusive that Lafayette's wife had to intervene to secure her place. By October Jefferson had rented a fashionable though unfurnished town house, the Hôtel Landron, where "wine, furniture, music, horses, and linen consumed his resources."[169]

Jefferson quickly became friends with the Adamses. Abigail found him "charming," and "an excellent man." Jefferson's relationship with young John Quincy was such that Adams declared Jefferson as much a father to the boy as he was. Indeed, Paris would prove one of the "richest" periods in Jefferson's life in private relationships. There was no political controversy to impose obstacles as there would be later, and he could be what he always wanted to be—"everybody's friend."[170]

But his diplomatic assignment proved more difficult. Setting up respectable commercial treaties was easier said than done, as

Adams and John Jay had already discovered. Many of the European countries had their own colonies with which they traded, to the exclusion of everyone else. And Britain, of course, was being impossible.

The subject of the Barbary pirates arose again, and Jefferson, unlike Adams, was adamantly opposed to paying a bribe for the safety of American ships. "Why not go to war with them?" Jefferson wrote to James Monroe, his young protégé in Virginia. "We ought to begin a naval power if we are to carry on our own commerce." He added, "I am of the opinion [John] Paul Jones with half a dozen frigates would totally destroy their [the pirates'] commerce."[171]

Unfortunately, Congress did not see things the same way and told the commissioners to pay the pirates a bribe of $80,000. That wasn't nearly enough, however, compared with what France and England paid, which was in the neighborhood of $300,000. Worried about the pirates' American captives, Jefferson persisted on their behalf and was at last told to pay the higher amount.

Distasteful as it was to him, Jefferson was willing to pay to save American lives from the horrors of slavery. The money did not arrive for almost five years, and by then Jefferson was ready to come home. He never forgot what he felt was an American "humiliation" at the hands of the pirates.

During his first winter in Paris Jefferson received devastating news. Lafayette, returning from America, brought letters from Jefferson's sister and her husband, who had been keeping his two younger girls. Whooping cough, "that most horrible of disorders," had struck their Virginia plantation. All of the children had caught it. Two-year-old Lucy Jefferson had died, as had one of her cousins. Polly Jefferson, who was then six, also came down with the highly contagious bacterial disease, but she recovered.

Jefferson was stricken with despair. He responded to his brother-in-law, thanking him for everything but saying that he simply had no words to describe his pain. Later he wrote, "The sun of happiness clouded over, never again to brighten." He sank into the same sort of deep melancholy that had accompanied his wife's death. For five months he refused all dinner invitations, wanting only to be alone. Occasionally, John and Abigail came to his home for supper, but Jefferson was in a most serious state of mourning.

Spring arrived, the Paris weather turned glorious once more, and Jefferson's spirits lifted. Word came that the queen, Marie Antoinette, had given birth to a prince, and all Paris exulted. An invitation arrived via Madame de Lafayette to attend a *Te Deum* at Notre-Dame, held to celebrate the royal birth; Louis XVI was to be prominent in the ceremony.

Jefferson attended, sharing a carriage with the Adams family. It was a lovely day and the music was certain to be uplifting. Throngs danced, sang, and cavorted in the streets, prompting Jefferson to remark drolly to seventeen-year-old Nabby Adams, within earshot of her parents, that "there were as many people on the streets as in the whole state of Massachusetts."

A few weeks later, great changes were announced for members of the American commerce commission. The commission itself was disbanded for its lack of progress. Franklin, suffering from gout and kidney stones, was ready to go home, and his wish was granted. Jay went back to America as secretary of foreign affairs. Adams received his appointment as ambassador to the Court of St. James's, while Jefferson was appointed to replace Franklin as the sole American ambassador to France. Jefferson was elated, and his spirits as nearly mended as they ever would be. His only concern was seeing to it that young Polly joined him and Patsy in Paris. The planning for her transatlantic crossing consumed nearly two years.

In the meantime, Jefferson had the obligatory audience with His Most Christian Majesty King Louis XVI, and he also met Marie Antoinette. But he wasn't particularly impressed with them—or, for that matter, with the ministers and courtiers who served them. Writing to his friend Gouverneur Morris, he said they "were really not worth knowing." He was more attuned to the exemplary French scientists and thinkers—notably the Duc de La Rochefoucauld, an eminent philosopher. Both Rousseau and Voltaire had recently died, but not before the latter had publicly embraced Dr. Franklin at the French Academy, kissing him on both cheeks.

Jefferson himself was highly impressed with the politeness of the French, but found their society "impure and purposeless." In dance halls, women kicked up their heels to reveal their undergarments. There was much unfaithfulness in all classes, and no one even gossiped about it. Nevertheless, he enjoyed the food and wine, sending casks of French brandy to friends in America (but also requesting that a few Virginia hams be shipped to him in France). In the gardens behind his home, he cultivated Indian corn, which he missed on his table as much as he did his native hams.

Jefferson also glimpsed the first signs of the industrial revolution in Paris. But as a stubbornly traditional agriculturist, he did not wish to see it reach American shores. "I consider the class of [industrialists] as the panders of vice, and instruments by which the liberties of a country are generally overturned," he stated. Yet he greatly enjoyed his Paris life and walked every day, weather permitting, in the lovely Bois de Boulogne. In 1784 he wrote to his fellow Virginians Madison and Monroe urging them to cross the Atlantic and spend the summer with him. The trip might be expensive, he said, "but would be a small price for knowledge of another world."

Jefferson's counterpart in the French government was the wily old Vergennes, with whom John Adams had struggled. While Jefferson did not find the French minister duplicitous, as Adams had, he nonetheless wrote to Madison that Vergennes's "devotion to the principles of pure despotism renders him unaffectionate to our government. But his fear of England makes him value us."[172]

There were the ever present trade questions for Jefferson to deal with, and he plunged into these issues with a mind toward securing favorable conditions for each of the colonies or regions. The American tobacco trade was in a shambles because the French had created a monopoly that allowed one quasi-government entity to set the buying price. Jefferson enlisted Lafayette's assistance in having a committee established to see what could be done about this. The marquis also helped smooth the commerce in whale oil between New England and France. The grateful inhabitants of Nantucket responded by donating milk to create a 500-pound cheese to be shipped to Lafayette.

Since his return from abroad, the marquis had become a distinctive Americophile. His abode "assumed American customs that bordered on affectation." His children were taught to speak (American) English, and his personal courier was dressed like an American Indian. In France, Jefferson noted, "There was nothing against [Lafayette] except suspicion of Republican principles." Jefferson held the young nobleman in high regard for his service in the Revolution and in assisting the American mission in France. If Lafayette had a flaw, Jefferson believed, it was "a canine appetite for popularity and fame."[173]

FRANCE IN THE MID-1780S was deep in crisis, financially and socially. The nearly constant wars it had been fighting for the past two decades had bled its treasury dry. The French middle class had been "reduced to the condition of peasants, and the peasants to that of starved and overworked helots." In the palace at Versailles, intrigue ruled as it had in Italy during the bewildering days of the Borgias. King and courtiers were spending money they didn't have and inventing ever more complicated schemes to levy taxes.

The American war had brought France to a crisis, sweeping away both its funds and its credit. As the Anglo-Irish politician and philosopher Edmund Burke pointed out, the "age of chivalry," or the ascendancy of royals, was "passing away" and in its place "a day of earnest—terribly earnest—men and women, was already sending up lurid harbingers of its approach."[174]

How much of this Jefferson understood at the time is unclear. Certainly he was aware of the poverty, as beggars were everywhere. And he had read the French philosophers who preached against the church and superstition, instead championing an age of liberty, science, and reason. An ever widening number of the educated French bourgeoisie—lawyers, journalists, academics, and others—had put aside blind loyalty and saw the excesses of the nobility clearly. Though they were not yet ready to make their move against the aristocracy, there was secret heretical talk of organizing a French constitution and a government of popular sovereignty such as existed in the United States.

In the spring of 1786 Jefferson decided to go to England for several weeks. He was not anticipating a pleasant visit, but at least he would be welcomed by his good friends John and Abigail Adams. Jefferson had conducted an ongoing personal correspondence with Abigail since the Adamses had left Paris, and John had kept up a continuous communication with Jefferson on matters of political and commercial interests.

Once in London, Jefferson accompanied Adams to a meeting with the minister from Tripoli to discuss the piracy question. Wearing a beard and dressed in Arab garb, the minister told the Americans it was "the duty of his countrymen to make war on sinners," meaning Christians. He then demanded far more in extortion payments than the United States could afford to keep American shipping safe. Jefferson was disgusted.

Meanwhile, the continued British intransigence on commerce had left Adams jaded. American ships still could not trade in the British West Indies nor enter ports in England, while the various American states, bowing to popular appeal, allowed English vessels into their ports to sell their wares.

Jefferson was furious at the anti-American invective and propaganda in the London newspapers. They were filled with tales of widespread anarchy (including Shays's Rebellion), poverty, and the inability of Americans to govern themselves. He felt the attacks came from envy and wounded pride, and he laid the force behind the continuing hostility against America squarely at the feet of George III. Jefferson believed that the king so terrified his ministers that none felt free to show the slightest deference or kindness to the United States. The merchants Jefferson spoke with were anxious to open a lively trade with the Americans, but their hands were tied. Jefferson gloomily predicted no relief from the situation because, as he told John Jay, "I do not expect a change of disposition during the present reign, which bids fair to be a long one as the King is healthy."[175]

His dissatisfaction with the British government notwithstanding, Jefferson was fascinated by Britain's achievements in engineering and science—particularly, the use of steam engines to run grist mills, as he believed that steam might one day be used to run ships. He also collected a number of instruments in London that were generally unavailable in America: a thermometer, a protractor, a globe telescope, a solar microscope, a hydrometer, and a camp theodolite, as well as a harpsichord. In April, Jefferson and Adams made a tour of English gardens; Jefferson made copious notes at such places as Blenheim, Hampton Court, Stowe, and St. Chiswick with a mind to applying their various designs and styles to the grounds at Monticello.

When Jefferson returned to Paris, he soon became close friends with the thirty-year-old portraitist John Trumbull, who had come from London to study French art and who had served as an aide-de-camp to Washington early in the Revolution. Trumbull in turn introduced Jefferson to a beautiful twenty-seven-year-old artist named Maria Hadfield Cosway, who was visiting Paris from Italy with her artist husband. That meeting took Jefferson on a romantic adventure that lasted the rest of his life. Born in Italy of English parents, Maria Cosway was married to the diminutive Richard Cosway, an acclaimed miniature portraitist who was known to be a libertine and was once described as looking "very like a monkey in the face." Their marriage was said to be one of convenience, Richard being twenty years her senior.[176]

Jefferson had been presented with ample opportunity to become involved with women while in Europe, but he was standoffish of their "voluptuous" style of dress and "female intrigue." But in the case of the talented, coquettish Maria Cosway, the American ambassador was "quite swept off his supposedly well-planted feet."[177]

Their chance meeting occurred at the Halle aux blés—the corn exchange in Paris—where Jefferson had gone with Trumbull to study ideas for a public marker he planned to erect in Richmond. He was smitten immediately by the slender, graceful woman with violet-blue eyes and blond curls. Jefferson somehow arranged for her and his party to spend the day together. They dined in the Paris suburb of St. Cloud and went sightseeing in the hills. He learned that she played the harpsichord, sang, and wrote music, spoke a number of languages, and was conversant in nearly all of the arts. After that they saw each other almost daily. Maria's husband was busy painting portraits and drumming up business and seemed not to mind his wife spending time with the distinguished American minister.

In any case, Maria was a known flirt who was sometimes described as being too free. The biographer James Boswell, best known for his *Life of Samuel Johnson,* charged that she "treated men like dogs." But her reputation seemed not to matter to Thomas Jefferson. The two spent day after day together in Jefferson's carriage as August became September. They visited sights along the Seine and gardens, forests, chateaux, statuary parks, libraries, and concerts in the far Parisian suburbs. Jefferson's principal biographer, Dumas Malone, wrote that no evidence exists of a physical romance, although affairs were generally condoned in French society. But Malone concedes as well that, as a biographer, he felt "it would be vain and cruel to attempt to draw aside the veil."

Jefferson and Cosway spent a glorious month together before a fateful fall put the American minister out of action. He called it a "folly," which suggests that he was trying to perform some stunt in front of Maria that went awry. Whatever the case, he either broke or dislocated his right wrist. A surgeon called to set the wrist bungled the job, and Jefferson spent the next two weeks in miserable pain. He wrote to Maria on October 5, using his left hand, shortly before her return to Italy: "I have passed the night in so much pain that I have not closed my eyes." "I would serve you and help you at dinner," she wrote, "and divert your pain with good music." In a note by messenger next day she told him, "I shall remember the charming days we passed together, and shall long for next Spring," when she would return.[178]

A day or so after Maria and her husband departed Paris, Jefferson, still writing left-handed, wrote her a lengthy philosophical letter styled as a "Dialogue between my Head and my Heart," in which he all but declared that he was in love with her but gave no hint that the relationship was anything other than a Platonic liaison.

For Jefferson, the affair seemed to augur a midlife crisis. Doubtless he was lonely after Martha's death—but French custom or no, he had been raised within a different code of conduct. In the "Dialogue between Head and Heart," he bared himself, his psyche, his soul, more than on any other occasion. If he was in love, and love without resolution was painful, he was willing to accept the pain along with the pleasure. He, too, looked forward to next spring.

IN FEBRUARY 1787, on the advice of his doctors, Jefferson traveled to Aix-en-Provence in the south of France to bathe his still ailing wrist in the warm spring waters. "I am now in the land of corn, wine, oil, and sunshine," he wrote to his secretary William Short, saying that if he should in future die in Paris, Short should take him back to southern France, where the sun would bring him back to life. On March 28 he wrote a long, plaintive letter to daughter Patsy at the convent school, dispensing advice, apologizing for leaving her behind. "No body in this world can make me so happy, or so miserable, as you," he told her. "To your sister and yourself I look to render the evening of my life serene and contented. It's [*sic*] morning has been clouded by loss after loss, till I have nothing left but you."

Next, Jefferson turned his carriage toward the north of Italy on an architectural tour. He was particularly taken with the Palladian styles inspired by the Venetian architect Andrea Palladio—especially his Villa Rotunda, whose style, Jefferson believed, might be incorporated into his beloved Monticello.[179]

The Paris to which Jefferson returned in early spring was seething with angry mobs gathered on street corners. Because of France's precarious financial situation, new taxes had been levied, many falling on the middle classes and the poor. Louis XVI had convened a meeting of the Assembly of Notables—an ancient legislative body consisting of nobles, ecclesiastics, and state functionaries—to advise him. All it succeeded in doing, however, was to expose the nation's bankruptcy.[180] The king instructed the Parliament of Paris to collect taxes, but that body refused, holding out for the cutting of state expenses and the creation of a constitution.

The king exiled its members to Troyes, a dark medieval town in the far north of France. Jefferson, who had become steeped in democracy over the past decade, was generally repelled by the authoritarianism of monarchical rule. Seeing it up close was even more distressing.

The mobs grew larger and more surly, marching the streets with placards and caricatures attacking the government. Work ceased. The king sent in the army to restore order, but dissatisfaction remained high and the reform party became stronger with each passing day. The king, who was "long in the habit of drowning his cares in wine, plunge[d] in deeper and deeper," Jefferson wrote John Adams on August 30. "The queen," he said, "crie[d], but sinn[ed] on."[181]

With the thin bubble of civil order threatening to burst, the king yielded. The Parliament of Paris exile was ended; the obnoxious taxes were repealed and others placed on the wealthy; and for a time the people were appeased. But Jefferson was convinced that the "worn-out monarchy had exhibited to the world a fatal indication of its weakness."[182] Given this, he was greatly pleased by the recent turn of events, which demonstrated that the king, who until just six weeks before had been omnipotent, was now forced to retract his abhorrent taxes "by the public voice."

It wasn't democracy, but it was the next best thing, Jefferson wrote John Jay. And he told another friend, "So much for the blessing of having kings . . . to besiege the throne of heaven with eternal prayers [a need exists] to extirpate from creation this class of human lions, tigers, and mammoths called kings, from whom, let him perish who does not say, 'good lord deliver us.'"[183]

As Paris seethed, eight-year-old Mary Jefferson, whom everyone called Polly, arrived in London and was given into the care of Abigail Adams. She barely had any recollection of her father, who had left for France when she was five, and she had become woefully attached to the man who commanded the ship that brought her over, a Captain Ramsey. Abigail wrote Jefferson that the old nurse he had expected to travel with Polly had become sick and that instead "she has a girl about 15 or 16 with her, the sister of the servant you have with you," referring to James Hemings. Teenage Sally Hemings was quite striking for her age, with fair skin and long straight hair that hung down her back. Captain Ramsey in fact seemed anxious to take her back with him, telling Abigail that Sally was "of little service." But Abigail interceded, assuring Jefferson that Sally "seems fond of the child [Polly] and appears good natured."[184]

AS JEFFERSON DEALT WITH HIS PERSONAL LIFE and conditions in Europe in that spring of 1787, Philadelphia became the scene yet again of momentous changes in America. James Madison, Jefferson's friend and political confidant, wrote to keep him abreast of the debates in the Constitutional Convention as they unfolded, but letters took a long time to cross and recross the Atlantic.

Still, from his Paris perch, Jefferson dispensed advice on the kind of government he felt the new nation should have. His chief fear was that somehow a monarch would emerge, and a governing body like the British Parliament would be created. Americans had become used to such a system in the previous two centuries, and Alexander Hamilton was said to believe in it. Exacerbating Jefferson's concerns were the rumors that abounded in London diplomatic circles; one was that a son of George III would be tapped for the job of monarch. And a British correspondent in America wrote to the British foreign secretary, "There is not a gentleman in the States between New Hampshire and Georgia . . . who is not desirous of changing [the present U.S. government] for a monarchy."[185]

In truth, no one with any standing was prepared to propose such a move—but that didn't stop Jefferson from worrying. In September the convention finished its work in Philadelphia, and George Washington sent Jefferson a draft of the Constitution it had created. He found much to like but much to dislike. James Madison had suggested that some sort of Bill of Rights should be included, spelling out in particular what rights the Constitution guaranteed. Jefferson heartily agreed. He wanted a declaration guaranteeing freedom of religion and the press, trial by jury, habeas corpus, and protection against illegal search and seizure.

But what concerned Jefferson most was the power that rested in the executive. In particular, he disliked the fact that the executive—the president—could be reelected ad infinitum, making that person much like a monarch who could serve for life.

Perhaps influenced by conditions in France, Jefferson wrote to a diplomatic official that autumn that "the tree of liberty must be refreshed from time to time with the blood of patriots and tyrants." To Madison the following month, he fulminated: "What country can preserve its liberties if its rulers are not warned from time to time that the people preserve the spirit of resistance. Let them take arms."[186]

Despite these sanguinary comments, Jefferson found more to like in the draft Constitution than to oppose; if the people of the various states ratified it, it was good enough for him. In the same letter to Madison, Jefferson said that if the states "approve the proposed Convention in all its parts, I shall concur in it cheerfully, in hopes that they shall amend it whenever they find it work wrong."[187]

With all the political excitement going on in America, Jefferson began to feel that he needed to go home for a while—if for no other reason than to squelch unpleasant rumors about him. His friend Francis Hopkinson— artist, poet, musician, and a deeply political creature—had written him in December: "Bye the bye, you have often been dish'd up to me as a strong Antifederalist, which is almost equivalent to what a *Tory* was in the days of the war . . . but I don't believe it."[188] Jefferson responded, sounding annoyed, "My opinion was never worthy enough of notice to merit citing, but since you ask it I will tell you. I am not a Federalist because I have never submitted the whole system of my opinions to the creed of any party of men whatever in religion, in philosophy, in politics or anything else where I was capable of thinking for myself . . . Therefore I protest to you that I am not of the party of Federalists. But I am much farther than that of the Antifederalists."[189]

POLITICAL EVENTS WERE QUICKLY EVOLVING in France. A bread shortage during the winter of 1788 sent mobs into the streets. A convention of the Estates-General had been called by the king, the first in nearly two hundred years. It was hoped that its three advisory bodies—Clergy (First Estate), Nobility (Second Estate), and Commoners (Third Estate)—could among them solve France's financial problems. But in late April riots killed several dozen people: the beginning of the violence that was to mark the French Revolution.

After meeting for several months, the Estates-General concluded it could not solve the financial problems and disbanded. At that point a group of commoners, known as the Commune, announced the formation of a National Assembly to govern the nation going forward. The king tried to defuse the situation by proclaiming a limited constitution, which granted citizens certain rights. It was too little too late.

The National Assembly seemed to grow more powerful daily. The streets were filled with joyous Parisian commoners, while at Versailles the king and his court were dismayed and frightened. The more the king conceded, Jefferson thought, the more the Assembly demanded. He admired its leaders, mostly lawyers, for their coolness and calmness. He believed their end goal was to strip the nobility of everything but their titles, and that didn't bother Jefferson.

The shortage of bread in Paris continued into the summer, and Jefferson, always thinking of American commerce, proposed shipping American flour and corn to France. The French finance minister Jacques Necker refused on grounds that the French harvest was just beginning. Jefferson was disappointed, but he was generally in one of his most optimistic and expansive moods concerning events in France, as they appeared to foretell a peaceful transition of power. "The Assembly," Jefferson wrote Thomas Paine in England, is "in complete and undisputed possession of the sovereignty . . . They have prostrated the government, and are now beginning to build one from the foundation."[190]

Lafayette, who was active in the Assembly, came to Jefferson for advice on how to establish a Declaration of the Rights of

Man, or a Bill of Rights. Jefferson was delighted to cooperate. He remained serenely confident that this transfer of power would be one of the miracles of the eighteenth century, despite reports of French and foreign troops marching on Paris. But with the arrival of the foreign troops, the mood of the crowds turned hostile, and three days later, on July 14, 1789, mobs stormed the Bastille prison. The French Revolution had exploded into motion.

Jefferson had seen the tensions building. Two days before the Bastille fell, his carriage ride took him through the Place Louis XV (now the Place de la Concorde). There he saw troops of German cavalry drawn up: the same brand of mercenary Hessians that had been unloosed on the American Patriots by George III. The Germans were being confronted by a screaming mob with a large pile of stones. As Jefferson passed, the crowd began throwing stones at the soldiers, causing them to retire. Ten days after the Bastille fell Jefferson wrote to Maria Cosway, in a morbidly playful mood, "We have been in the midst of tumult and violence. The cutting off of heads is become so much á la mode, that one is apt to feel of a morning whether their own is on their shoulders."[191]

In the weeks to come many chateaux in the countryside were set on fire. The nobility, aristocracy, and high-ranking clergy began to flee the country. Partisan soldiers sent by the Commune sought to hunt them down for trial and punishment.

IN THE SPRING OF 1789 Jefferson was finally granted the leave of absence he'd asked for months before. He was going to take his daughters home for good, though he ultimately planned to return. Because of the extensive baggage they would carry, he wanted a ship that would take them to a Virginia port, so he had to wait considerably longer in France even as the revolution progressed.

Finally, on September 27, 1789, Jefferson left Paris. With him were Patsy and Polly and the slaves James Hemings, now an accomplished French chef, and his sister Sally. As fall descended on the Atlantic, they set sail in the *Clermont,* bound for Norfolk, Virginia. They would return to a United States now governed by its first constitutionally elected Congress and its first president—George Washington.

Several months earlier James Madison had written Jefferson, asking if he would serve in some position in Washington's new administration. At the time Jefferson had demurred, saying that when he had completed his duties as ambassador to France he intended to return to Monticello and retire to the life of a country gentleman. But politics beckoned. There was a fresh excitement in the air, with a new government to guide the fledgling nation. Jefferson saw danger too; he still felt the federal government might assume too many powers. There must be counteracting forces, Jefferson reasoned, someone to stand for liberty.

When he arrived in Norfolk on November 23, 1789, Jefferson was surprised to find that some newspapers were reporting that Washington had nominated him as secretary of state and the Senate had confirmed him. The people of Norfolk treated him like "royalty," but Jefferson was disconcerted by the pomp and didn't fully believe what appeared in newspapers. He and his entourage, accompanied by a huge baggage train, made their way to Eppington, the house where Polly had lived before coming to Paris. They stopped there for a few days so that Polly could enjoy the company of her aunt Elizabeth Epps, who had been her surrogate mother for five years.

At Eppington, Washington's nominating letter caught up with Jefferson. He might have assumed that his name would be prominently mentioned as secretary, but he was deeply concerned at the responsibilities he felt the office implied. He understood that of the three administrative departments of the federal government—War, Treasury, and State—the State Department would be responsible not only for foreign affairs but for the entire domestic administration as well. Jefferson felt comfortable enough with foreign diplomacy, but far less so in the domestic realm, which he believed would easily draw disapproval. He wrote to Washington that he feared "criticisms and censures of a public . . . sometimes misinformed and misled." He said he would prefer to remain as ambassador, but added, "It is not for an individual to choose his post."[192]

The question of his appointment was still unresolved when Jefferson arrived at Monticello two days before Christmas. His slaves were so overjoyed at his return that they ran down the mountain, unharnessed the horses, and pulled Jefferson's carriage over the last ridge. Their reception was "unlike any other that [Patsy] had ever witnessed." There was laughter, crying, singing, and praying among the bondsmen. They carried him into the house and kissed his hands and feet. Over the holidays, a steady stream of neighbors came to welcome him home.[193]

Madison, too, arrived to discuss Jefferson's appointment. He did not believe that domestic matters would amount to more than a "trifle" and if necessary the two duties could be separated, as they were in Britain, which had a foreign secretary and a home secretary.

At length came a firm but polite letter from Washington. "I consider the office of Secretary for the Department of State as very important on many accounts: and I know of no person, who in my judgment, could better execute the duties of it than yourself," he stated. He added that the public reaction to Jefferson as secretary of state had been overwhelmingly favorable.[194] The letter left no question that Jefferson was the man Washington desired for the post. Jefferson dutifully laid aside his desire to return to France as ambassador and his qualms over public opinion—which had so far been "a major factor in his ultimate political success"—and bowed to the wishes of the president.[195]

Two major events in Jefferson's life occurred in February 1790. The first was Madison's formal break with his fellow *Federalist Papers* author Alexander Hamilton, which occurred when Madison opposed Hamilton's bill for the federal government to assume the debts of the states. It was the beginning of Madison's turn away from the growing move for a strong federal government and toward Jefferson's belief in states' and individual rights.

The second was of a personal nature. Jefferson's seventeen-year-old daughter Martha, his beloved Patsy, was to wed her third cousin, twenty-one-year-old Thomas Mann Randolph Jr. Exactly how the romance began is unclear. Mann may have visited Patsy in Paris, while he was a student at the University of Edinburgh, or perhaps he and Patsy met during the long trek from Norfolk to Eppington to Monticello. In any case, Jefferson was delighted with the match, though it must have been a wistful time for him. Patsy had been a close companion while they were in Paris, visiting him from the convent school on weekends and conversing on many subjects as she grew older and more worldly. Described as more handsome than beautiful, she was tall and slender, with exquisite manners and an acute, inquiring mind.

After the wedding Jefferson took stock of his personal affairs. He had lands of more than 10,000 acres and two hundred slaves, both of which could be used as collateral for a loan he badly needed. His fields had deteriorated in his long absence, but because he was leaving again for his new post he arranged for a friend and neighbor, Nicholas Lewis, as well as his new son-in-law, to look after Monticello. In March 1790, Jefferson packed once again and headed north to New York, the seat of the first official United States government.

On arrival, Jefferson immediately paid a visit to the president. There was much to go over, and he and Washington met for several days running. Washington had deep respect for Jefferson's mind and virtues, as he had heard high praise of him from Lafayette and others. Jefferson's response to Washington, meanwhile, was more than cordial; it was reverent. He told Madison that Washington's person was fine, his stature exactly right, his deportment easy, erect, and noble, that he was the best horseman of his age and the most graceful figure that could be seen in any age."[196]

Despite his strong admiration for Washington, Jefferson soon came to view Alexander Hamilton as a political archenemy whose ideas of government clashed with his own— particularly regarding the power of the executive branch. He even disliked the fact that the Constitution did not limit the presidency to one or two terms, instead allowing a president to run for office in perpetuity. Jefferson was convinced that the Federalists, and particularly Hamilton, had a penchant for accumulating power and would destroy the fruits of their revolution—the most prominent one being liberty—and make the nation a mere spinoff of Great Britain.

Jefferson later hired a clerk-translator at his Department of State, Philip Freneau, to publish anti-Federalist articles in Freneau's paper, the *National Gazette.* Hamilton, meanwhile, was sponsoring a rival newspaper, *Gazette of the United States,* edited and published by a John Fenno, whose views coincided with the Federalist philosophy. Although there were laws in most states against defamation, or libel, they were treated somewhat loosely by the press, whose writers knew how to skirt the letter of the law by innuendo, insinuation, ambiguity, and other artful dodges.

The infant years of the republic were rife with overblown fears, bias, and fierce political hatreds among men who wished only the best for their country. But because they were grappling, often in the dark, with how to hold the nation together, they were terrified of making some mistake that would set the course of the newly formed United States on a poor or even fatal course. Like a band of castaways sailing into uncharted waters without a compass, they had only their theories, suppositions, intuitions, and prayers to guide them. Hamilton, John Adams, and to a lesser extent John Jay—all northerners—deeply espoused their Federalist beliefs, while the Virginians Jefferson and Madison held firmly to their Republican ideals.

Jefferson worried that Congress was nearly paralyzed by the extreme differences between southern and northern men, which had led to the "bitterest animosities." Fearing that this regionalism might break up the Union, he proposed a compromise deal that satisfied Hamilton's support of the debt assumption act and regional concerns regarding the capital city's permanent location.

But his efforts to be conciliatory with the Federalists ended when Jefferson learned from Madison that speculators were "exploring the interior and distant parts of the Union in order to take advantage of the ignorance of the holders" of public debt.[197] In those areas newspapers were a rarity, so bad actors could buy up old government securities from unsuspecting owners for a shilling or two to the pound, then sell them to the federal government for eight or ten shillings a pound.

Jefferson tied this to Hamilton's debt assumption bill and was outraged, claiming he'd been "duped" by the secretary of the treasury. He lambasted the "corrupt bargain" that somehow cheated innocent veterans and others holding what had been until that time nearly worthless government paper. He invented phrases describing the Federalists as "a stock-jobbing herd," and "corrupt squalor," and "votaries of the Treasury." Jefferson hated speculation above almost all things, always maintaining that the life of the simple farmer was the future of the American nation.

In foreign affairs, Jefferson's first skirmish involved the thing that all diplomats abhor: war. During the summer of 1790, a controversy had arisen between Britain and Spain over the Spanish seizure of two British ships, the *Princess Royal* and the *Argonaut,* at a place called Nootka Sound on the coast of Vancouver Island. Both Spanish and British explorers had claimed the place, and the seizure provoked outrage in London's political circles. Goaded by the English press, there was even talk of war with Spain.

Jefferson saw this as a serious problem for America. If there was such conflict, Britain could use the occasion to transport its troops in Canada to seize the territory of Spanish Florida, which ran from Key West along the coast of the Gulf of Mexico to New

Orleans. Such an action would give Britain a vast new foothold on the American continent, disturb the balance of power, and pose a significant new danger to the United States.

Jefferson's solution was to send an offer to Spain. In exchange for Spain ceding to America navigation rights on the Mississippi River and all of Spanish West Florida, America would guarantee that Spain would control all the lands (except New Orleans itself) west of the Mississippi. Jefferson saw no harm in this, as he believed it would "be ages" before Americans would want to move west of the Mississippi. Spain, however, refused the offer.

Jefferson had also suggested to Washington that if the British attempted to seize Spanish Florida, the United States should go in on the side of Spain. In the end, the affair defused itself, but it highlighted Jefferson's mind-set at the time: he was willing to give away huge expanses of land and even go to war to keep the British out of America.

In September 1790 Congress opened its fall session in Philadelphia, which was to be the nation's capital for the next ten years. Jefferson had rented a handsome house on High (Market) Street three blocks from Washington's presidential residence. He had it elaborately remodeled at his own expense, adding a library, stable, and a "garden house," where he could have total privacy.

Jefferson had invented a new word for his political enemies—"monocrats"—so convinced was he that they were in favor of installing a monarch or a dictator as president. He did not publicly rail against them. To the contrary. True to his personality, he tried to remain on a friendly personal basis with them, as well as they did with him. These men were often in close social circles in Philadelphia, as they had been in New York, finding themselves on many occasions seated nearby one another at a dining table or mingling at dances and balls.

Instead of confronting them, Jefferson worked, as usual, behind the scenes, sending letters and notes to Washington and Madison or writing essays opposing or favoring this policy or that for Freneau's *National Gazette*. Hamilton, though more outspoken, usually followed the same approach. To an uninformed visitor observing the cabinet of President Washington, all might have appeared serene. In truth, a war was being waged for the very soul of America.

Jefferson hosted a friendly gathering at his home for fellow cabinet members, and the after-dinner conversation turned to politics—in particular, to the British form of government. John Adams remarked, "If some of its defects & abuses [of the British system of government] were corrected, it would be the most perfect constitution of government ever devised by man."[198] The comment appalled Jefferson, who was further incensed when Hamilton chimed in that "It was the most perfect model of government that could be formed; & that the correction of its vices would render it an impracticable government."[199]

Earlier that evening, Hamilton had asked about a collection of portraits that hung on Jefferson's dining room walls, inquiring as to who the men portrayed were. Sir Francis Bacon, Isaac Newton, and John Locke, Jefferson said. "I told him they were my trinity of the three greatest men the world had ever produced."[200] Hamilton thought for a moment while absorbing this appraisal, then declared, "The greatest man . . . that ever lived was Julius Caesar."[201] To Jefferson this was more evidence that Hamilton and Adams, the two Federalist monocrats, were bent on installing a British-style system of government in the United States, with some kind of king or strongman as its leader.

As the guests were leaving, Jefferson contemplated the differences between Adams and Hamilton. Reflecting many years afterward, he concluded, "Mr. Adams was honest as a politician as well as a man; Hamilton honest as a man, but, as a politician, believing in the necessity of either force or corruption to govern men."[202]

In February 1792, the final year of Washington's first term as president, Thomas Jefferson rushed to the executive office one afternoon just before 3 p.m., the hour when Washington began seeing visitors from the general public. Jefferson wanted Washington to remove the postal service from the Treasury Department and put it under his own supervision at the State Department. He argued that such a move would increase the efficiency of the service by "doubling the 'velocity' of the post-rider" from fifty to one hundred miles a day.[203]

By the time Jefferson had made his point, the three o'clock hour had arrived and Washington asked him to breakfast next morning. There, he once more stated his case, adding for Washington's edification that "the Treasury already possessed enough powers as to swallow up the whole" presidency. But, he reassured Washington, he had "no personal interest," but only "to place things on a safe footing" for the good of the people. And as if to add emphasis, Jefferson informed the president that he had no further political aspirations and intended to leave office as soon as Washington did.[204]

Washington, in a poignant moment, began to unburden himself of his exhaustion and exasperation as the chief executive and told Jefferson he did not intend to seek a second term. He was feeling old, he said, in body and in mind. Also, he feared that seeking a second term would give some a chance to say that, "having tasted the sweets of office, he could not do without them."[205] Yet, the president continued, he was also fearful that if his cabinet members, Jefferson among them, all began leaving as well, "This might produce a shock in the public mind of dangerous consequence."[206]

Jefferson reviewed his own path to becoming secretary of state, telling Washington, "No man had ever had less desire of entering into public offices than myself." Washington absorbed this moment of candor between himself and his fellow Virginia aristocrat, then confided a private anxiety to Jefferson. "The government had set out with a pretty good general good will of the public," he said. "Yet symptoms of dissatisfaction had shown themselves far beyond what [I] could have expected, and to what height these might arise in case of a great change in the administration could not be foreseen."[207]

Jefferson saw his opening and used the occasion to jab at Alexander Hamilton. There was, he told Washington, "only a single source of these discontents." The Treasury Department was at fault, "deluging the states with paper money instead of gold and silver," and in so doing abetting speculation to the detriment "of [other] useful industry." He further complained that the Federalist lawmakers "had feathered their nests with paper," and were planning a time "to let us know whether we live under a limited or an unlimited government."[208]

Two months later Jefferson was haranguing Washington once more, this time regarding the Treasury Department's proposal to pay off the interest on the national debt by borrowing more money and by levying a tax on alcoholic spirits, the "whiskey tax."

In a letter to Washington, Jefferson seemed to complain that Hamilton was inflating the currency by printing more money than was backed by actual gold or silver. He told the president, "That all the capital employed in paper speculation is barren and useless, producing, like that on a gaming table, no access to itself, and is withdrawn from commerce and agriculture . . . It nourishes in our citizens habits of vice and idleness instead of industry and morality."[209] Then he got around to his principal argument, which remained the same: "That the ultimate object of all this is to prepare the way for a change, from the present republican form of government, to that of a monarchy, of which the English constitution is to be the model. That this was contemplated in the [constitutional] convention, is no secret," Jefferson maintained, referring to Hamilton's June 1787 speech in which he had said the "English model [is] the only good one on this subject."[210]

Jefferson went on to charge that the Federalist members of Congress, who held the majority, were making money from Hamilton's monetary system. "It will be the instrument for producing in future a king, lords, and commons," Jefferson said, adding that its goal was to use "the new government merely as a stepping-stone to monarchy."[211]

Warming to his subject, Jefferson then issued a warning for the worst-case scenario—secession. He intimated to the president that under the Hamilton system the people of the southern states, in order to annually finance their large plantations, were the borrowers in the country and were being fleeced by northerners, who were the lenders. "I can scarcely contemplate a more incalculable evil than the breaking of the Union into two or more parts," Jefferson groaned. "This is the event at which I tremble," he said, mentioning "violence or secession" as distinct possibilities.[212]

There was a way clear of this tragedy, Jefferson said: for Washington to agree to serve another term as president. "The confidence of the whole of the Union is centered in you," Jefferson told him, "in your being at the helm." It wouldn't even be necessary for Washington to serve a full four-year term. "One or two sessions [of Congress] will determine the crisis; and I cannot but hope that you can resolve to add one or two more to the many years you have already sacrificed to the good of mankind[213] . . . North & South will hang together, if they have you to hang on," Jefferson concluded.[214]

How much Jefferson's pleas affected Washington's ultimate decision to seek a second term cannot be known for certain; Washington did not speak of it. But it is fair to assume that the secretary of state's words did not fall on deaf ears. Possibly the answer lies in Jefferson's own appraisal of Washington's character. "He never acted until every circumstance under consideration was weighed. Hearing suggestions, he always did what was best."

WHILE JEFFERSON BATTLED to save his young country, France slumped into anarchy. Thousands were slain by mobs or by the army, and the streets ran red as severed heads were marched all over the city on pikes. The Jacobins—Robespierre, Danton, Marat, and others—were in the ascendancy, and they called for the blood of traitors, by which they meant the aristocrats. Lafayette and his wife fled the country, but he was subsequently caught and imprisoned for about five years in the revolutionary zealotry against aristocrats. In January 1793 Louis XVI was executed in a great public ceremony; nine months later his wife Marie Antoinette followed him to the guillotine.

John Adams was initially sympathetic to the revolution but was convinced from the outset that the kind of broad democracy espoused by the French revolutionaries was doomed. He and Hamilton became appalled by the reports of violence and bloodshed in France—but Jefferson sometimes seemed to exult in them, scolding anyone who was unenthusiastic. He considered the French Revolution a "beautiful" event, akin to the American Revolution; he compared the Jacobins with the American Republican Party, which is what Jefferson and the other anti-Federalists had taken to calling themselves.

Americans were generally slow to change their attachment to the French, who had stood by them and whose active assistance had materially affected the great victory at Yorktown. Then, too, the idea of a nation fighting for its liberty was an ideal ingrained in the American character. Many of the Democratic-Republican clubs that had followed in the wake of Citizen Genêt were still operating as chaos spread in France. But as reports of the brutality there grew, public opinion turned decidedly against the new regime. Alexander Hamilton called it "a horror," and "one of the most degrading things that ever disparaged the understandings of an enlightened people." In a Philadelphia speech in 1794 he deemed the French Revolution "a political convulsion that in a great or less way shakes the whole civilized world."

Jefferson would doubtless have agreed with this last appraisal, although not in the sense that Hamilton meant it. Jefferson remained steadfast in his support of the revolutionaries, and in a letter to the American chargé d'affaires in Paris, written just weeks before the murder of the king, he had explained: "In the struggle which was necessary, many guilty persons fell without the forms of trial, and with them, some innocent. These I deplore as much as any body . . . but I deplore them as . . . [if] they had fallen in battle. It was necessary to use the arm of the people, a machine [the guillotine] not quite so blind as balls and bombs, but blind to a certain degree.[215]

". . . The liberty of the whole earth was depending on the issue of the contest, and was ever such a prize won with so little innocent blood? My own affections have been deeply wounded by some of the martyrs to this cause, but rather than it should have failed, I would have seen half the earth desolated."[216]

Washington did not share his views. When, two weeks after the king's execution, the Jacobin government declared war on Britain, the president immediately issued a proclamation declaring that the United States would remain neutral. This in turn set off the Republicans, who charged that Washington had exceeded his powers and that only the legislature could rule "on the subject of war and peace." The matter was debated in the press, much to Washington's consternation, but then the opposition died away.

Jefferson and the Republicans continued squabbling with Hamilton and the Federalists, despite Washington's pleas for harmony. Jefferson was letting his emotions get the better of him, almost to the point of paranoia. He had come to despise his job and his continued presence in Philadelphia, where "the laws of society oblige me to move in always exactly in the circle which I know to bear me particular hatred, that is to say the wealthy aristocrats, the merchants connected closely with England [and] the newly created paper fortunes," he told Washington.[217]

Despite Washington's formal request that he stay on at least until the end of the next congressional session, Jefferson had had enough, and on the final day of 1793 he tendered his resignation. The next day, Washington accepted it with regret, adding that, "I could not suffer you to leave your station without assuring you that the opinion, which I had formed of your integrity and talents . . . has been confirmed by the fullest experience . . . Let a conviction of my most earnest prayers for your happiness accompany you in your retirement."[218]

With that, Jefferson departed Philadelphia and returned to his beloved Virginia mountaintop. He was fifty years old. A week after Jefferson's departure, Adams wrote to Abigail, "Jefferson went off yesterday and good riddance to bad ware. I hope his Temper will be more cool and his Principles more reasonable in retirement than they have been in office. He has talents, I know, and integrity I believe, but his mind is now poisoned with passion, prejudice, and faction."[219]

Despite the opinion of Adams and other Federalists, in the weeks following his resignation Jefferson received dozens of letters of congratulations and hopes that he would someday return to public life. He answered one of these, from the former revolutionary general Horatio Gates, in the negative, citing politics, "which I have ever hated in both theory and practice. I thought myself conscientiously called from those studies which were my delight by the political crisis of my country . . . In storms like those, all hands must be aloft. But calm has been restored and I leave the [ship] with joy to those who love the sea."[220]

At Monticello, Jefferson threw himself into a busy routine of tending to the farm and buildings. He told friends he stayed in the saddle most of the day. He soon embarked on a major renovation of the entire plantation, including Mulberry Row, the slave quarters. But it was the main house that received most of his attention. Declaring that architecture was his "delight," Jefferson had much of Monticello pulled down and over the next decade and a half he erected an elegant structure twice the size of the original. He selected a Palladian architectural style from places he had visited in France and Italy, drew the plans, and supervised the construction.

He also built new cabins for the slaves and added a blacksmith shop, carpentry shop, stables, sawpit, smokehouse, wash house, dairy, and a nailery in which young enslaved boys produced up to 10,000 nails a day. In their cabins, women spun cloth from cotton and sewed clothes for the family. Like many plantations, Monticello was a self-contained town that grew its own vegetables; raised its own cattle, hogs, sheep, and fowl; and bred its own horses.

Jefferson loved hunting and fishing. He wrote a letter to one of the directors of the Rivanna Company that had been organized to improve the river for barge traffic, saying, "Every American who wishes to protect his farm from the ravages of quadrupeds and his country from those of biped invaders" should be "a gunman."[221] "I am a great friend to the manly and healthy exercises of the gun." He told his fifteen-year-old nephew Peter Carr that "Games played with the ball . . . are too violent for the body and stamp no character on the mind. Let your gun therefore be the constant companion of your walks."[222] Jefferson kept a good collection of guns, including eleven pistols, a musket, a double-barrel shotgun for fowling, and two Austrian-made Girandoni air rifles—a futuristic multishot weapon.

His slave Isaac Jefferson recalled that Jefferson hunted partridges, squirrels, and rabbits. "Old master wouldn't shoot partridges settin, wouldn't take advantage of 'em . . . would'nt shoot a hare setten 'nuther, skeer him up fust."[223] Apparently Jefferson didn't hunt deer, preferring to watch them feed in Monticello's deer park, and if ever hunters were found there, he "used to go down tar wid his gun and order 'em out."[224] Jefferson also found great joy in fishing "below the old dam" in the Rivanna for trout and bream. But mostly he enjoyed the solitude he found in his long rides through the woods of his mountain retreat.

He was pleased to have his daughter Patsy and her husband, Thomas Randolph, still living at Monticello. They had taken care of the plantation while he was in Philadelphia, and the couple now had two children, Thomas Jefferson Randolph and Ann Cary Randolph. Jefferson delighted in playing with the children, and proudly talked of them in letters to friends.

When domestic preoccupations were not on Jefferson's mind, politics were. He hungered for news and digested the mail as quickly as possible after it arrived. Madison and James Monroe, his two most faithful correspondents, wrote regularly.

Soon after Jefferson retired, John Adams had also written, somewhat hypocritically, "I congratulate you on the charming opening of the spring and heartily wish I was enjoying of it as you are upon a plantation, out of the hearing of the din of politics and rumours of war."[225] The rumors of war were too true. Great Britain was as surly and provoking as ever since losing the colonies in the Revolution. It had come to Jefferson's attention during his last days as secretary of state that the British were inflicting serious depredations on American shipping in the West Indies. This had been authorized by the British cabinet as a war measure in its latest struggle with France. The produce of the French Caribbean colonies was immensely profitable, and much of it was conducted to its final destination by American ships. Britain decided to put a stop to that and seized hundreds of U.S. ships, confiscating their cargos.

When word of this reached the press, Americans were outraged and many called for war against Britain. Washington, however, resisted these passions. He sent John Jay, who was presently serving as the U.S. chief justice, as a special envoy to England to see if matters could be rectified. Meanwhile, Congress passed the Navy Act of 1794 in March of that year. This led to the rebirth of the U.S. Navy and to the construction of six warships—including the soon-to-be-famed USS *Constitution*—to deal with the Barbary pirates, and with the British if necessary.

Jefferson was much pleased that a navy was being formed; he had wanted to go after the Barbary pirates for years. He was less sanguine about a war with Britain, but he told James Monroe that in Virginia "the spirit of war" ran high.

WAR WITH ENGLAND did not come to America. Instead, in the late autumn of 1794, the Jay Treaty arrived, setting off a national controversy of unprecedented dimensions. Chief Justice Jay had been sent to London by the president to negotiate a mutual agreement—devised by Alexander Hamilton—whereby both the United States and Great Britain would enter into trade with each other and avert war. The British were now more amiable to dealing with the Americans, so as not to drive them into the French orbit, and in his main mission Jay succeeded.

But for Jefferson, Madison, and the Republicans Jay had given up too much to the British. The Republican press whipped this notion into the magnitude of a national humiliation and sellout to the British. There were calls for Jay's impeachment, and even Washington's. Jay was hanged in effigy in a number of cities. There were organized Republican protests, especially by the Democratic-Republican clubs, who hated the British and favored the French. The country was divided so bitterly that the ranks swelled in both Federalist and Republican Parties in each of the states.

The principal issues Jay had been instructed to negotiate were these: a commercial treaty between the two countries that would avoid war; cessation of the impressment of American sailors on the high seas; compensation for the 250 American ships seized by the British in the West Indies; compensation for several thousand slaves taken by the British during the Revolutionary War; the opening of the West Indies to American trade; and British withdrawal from forts they continued to occupy in the Northwest Territory (mainly in Michigan and Ohio, where the British were selling modern weapons to the Indians). The British maintained they had continued to occupy the forts, in violation to the Treaty of Paris, because the Americans had violated the treaty by failing to prevent states from seizing the property of Tories and failing to pay prewar debts to British merchants.

Under the terms of the new Jay Treaty, the British would pay American shipping merchants $11,650,000 in damages and the United States would pay the British £600,000 for past debts that American states had refused to pay. The British agreed to vacate their forts in the Northwest and in New York. Styled "A Treaty of Amity, Commerce, and Navigation," the agreement was to be of ten years' duration.

Two items seriously rankled the southern states: Jay, a New Yorker who opposed slavery, dropped the quest for a claim to compensation for British-confiscated slaves (many if not most of whom were resold in the West Indies), and he did not pursue an agreement to limit the amount of American (southern) cotton that could be exported for trade. These were the kinds of things that had led to Jefferson's 1792 warning to George Washington: the rift was growing ever wider between North and South, which could lead eventually to secession and civil war.

The war of words over the Jay Treaty continued in the newspapers in June 1795, when Washington submitted the treaty to the Senate for ratification. The agreement may have been a compromise between the United States and Britain, but it was not one between the Federalists and the Republicans. The latter party wanted the U.S. government to support France in its war with Britain, and not to trade with an enemy who represented the height of aristocracy. Hamilton, Jay, and even Washington were denounced as monarchists and traitors.

The Federalists countered that the treaty had averted war at a time when the United States was totally unprepared for one, and that it would give a powerful boost to American commerce and the economy. Washington, who was determined to keep America neutral in the European conflict, added the weight of his enormous prestige by signing the treaty after it was ratified. In the end, the Federalists' argument prevailed, and the treaty was ratified in the Senate by the necessary two-thirds vote of twenty to ten.

Madison then began to argue that the treaty must also be approved by the House, because it involved funding and commerce, but that claim was rejected in the Supreme Court. After being likewise ratified by the British, the treaty went into effect February 29, 1796. This immediately precipitated the very real prospect of war with France.

Three months later, Jefferson was fully engaged again in the political fray, struggling with whether to let his name be put up in that fall's presidential election. The issue of who would succeed George Washington was a tremendous one, fraught with terrible implications for the country's future. Jefferson was determined to have a Republican in the White House, but he was also tormented by the idea of exposing himself to the most critical public scrutiny of any figure in the land.

He was fifty-three years old and enjoying the comfort, beauty, and privacy of his mountaintop; the notion of once more reentering the hurly-burly of politics was immensely difficult for him. Yet during the past several years he had stepped up his interest in that exact subject, subscribing to several political newspapers, increasing his correspondence with Madison and Monroe, eagerly badgering visitors to Monticello about foreign and national affairs.

Then in August 1796 Jefferson received a short letter from Tennessee senator William Cocke, who had "the pleasure to inform you that the people of this State of every description express a wish that you should be the next President of the United States, and Mr. Burr, Vice President." Jefferson waited a considerable period to respond—almost to election time. And even then he was either still clearly conflicted or overcome by false modesty.

It was always a "great pleasure," he wrote, to learn that, "I am recollected with approbation to those [I serve]." Then Jefferson drifted off on another of his nautical analogies. "Our acquaintance commenced on a troubled ocean," he told Cocke. "My bark has at length entered port less shattered than I expected, and I wish not to hazard it again." [226] But, he added, "I have not the arrogance to refuse the honorable office you mention to me; but I can say with truth that I would rather be thought worthy of it than to be appointed to it. For well I know that no man will bring out of that office the reputation that carries him into it."[227] What Cocke made of this convoluted reply is not known.

Like almost everything else in the new democracy, presidential elections were baffling. Candidates did not campaign—in fact, they didn't even announce their candidacy, but acknowledged their acceptance of it after their names were put forward by others. Or they maneuvered to have others put forward their names.

Jefferson's name was put forward and, despite Washington's stern warning in his Farewell Address against forming "factions," adherents of the two political parties immediately began attacking one another. Jefferson was portrayed as a coward in 1781 when, as governor, he left Monticello as Banastre Tarleton's dragoons were closing in on him. He was said to have fled in "haste and confusion," leaving public records to be destroyed. The charge was as ridiculous as the one leveled by Jeffersonian Republicans claiming that John Adams was a monarchist who wanted to form a hereditary chief executive and Senate-for-life.

Madison warned Jefferson that he should be prepared to accept the vice presidency should John Adams win. That was fine with Thomas Jefferson. "It is not the less true, however, that I do sincerely wish to be second on that vote rather than the first."

Hamilton, now out of government, was involved in various machinations that could throw the election into chaos. One such prospect was that the electoral vote would be tied, putting the ultimate decision into the hands of the House of Representatives. Jefferson generously told Madison that if it should come to that, he wanted the House to choose Adams. "He has always been my senior from the commencement of our public life," Jefferson told Madison, "and the expression of the public will being equal, this circumstance ought to give him the preference."[228]

The electoral vote was tallied on February 8, 1797. John Adams beat Jefferson by three votes—71 to 68. Jefferson was well satisfied. "On principles of public respect I should not have refused [the presidency]: but I protest before my God that I shall, from the bottom of my heart, rejoice at escaping."[229]

The prospect of war with France looming. And now there was talk in the northern press of those states seceding from the Union, because the constitutional provision that counted slaves as three-fifths of a person gave southerners an unfair advantage at the polls. Jefferson found himself grateful that he had lost the presidency at this time. "This is certainly not a moment to covet the helm," he said.[230]

On March 4, 1797, Adams and Jefferson were sworn in at a brief ceremony at Congress Hall in Philadelphia. George Washington seemed exceedingly pleased as Adams took the oath and whispered to him gloatingly right afterward, "Ay, I am fairly out and you fairly in! see which one of us is happiest." For his part, Jefferson told Madison, "The President is fortunate to get out just as the bubble is bursting, leaving others to hold the bag." The presidency, he said, "is but a splendid misery."[231]

In a private conversation at the presidential mansion, Adams told Jefferson that he wanted his vice president to participate heavily in the decision-making process, rather than repeating his own experience under Washington of being completely ignored. Jefferson wrote later, "He never after that said one word to me on the subject, or ever consulted me on any measures of the government."[232]

CHAPTER SEVEN

In 1797, at the age of sixty-one, John Adams finally found himself in the presidency. He had spent two four-year terms as vice president, during which he complained to Abigail, "My country in its wisdom contrived for me the most insignificant office" ever conceived by man, and that he "can do neither good nor evil."[233]

When George Washington left office, he handed President Adams a smoothly running ship, with one exception: French depredations on the American merchant fleet. The French were furious that the United States had concluded the so-called Jay Treaty with Britain, with whom France was at war. They had become further outraged when, after the revolutionaries deposed and executed Louis XVI and Marie Antoinette, the States stopped repayment of its Revolutionary War debts to France, claiming that the debt was owed to a "previous regime."

In retaliation, revolutionary France began attacking and seizing U.S. merchant ships in the Caribbean Sea, where the French maintained eight colonies, including the soon-to-be-infamous Devil's Island. French privateers also ranged the length of America's Atlantic coast, preying on merchant vessels. Nothing could be done to stop them, because the United States had foolishly disbanded its navy after the Revolutionary War and sold its last warship more than a decade earlier.

George Washington had kept the country neutral during the Franco-British war, and John Adams intended to do the same. Before he left office, Washington had sent South Carolinian Charles Cotesworth Pinckney as ambassador to France, but the French government refused to receive him. In February 1797, Secretary of State Timothy Pickering informed Congress that more than three hundred American merchant ships had been seized by the French. In an effort to defuse the situation, Adams appointed a three-man commission to go to France and see if negotiations could be restarted. Alexander Hamilton approved the move but told Adams that unless there was a Republican of some note among the three, the French would not consider the commission as representative. Both Madison and Jefferson were offered the post, and both turned it down. In the end, Elbridge Gerry of Massachusetts was chosen as the Republican member of the delegation, along with the Federalists Pinckney and John Marshall.

Meanwhile, Adams's own vice president Jefferson had several secret conversations with the French consul in Philadelphia, Joseph Létombe, advising him that France should attack and subjugate Britain. Predicting that Adams would be ousted after one term, Jefferson called him "vain, irritable, stubborn . . . and still suffering pique at the preference accorded Franklin over him in Paris." And, he told the French consul, when the American commission came to Paris, the French government should listen to them and "then drag out the negotiations at length," which is just what happened.

The commissioners arrived in Paris in August 1797 and were met by the unctuous minister of foreign affairs, Charles Maurice de Talleyrand-Périgord, known simply as Talleyrand. He shifted the negotiations to a panel of three junior diplomats, who became notorious for their American diplomatic code names X, Y, and Z. They imposed a number of excruciating demands on the Americans: an enormous loan to the French government; a withdrawal of some bellicose remarks President Adams had made to Congress about the behavior of France; reparations for damages to French ships by American privateers; and finally and most egregious, the payment of large bribes to them personally before any consideration of negotiations could begin. Thus began the infamous XYZ Affair.

The two Federalists on the commission were appalled and indignant and wished to end the mission immediately, but Republican Elbridge Gerry recommended that they play along with the demands to see if they could arrange a meeting with a French official who was less avaricious. The commissioners remained in France seven more wasteful months. John Marshall wrote a full account of the indignities that the Americans suffered from the intransigent French diplomats, including the bribes. The undertaking seemed a total failure. On March 4, 1798, the report was read by President Adams.

In March, Adams delivered a temperate but firm message to Congress in which he outlined the failure of the mission to Paris but deliberately neglected to mention the infamous bribe demands by the French diplomats. Jeffersonian Republicans, who favored close relations with France, denounced the Adams administration, demanding that Adams release all relevant papers involved in the mission, confident that they would show France in a better light. Republicans were dumbstruck, however, when Adams complied, revealing the French infamy in the XYZ Affair. When the XYZ documents were made public, Americans were outraged at the insulting, shabby, and corrupt behavior of the French government.

Adams was push-pulled by the divisiveness in the country. As France grew ever more bellicose, Hamilton advocated constant vigilance against war by preparing for it in advance. Jefferson thoroughly rejected the notion of a standing army, believing, despite his own personal experience during the Revolution, that state militias were adequate to defend America's shores. Hamilton's experience during the war had been that militias were undependable against seasoned, professional soldiers. But Jefferson prophesied that a standing army could be used to suppress opposition views.

BY JULY 1798 THE COUNTRY was taken with war fever, and Hamilton's arguments won out. Adams declared that the United States needed to be placed in a more "defensive posture." Congress complied, passing bills that created a provisional 10,000- to 12,000-man army and a Department of the Navy, as well as a Marine Corps. Money was appropriated to build immediately three twenty-two-gun frigates, with another eighteen warships contemplated in the near future. Many merchant vessels were also armed.

A trade embargo with France was instituted, and the earlier treaties with France rescinded. War seemed on the horizon. But luckily for the United States, France was already at war with most of the civilized world, fighting in some way or other not only Britain, but Spain, the Netherlands, Austria, Prussia, Italy, and Luxembourg. France had also committed large numbers of troops to an invasion of Egypt, led by Napoleon Bonaparte, and to Ireland, in an attempt to foment an Irish rebellion against England. In other words, France had her hands full when the so-called Quasi-War with America broke out.

Adams approached George Washington, then sixty-six, to once again serve his country and organize the new U.S. Army. Washington agreed to make his presence known only if the troops had to march. Otherwise, Washington said, the new army should be under Alexander Hamilton. Adams did everything possible to dissuade Washington from this scenario—not the least because Hamilton had been born on a Caribbean island and not in America, a complaint Adams had long held against the ex–secretary of the treasury. In the end, and over Adams's objection, Washington's wishes prevailed.

As the military preparations proceeded, the Republicans loudly objected. The revelation of bribery and other diplomatic misdeeds by the French had done nothing to stanch their conviction that the Adams administration was deliberately trying to provoke war with France. Jefferson didn't put it past Talleyrand to have attempted extortion, but he believed the French government knew nothing about it. Madison accused Adams of employing lies against the French to incite war.

All reason seemed to have fled the body politic—and not only on the Republican side, for as Jefferson and his cohorts continued with their outrageous charges, the Federalists' suspicions deepened as well, until each side seemed headed toward some advanced stage of political paranoia. Jefferson noted an increasing incivility, as he wrote to the prominent South Carolinian and future governor Edward Rutledge, "Men who have been intimate all their lives cross the street, to avoid meeting and turn their heads another way, lest they should be obliged to touch their hat." It was in this unhappy atmosphere that the Quasi-War proceeded.

As a direct consequence of the war, the Federalist-controlled Congress had also passed four laws collectively known as the Alien and Sedition Acts. Adams had nothing to do with engineering the acts, but he did sign them into law when he could have vetoed them. Justified as a "security" measure, they allowed, among other things, the president to deport foreigners he found "dangerous," although no precise definition of that term was specified.

The new laws also raised the time it took to apply for U.S. citizenship from five to fourteen years. This, some charged, was aimed at suppressing the Irish vote, because the Irish loathed the British and generally voted Republican. The crowning feature of the legislation, the Sedition Act, set criminal penalties for speaking or publishing "any false, malicious, or scandalous" writings against the United States government or Congress, "with intent to defame . . . or bring them . . . into contempt or disrepute." Maximum sentences were fines of up to $2,000 (about $40,000 in today's dollars) and two years in prison.

One of the first people arrested was Benjamin Franklin Bache, editor and publisher of the pro-Jefferson *Philadelphia Aurora,* who had described President Adams as "querulous, bald, blind, crippled, toothless Adams." A yellow fever epidemic took Bache before he could be tried. The most that many violators were guilty of was hyperbole, but the Federalists maintained that the acts were necessary for national security (especially considering the ongoing hostility with France), and to prevent anarchy at home.

Nevertheless, Jefferson and Madison were so appalled by the acts that they secretly authored protests that were nearly as bad, if not worse. The two men covertly drafted the Kentucky and Virginia Resolutions, which called for state "nullification" of any federal law the state found unjust; the resolutions even threatened armed insurrection and civil war. Hamilton considered the resolutions "a regular conspiracy to overturn the government."

The one bright note on the horizon in these troubled times came from the war front. With completion of the frigates and other ships and the arming of merchantmen, the tide began to turn in the Americans' favor. As more newly built warships entered the fray, many French privateers, as well as French navy warships, were either captured or sunk. The Quasi-War lasted two years and resulted in the capture or destruction of nearly a dozen French warships or privateers at a minimal cost to the United States.[234]

IN THE SPRING OF 1800, with the presidential election bearing down, Adams knew there was severe and growing pressure on his administration, in part due to the public rancor over the Alien and Sedition Acts. Four years before, James Callender, a scandalmongering journalist and drunkard who had been forced to flee his native Scotland, had landed in Philadelphia. There he began to attack Federalists, particularly Alexander Hamilton, and soon earned a reputation as one of the most "virulent propagandists of his generation." Now, still writing propaganda for the Republicans, Callender called Adams's presidency "one continued tempest of malignant passions." Claiming that Adams was actually mentally unbalanced, Callender recited a story about how Adams, in a fit of pique in his office, tore off his wig, "dashing and trampling [it] on the floor."[235] Even though American commissioners were negotiating in Paris to maintain peace, Callender claimed that Adams's "sole objective was to make war on France. The choice was clear—Adams and war or Jefferson and peace."

All of this slander was executed with Jefferson's explicit approval. Callender was ultimately arrested under the Sedition Act, tried, and imprisoned for nine months. Jefferson was content to let him stay in jail, satisfied that his published screed would assist in Jefferson's election. "Such papers cannot fail to produce the best effects," he said.[236]

It was around this same time that Adams decided his cabinet contained disloyal people who were working with Alexander Hamilton. In this he was correct. Both Secretary of State Timothy Pickering and Secretary of War James McHenry were in Hamilton's orbit, and had been since they took office. They were in almost constant contact with the former treasury secretary, who had reentered the public arena as a military man.

Hamilton had known that McHenry was incompetent as war secretary, but he kept silent because he knew he could control him. Both Pickering and McHenry had urged Adams to declare war on France, but the president had determined to try negotiating instead. Adams had begun to suspect their duplicity, then became convinced of it. For that reason, he rarely consulted his cabinet before acting; that in turn led to more rumors of incompetence and willfulness.

On May 5, McHenry went to Adams's office on some minor matter and in the course of conversation said something that displeased the president. That set Adams off on the subject of

Hamilton, "a man devoid of every moral principle—a bastard and . . . a foreigner." He accused McHenry of conniving with Hamilton to undermine his programs. Then, to McHenry's astonishment, he declared that Jefferson would make a better president than Hamilton. Adams began berating the startled McHenry, charging him with a laundry list of (mostly insignificant) failures at his job, and at last sputtering, "You can not, sir, remain longer in office," probably leaving the secretary of war to wonder if the president was going to tear off his wig and stomp on it. When McHenry said he would resign, Adams's wrath seemed to deflate. He gathered himself and apologized. McHenry later set down his version of the encounter in which he described Adams: "At times he would speak in such a manner . . . to persuade one that he was actually insane."[237]

Unlike the vituperative confrontation with McHenry, Adams wrote his secretary of state a simple letter saying his services were no longer needed. Astonishingly, Pickering declined to resign, saying he did not feel it was his "duty" to resign. Adams fired him and installed instead John Marshall, the respected Virginia congressman who had been a peace commissioner during the XYZ Affair. To fill the post of secretary of war he picked Senator Samuel Dexter of Massachusetts.

That all happened in the spring of 1800, just before the federal government moved to the new capital of Washington. Congress would have control over this Federal District and thus no longer would be subject to the whims of state governors, who might or might not offer proper protection to its delegates.

Before he left Philadelphia, though, Adams had another dilemma to attend to—deciding whether three German-speaking Pennsylvania farmers should be hanged for treason. These men had been convicted of inciting a revolt against government collection agents who had been trying to enforce federal property taxes levied by Congress to pay for the new provisional army. Americans were touchy when it came to being taxed. There had already been three rebellions over taxes: Shays's and the Whiskey Rebellion and, of course, the American Revolution itself. The current disturbance had been dubbed the Fries Rebellion, Fries being one of the condemned. It was alleged that the three farmers had organized a protest by large armed mobs to intimidate government agents.

To quell the rebellion, Adams had sent federal troops and militia; dozens of protesters were arrested but only the three farmers were sentenced to death. On this issue, Adams had made a point of consulting his cabinet, and they were unanimous in the opinion that the culprits should be made an example of and hanged. But Adams decided otherwise. After reading the trial testimony, he concluded that what the farmers had incited was not a "rebellion" but more in the nature of a "riot." He commuted their sentences.

Adams left Philadelphia for Washington at the end of May, traveling in a carriage through the lush cornfields of southern Pennsylvania and Maryland, and reaching Washington on June 3. It quickly became obvious that the city was only half finished, if that. The Capitol was without its dome, and though the sandstone-blocked President's House (the future White House) was built, much of the inside remained unfinished. Slaves were at work everywhere, which might have given pause to Adams and other New Englanders. The Treasury building was the only one that was finished.

The city, such as it was, consisted of a few cheap hotels and some boardinghouses that would house federal workers and congressmen when they began to arrive at the middle of the month. Much of the surrounding land had been cleared and a vast expanse of tree stumps stretched to the Potomac River. It was new, all new, carved from a marshy wilderness. With Adams's penchant for good order, he might have been expected to be displeased, but he was not. "I like the Seat of Government very well," he told Abigail, "and shall sleep, or lie awake next winter in the President's House . . . The establishment of the public officers in this place has given it the air of the seat of government and all things seem to go on well."[238]

Adams was joined by John Marshall and Secretary of War Dexter and stayed for ten days, finding time to travel across the river to Mount Vernon, where he paid a visit on Martha Washington, "who very kindly inquired after your health and all your children's," he wrote Abigail.[239]

OVERSHADOWING THE LAST DAYS OF SUMMER and the coming fall was the election of 1800. At that time, voting was not a one-day affair. Instead, each state chose its own election day, and the voting lasted for months. Partisan feelings ran higher than ever. There remained the threat of secession by New England if Jefferson was elected. The historian David McCullough writes that it "rapidly became a contest of personal vilification surpassing any presidential election in American history . . . Whether Adams or Jefferson was the most abused would be hard to say." Jefferson was accused in Federalist pamphlets and papers of atheism, libertinism, Jacobinism; of being a shameless debtor; and of advocating states' rights over the

Constitution. And there were whispers and rumors that Jefferson slept with his slave women.

Adams was pilloried as a bald, toothless, incompetent grump, a madman, a monarchist, corrupt, and insane, and, richest of all, he was accused of sending Charles C. Pinckney, late of the XYZ Affair, to England to fetch them each two wenches for immoral purposes. To this last, Adams addressed himself to his longtime law partner and correspondent William Tudor, "Now I declare upon my honor, if this is true Gen. Pinckney has kept them all four to himself and cheated me out of my two."[240]

On November 1 Adams returned to the President's House, accompanied only by his carriage driver and secretary. Carpenters, painters, and plasterers were still busily at work in the mansion, the largest personal home in the country at the time. A bed, a few pieces of bedroom furniture, and an office desk and chair were set up for him on the second floor. On November 16 Abigail arrived from Quincy. She found the President's House overwhelming—"A castle of a house . . . Not one room is finished," but it is "built for ages to come," she wrote her sister a week after her arrival. "It is habitable by fires in every part, thirteen of which we are obliged to keep daily or sleep in wet or damp places. I had much rather live in the house at Philadelphia."[241] Yet Abigail was impressed by the surrounding countryside, "romantic but wild—a wilderness at present." She was less impressed by a visit to Georgetown, where most of the better homes and shops were. "It is the very dirtiest hole I ever saw," she said, "for a place of any trade or respectability of inhabitants."[242]

It didn't take long for Abigail to conclude that slavery was an inefficient and wasteful institution. After observing a group of enslaved men at work, she wrote her doctor in Massachusetts, saying that "Two of our hardy N[ew] England men would do as much work in a whole day as the whole 12 [slaves]."[243] She held an even poorer opinion of the lower class of whites, who "are a grade below the Negroes in point of intelligence, and ten below them in point of civility. They look like the refuse of human nature."[244]

By mid-December the Adamses had suffered two blows. Their son Charles, an alcoholic and estranged from his father, had died of cirrhosis of the liver at the age of thirty. And it was clear that Adams had been voted out of office. The contest, still undecided, had devolved to a battle between Jefferson and Burr, to be decided by the House of Representatives. It would take a week before the tie was broken in Jefferson's favor.

On New Year's Day 1801, knowing they would be departing Washington, the Adamses held their first reception at the President's House. Later that week, they invited Jefferson to dinner. Rumor had it that Adams and Jefferson hated each other and would not speak, but it wasn't so. "Mr. Jefferson dines with us," Abigail wrote her son Thomas, "and in a card of reply to the President's invitation he begs him to be assured of his homage and high consideration."[245]

A month later, when Abigail was preparing to leave Washington permanently for Massachusetts, Jefferson accepted an invitation to tea, "in order to take leave and wish me a good journey." The Adamses' relationship with Jefferson was certainly not what it had been in Paris but it was cordial, and unquestionably civil.[246]

Before adjourning, the lame-duck Federalist Congress passed one of the most controversial laws in U.S. history—the Judiciary Act of 1801. For several years John Adams had been trying, unsuccessfully, to expand the federal judiciary so as to relieve

Supreme Court justices from having to ride circuit—to go in person to far-flung parts of the country to resolve local disputes of a constitutional nature. A few weeks before Jefferson's inaugural, Congress finally passed the act Adams had fought for, reducing the number of justices from six to five and relieving them of riding circuit. Instead, it created sixteen federal judgeships and forty-two justices.

To the dismay and consternation of Republicans, Adams began appointing Federalist attorneys to these posts, all or most of whom were well qualified. Still, it looked like a last-minute dirty trick that the Republican press dubbed the "Midnight Judges Act," calling up an image of Adams staying up into the wee hours appointing judges. In truth, the act was necessary. The country was growing, and there were more people suing in the federal courts. But the Jeffersonian Republicans didn't see it that way, and they threatened to undo the legislation once they took office.

One appointment Adams made turned out to be among the major accomplishments of his career. That was the selection of John Marshall as chief justice of the United States. Marshall had been a Virginia legislator in Congress, a commissioner in the XYZ Affair, and Adams's secretary of state for at least five months. Once confirmed by the Federalist-led Senate, Marshall could not be removed by the Republicans. Through the next tempestuous thirty-four years, John Marshall guided the Supreme Court with a wise and steady hand, passing down reasoned, far-ranging opinions that form the foundation of today's body of laws. He also firmly established the judiciary as an equal partner in the tripartite government ordained by the Constitution.

AT 4 A.M. ON INAUGURATION DAY, March 4, 1801, Adams left Washington. Many saw it as an act of sullenness or an old man's bitter rudeness. Many felt it would have been better for the country had he stayed and welcomed his successor, the third president, Thomas Jefferson. McCullough suggests that there was no precedent for a defeated president to attend an inaugural for the winner, or even perhaps that Adams wasn't invited to the inauguration.

He might have constructed a fair epitaph for his administration when he wrote to a friend shortly before leaving office: "After the 3rd of March I am to be a private citizen . . . I shall leave the state with its coffers full, and the fair prospects of a peace with all the world smiling in its face, its commerce flourishing, its navy glorious, its agriculture uncommonly productive . . . O, my country! May peace be within thy walls and prosperity within thy palaces."

It took Adams a week by stagecoach to reach Quincy and his beloved Abigail and Peacefield.[247] His old law partner had asked if he wanted to resume their practice in Boston, but Adams had answered in the negative. "I am just going to be old farmer John," he said. For his remaining twenty-five years he lived at his Quincy farm, surrounded by family and rarely leaving the area. But he wrote voluminously, including wide-ranging correspondence and an autobiography.

In late 1811 one of Thomas Jefferson's neighbors was traveling in New England and visited the Adamses at Peacefield. The neighbor reported that Adams said, "I always loved Thomas Jefferson, and still love him." On hearing that, Jefferson's response was, "That is enough for me." Letters between the two old friends and adversaries resumed on a wide variety of topics, from philosophy to religion, to aging, to their individual reasoning about how the Constitution was made, what it meant, and the way the federal government had developed from it.

In 1818, Abigail died of typhoid fever; she was seventy-three. Her health had been poor in her last years, and she grieved the loss of her daughter Nabby, who had been taken by cancer in 1813. Abigail did not live to see her son John Quincy elected the eighth president of the United States, but John did.

The following summer, John Adams died during a rainstorm at the age of ninety. At his death a final boom of thunder sounded, followed by a stream of sunlight. According to John Quincy, his father's last words were, "Thomas Jefferson survives!" But Adams was wrong. Jefferson—his friend, nemesis, and compatriot—had passed away six hours earlier at Monticello. Both Patriots died on July 4, 1826—fifty years to the day after the Declaration of Independence heralded a new age.

CHAPTER EIGHT

In May 1794 Alexander Hamilton was exonerated by congressional investigators on charges of corruption in office. The charges had been brought by Virginia congressman William Giles, a determined ally of Madison and Jefferson. As usual, the Republicans were making it as difficult as they could for the treasury secretary, but the committee of investigators they dominated "could not deliver the comeuppance it craved."

With the Republicans now a majority in Congress, Hamilton had intended to retire, but he told Washington that because of the continuing dangers of a war with France he would stay on if asked. Washington asked, and Hamilton soldiered on in Treasury in an increasingly strengthening U.S. economy. Then, on August 1, western Pennsylvania exploded in riotous insurrection. Some 7,000 angry farmers congregated outside Pittsburgh at Braddock's Field to hear a firebrand named David Bradford harangue them with exhortations to take up the French model of the Jacobins and create "a committee of public safety," complete with guillotine and an attack on the arsenal at Pittsburgh to obtain military weapons. The so-called Whiskey Rebellion had broken out in full fury.

Western Pennsylvania, more than most areas, had simmered for three years, ever since Hamilton had persuaded Congress to impose a government excise tax on alcoholic spirits. Most of the Pennsylvania men, in addition to tending regular crops and livestock, used their excess barley or corn to distill whiskey that they used as barter or sold across the Alleghenies. The tax, they said, was unfair because it singled them out above all others and ate into their meager profits.

There had been prior incidents of increasing violence since the tax was imposed. Threats were made against government revenue agents, and some agents were beaten, kidnapped, or tarred and feathered; whiskey makers who paid the tax found their stills burned. The chief government whiskey inspector in the area, Col. John Neville, a veteran of the Revolution, found his house in western Pennsylvania surrounded by furious rebels, who burned his fences, crops, barns, and stables. He escaped, but barely. Local militia who had been summoned to quell the disturbance were unable to cope with the demonstrators.

When word of this disorder reached Alexander Hamilton, he was outraged; he saw it as a threat to the country. Bradford was reported to have bragged, "We will defeat the first army that comes over the mountains and take their arms and baggage."

Hamilton gathered as much information as was available and composed a lengthy letter to Washington, laying out the depredations his agents had endured, as well as reports of the large gathering of thousands and the threats issued near Pittsburgh. If allowed to grow, the treasury secretary concluded, such a treasonous plot might possibly overthrow the federal government. He suggested a massive show of government force to cow the rebels into submission or to overwhelm them if they responded with violence. Secretary of War Henry Knox concurred. Washington asked for and received from the Supreme Court a declaration of anarchy in the area across the mountains.

Hamilton also recommended that an army of 12,000 men be drawn from the state militias of Virginia, Maryland, and New Jersey. Secretary of State Edmund Randolph worried that the use of force would probably "unify" the rebels, so Washington embarked on a compromise. He issued a proclamation giving the insurgents until September 1 to disburse; if they did not, he would bring in the military. He also sent a three-man peace commission to Pittsburgh to parley with the insurgents.

The conciliatory approach failed miserably. It only encouraged the rebels, who saw it as a sign of weakness. The peace committee reported that the rebels were violent, threatening, and determined to resist the excise tax "at all hazards."

The September 1 deadline passed with the whiskey makers intransigent as ever. By September 9 Washington was fed up. Earlier he had declared, "If the laws are to be trampled upon—with impunity—and a minority . . . is to dictate to the majority, there is an end, put at one stroke, to Republican government; and nothing but anarchy and confusion may be expected thereafter." Washington ordered his army of about 12,000 state militiamen to march into western Pennsylvania, with himself at its head and Hamilton as second in command.[248]

That position had befallen Hamilton when Secretary of War Knox told Washington that he had to go to Maine on urgent real estate business. Under the administrative setup of the cabinet, the treasury secretary was to run the War Department in the absence of the war secretary.

Hamilton was delighted to be in the field again, despite his own personal crisis. His wife Eliza, who was at the end of a difficult pregnancy, had written that their two-year-old son, John Church Hamilton, had fallen deathly ill and the only treatment doctors could prescribe was laudanum, an opiate. In between arranging for tents, horses, uniforms, and other military accouterments for the militia regiments, Hamilton managed to write letters home at least once and sometimes twice a day.

Washington, now sixty-two, was to ride in a carriage to the army rendezvous at Carlisle, Pennsylvania. Hamilton would join him there so the two could discuss tactics. Washington said that if the rebellion seemed to be waning, he would go no farther than Carlisle, which was about 200 miles from western Pennsylvania. But if the violence and revolt were ongoing he would continue with the army.

Hamilton worried about the training, devotion, discipline, and efficiency of the state militias, as their performance had frequently disappointed him during the Revolution. He remained convinced that the federal government needed a standing professional army that could be called upon to defend the nation against invasion by foreign powers or rebellion within. "In the expedition against the western insurgents," Hamilton told a friend, "I trembled every moment lest a great part of the militia should take it into their heads to go home."[249]

He need not have worried. The militias behaved splendidly—even if lacking in high military discipline—marching across the Alleghenies into Pittsburgh and beyond in the crisp autumn air. Hamilton wrote a note to his sister-in-law, "I am thus far my dear Angelica on my way to attack and subdue the wicked insurgents of the west. But you are not to promise that I shall have any trophies to lay at your feet. [Our] large army has cooled the courage of those madmen, and the only question seems now to be how to guard against a return of the phrenzy."[250]

It was true—most of the rebels faded into the countryside at the appearance of Washington's large force, although Washington himself had returned to Philadelphia after reviewing the army at Carlisle. Hamilton was given one wing of the army to command, and Gen. Daniel Morgan, of Revolutionary War fame, the other.

Over time, some fifty of the rebellion's leaders were arrested. Of these, most were released due to mistaken identity, insufficient evidence, lack of witnesses, and other legal impediments. Two men, however, were convicted of treason and sentenced to be hanged, but Washington pardoned them. Thus, the Whiskey Rebellion ended not with a bang but with a whimper.

Its aftermath, however, reverberated through the government, the press, and political circles everywhere. William Findley, a Republican congressman from western Pennsylvania, wrote a book in 1796 accusing Hamilton of deliberately provoking the rebellion, saying that the treasury secretary was against small businesses like private distillers and wanted whiskey made in large factories. The Republicans blasted Hamilton for pushing his way into a major army command and lambasted Washington for agreeing to it. They claimed that Hamilton was pushing for a large standing army in order to take over the federal government. Madison told James Monroe that political talk in Philadelphia was that "a standing army was necessary for enforcing the laws."[251]

President Washington made a full report to Congress on the Whiskey Rebellion, in which he censured the many Democratic-Republican societies in various regions for abetting the insurrection.

This in turn infuriated the Jeffersonians, prompting Madison to tell Monroe, who was currently winding up a tour as the U.S. minister to France, that Washington's effort to connect the Democratic-Republican societies "with the odium of the insurrection . . . was perhaps the biggest error of his political life."[252] For his part, Hamilton wrote his sister-in-law that, "In popular governments 'tis useful that those who propose measures [the whiskey tax] should partake in whatever dangers they may involve. 'Twas very important that there should be no mistake in the management of the affair—and I might contribute to prevent one . . . The insurrection will do us a great deal of good and add to the solidity of everything in this country."[253]

Despite the controversy of the Whiskey Rebellion, its utter vanquishing demonstrated that the federal government not only could but would use overwhelming force to put down popular uprisings when necessary to enforce the laws of the land.

With the rebellion put down, Hamilton resigned his post as the nation's first treasury secretary. He felt it was time to move on, that he had done what he could to enable America's success, despite the political winds that had thwarted him. He had fashioned a plan for national finance and solvency, and set about putting it in motion as soon as he took office. In those critical first years under a constitutional government, he had kept the country afloat and creditworthy. Juggling the nation's debts like a circus performer, he had used some European loans to pay off other loans and opened America's first national bank, a primitive forerunner of the Federal Reserve. Now, Hamilton was ready to relinquish the burden of keeping the new nation afloat. At forty, he looked forward to the decades ahead with his family and his law practice.

★★★★★

HAMILTON'S OPTIMISTIC PLANS were quickly shattered by the scandalmongering James Callender. Somehow the papers that James Monroe had left with the clerk Beckley regarding Hamilton's affair with Maria Reynolds had come into Callender's possession, and in 1797 Callender exposed the affair to the world. He also renewed accusations that Hamilton had been dishonest with the government's money. Both Reynoldses and their duplicitous accomplice Jacob Clingman were interviewed and quoted. Maria Reynolds asserted that there had been no affair between her and Hamilton, saying not only that had Hamilton made the whole thing up, but that he was also a crook.[254]

The notion of being fingered as a crook was Hamilton's worst nightmare—worse, even, than being exposed as an adulterer. On that last front he had received some hopeful news from his brother-in-law John Church, who informed him by letter that Eliza had learned of the accusations, but they did not trouble her.

Ignoring the advice of his friends, the infuriated Hamilton insisted on defending his reputation and his honor against charges of financial corruption. He published a lengthy explanation almost in the form of a legal brief, laying all things bare, including the amorous affair with Reynolds. This became known as Hamilton's confessional "Reynolds Pamphlet."

Hamilton's actions make better sense when viewed in a historical light. Granted, the allegations against him were made by a salacious scandalmonger, but as the first secretary of the treasury Hamilton felt that, if the world's only free democracy could not depend on honesty from the individual largely responsible for its financial health, how would that look?

Though he was willing to own his indiscretion, Hamilton had harbored a slow-burning fury at James Monroe. He blamed Monroe for releasing the Reynolds papers that Monroe, five years earlier, had vowed would be kept secret and secure. When Callender's scandalous story had broken, Hamilton had immediately written to the three legislators he had met with about the accusations, asking that they affirm they found no wrongdoing or financial corruption on Hamilton's part. Two of the congressmen, Frederick Muhlenberg and Abraham Venable, confirmed this, but Monroe was slow to respond.

The previous year, in late 1796, Washington had recalled Monroe as minister to France at Hamilton's urging. The president had dressed Monroe down and called him a "mere tool" of the French government. Echoing this, Callender's defamatory pamphlet against Hamilton declared, "The unfounded reproaches heaped on Mr. Monroe form the immediate motive to the publication of these papers."[255]

When Hamilton did not hear from Monroe after he sent his first letter, he became more suspicious and wrote a second in which he demanded that Monroe repudiate the accusations of financial corruption laid out in Callender's pamphlet. "And I shall rely on your delicacy that the manner of doing it will be such as one gentleman has a right to expect from another," meaning that he wanted an unequivocal denial by Monroe as to the veracity of Callender's assertions. But Monroe did not reply to that letter either.

On July 10, Hamilton learned that Monroe had arrived in New York to visit relatives. He immediately sent an abrupt note fraught with intimidation: "Mr. Hamilton requests an interview with Mr. Monroe at any hour tomorrow forenoon which may be convenient to him. Particular reasons will induce him to bring a friend to be present at what may pass. Mr. Monroe, if he pleases, may have another."[256]

Monroe could certainly smell the possibility of a personal challenge in this icy language, but replied that he would see Hamilton and his friend at his lodgings at ten o'clock the following morning. It would be the most appalling confrontation recorded between two of America's Founding Fathers.

Hamilton had chosen his brother-in-law John Church to accompany him. Monroe had in attendance New York businessman and Republican activist David Gelston, who wrote a vivid, minute-by-minute account of the face-off between the two titans of American politics.

Hamilton arrived "much agitated upon his entrance to the room," Gelston wrote; in fact, seeing Monroe, Hamilton became nearly beside himself and struggled for control. He opened with a long recitation of the December 1792 meeting, saying he recalled that Monroe and the other two congressmen had told him he was cleared of any suspicions of improper financial dealings and that they promised to keep the records of the investigation confidential.[257]

Monroe asked coldly, "What all that meant & said if you wish me to tell you anything relating to this business all this history is unnecessary." Hamilton, still visibly agitated, addressed Monroe, saying he would "come to the point directly." According to Gelston, "some warmth appeared in both Gentlemen."[258] Hamilton said he had written to Monroe, Venable, and Muhlenberg and had "expected an immediate answer to so important as subject, in which his character [and] the peace and reputation of his family were so deeply concerned." Monroe condescendingly told

Hamilton, "If he . . . would be temperate or quiet for a moment . . . [Monroe] would answer him candidly." Hamilton replied that he "should like to hear it."[259] Barely able to conceal his rage, Hamilton glared at Monroe in silence. It was obvious the two men could not stand each other.

Monroe said he had intended to answer Hamilton's letter but had wanted to consult first with Muhlenberg and Venable; when he went to their lodgings, however, he found they had left town. So far as Callender's writings were concerned, Monroe said he had given the papers of the investigation to a Virginia friend (the clerk Beckley, though Monroe did not identify him) and believed they had "remained sealed" until Callender revealed them in print.[260] Able to contain his wrath no longer, Hamilton fairly spat at Monroe, "Your representation is totally false!" Both men "instantly rose," and Monroe lashed out, "You say I represented falsely, you are a scoundrel!"[261] The men were inches apart, glowering. "I will meet you like a gentleman," Hamilton declared. "I am ready, get your pistols!" Monroe retorted.[262]

Both Church and Gelston leaped to their feet and jumped between the two antagonists, pushing them apart, with Church crying, "Gentlemen, gentlemen."[263] Hamilton and Monroe took their seats, with Hamilton still in a rage but Monroe disdainful and "quite cool." He repeated his innocence in the release of the papers, and told Hamilton that if he would calm down he, Monroe, would try to explain his actions. At this point Gelston intervened, suggesting a compromise. Monroe, Gelston said, had answered Hamilton's suspicion about leaking the papers to Callender and that it would be only fair to let Monroe meet with Muhlenberg and Venable in Philadelphia to answer the rest of Hamilton's queries.[264] Hamilton grudgingly assented and the interview came to a close, but the animosity was far from settled.

Monroe returned to Philadelphia and, along with Muhlenberg (Venable was out of town), sent Hamilton a letter confirming that they had believed Hamilton's version of the Reynolds affair and had confidence that he had not acted corruptly.

There the matter might have rested, but Hamilton roiled it once more. He demanded that Monroe repudiate a memo found in the Hamilton file dated several days after the three congressmen interviewed Hamilton. In it, Monroe is far less certain of Hamilton's innocence. Monroe replied evasively, saying that his memo was "not intended to be a judgment on the facts." But he told Hamilton that he could not affirm that Hamilton was innocent of corruption, because it "depends upon the facts and circumstances which appear against you and upon your defense." In other words, Monroe was trying to goad Hamilton to make the matter public. A furious Hamilton told Monroe, "As a man of honor and sensibility you should have come forward in a manner that would have shielded me completely from the unpleasant effects brought upon me by your agency," by which he meant that Monroe had entrusted custody of the papers to an untrustworthy person. He proceeded to brand Monroe "malignant" and accused him of "dishonest motives."[265]

A flurry of letters with ever increasing hostility ensued for the next several weeks. Hamilton continually tried to press Monroe to recant his letter suggesting Hamilton's guilt, while Monroe's replies were a masterpiece of evasive convolution. At last, on August 4, Monroe received from Hamilton a letter that seemed to again suggest a duel. He responded, "If . . . you meant this last letter as a challenge to me, I have then to request that you say so, and in which case I have to inform you that my friend [Colonel] Burr who will present you this, and who will communicate with you on the subject, is authorized to give you my answer, and to make . . . arrangements."[266]

Aaron Burr as counsel (and, if necessary, second on the field of honor) tried to dissuade Monroe from carrying the matter further. Though he had now become a staunch Republican, Burr did not believe Hamilton was dishonest. He told Monroe that the correspondence with Hamilton should be burned, and Burr's counsel was conveyed to the former treasury secretary. The Hamilton biographer Ron Chernow points out that if Burr had harbored a hatred for Hamilton at that time, he "could have egged on Monroe and engineered a duel in which Hamilton might have died. Instead he had the grace and decency to plead for fairness."

The publication of Hamilton's own pamphlet confessing to the affair but denying corruption riled Monroe, who felt it insulted his honor. Monroe sent Burr to Hamilton with a letter saying, "You ought either to have been satisfied with the explanations I gave you, or to have invited me to the field." Hamilton nearly sent a note accepting a duel, but then thought better of it. The affair between the former secretary of the treasury and the future president mercifully sputtered to a close.[267]

What Burr made of Hamilton's refusal to take up Monroe's half-dropped gauntlet is not known—but there is the possibility that it caused him to conclude that Hamilton wouldn't fight. What Burr thought of Monroe is another matter. Years later, he described Monroe as "Naturally dull . . . extremely illiterate; indecisive to a degree that would be incredible to one who did not know him; pusillanimous and, of course, hypocritical; has no opinion on any subject and will always be under the government of the worst men."[268]

HAMILTON HAD LONG SUSPECTED the motivations of the French and warned that the military autocrat Napoleon, who had been busy carving up Italy, was potentially rising as the nation's leader. Beginning in early 1797, he published a series of "Warnings" in the *Gazette of the United States* in which he predicted that France would become "the terror and the scourge of nations." Writing under the pseudonym "Americus" in his "Warning no. 1," Hamilton anticipated that "the specious pretence [by France] of enlightening mankind . . . is the varnish to the[ir] real design of subjugating" other countries.[269] France had predictably retaliated against the United States for approving the Jay Treaty by turning loose its privateers on American ships bound for British ports; by early 1797 it had captured more than three hundred American merchantmen.

John Adams had just taken office as the country's second president, with Jefferson as his vice president, when word came from France that Charles Pinckney, the minister sent to Paris to replace James Monroe, had been expelled over the Jay Treaty. In his "Warnings," Hamilton carefully specified that all diplomatic channels should be exhausted before the United States resorted to war. At the same time, he recommended to Adams that a provisional army of 25,000 men be raised, as well as a much stronger naval force, including frigates and ships of the line. Merchant ships should be armed and sail to Britain in convoys, escorted by frigates.

The American coast, Hamilton warned, was extremely vulnerable to invasion by a power such as France, which had built itself into the strongest military nation in Europe. The interest of France, Hamilton told Secretary of State Timothy Pickering, was "to punish and humble us—to force us into a greater dependence . . . We shall best guarantee ourselves against calamity by preparing for the worst."[270]

When negotiations with the French later stalled, Hamilton continued to offer advice to Pickering, counseling, "The attitude of calm defiance suits us."[271] At the same time, he pushed for the construction of ten large ships of the line and "the increase in our military establishment to 20,000 & a provisional [reserve] army of 30,000," along with an increase in each state's militia. Moreover, Hamilton called for the navy to capture all privateers within 60 miles of the American coast.[272]

By July 1798 diplomacy with France had failed, and the country was on its way to war. When Congress passed legislation creating a standing army of twelve infantry regiments and six cavalry companies (about 12,000 men), as well as a Department of the Navy, Adams blamed Hamilton's influence in Congress for such a large military buildup. Still, he needed a commander, and when George Washington insisted that Hamilton be placed in daily charge of the army Adams reluctantly agreed. Hamilton took charge of the army with the rank of major general. The political situation had become so highly charged that Hamilton believed if the French invaded Jeffersonians by the thousands would flock to the enemy army, as the disloyal Tories had to the British during the Revolution.

During the winter of 1798–99 Hamilton plunged into the task of organizing the provisional American army. With the assistance of only one aide-de-camp—his nephew Philip Church—he designed uniforms for various ranks, huts for officers and men, a drill manual and a manual of arms, and plans and a curriculum for a military academy at the old West Point fort on the Hudson. Before long Hamilton was issuing directives to the inept secretary of war, his old friend James McHenry.

As the army began to form up, Hamilton worried at the growing desertions. This was traced to a lack of pay and provision for uniforms that led directly to dalliance and mismanagement in the War Department. Hamilton approached his successor at Treasury, Oliver Wolcott Jr., to correct the problem. Hamilton's officiousness led his Republican enemies to begin calling him a "second Bonaparte."

At some point in late 1798 Hamilton came under the influence of a soldier of fortune named Francisco de Miranda, a Venezuelan who had fought on the American side during the Revolution. Miranda had an expansive scheme to liberate both North and South America from European colonists, chiefly Spanish and Portuguese. He had arrived in New York in 1784 and propositioned Hamilton with a scheme to expel the Spanish from Florida and Louisiana, as well as from Central and South America. Their treasures, Miranda said now, had been channeled through the Spanish throne to the French ever since Spain's forced alliance with France in 1792.

Miranda had been a soldier of fortune in Europe, fighting for the British and then the French until he became disenchanted with the French Revolution. Its leaders, Miranda said, were crooks and hypocrites. He conveyed these sentiments in letters to Hamilton, who had initially seen him as an adventurer. But when Hamilton took control of the army, he found he was drawn to

Miranda's outré notions. He told Miranda that while any military plans would have to include an endorsement by the U.S. government, he could foresee a British fleet and American ground troops ejecting the Spanish from their U.S. and South American territories, liberating them for democracy.

In the end, Hamilton became so enthralled with the idea that he began suggesting it to various congressmen. Eventually, of course, this got back to President Adams, who saw it as foolish. "I do not know whether to laugh or weep," Adams complained to Elbridge Gerry. "Miranda's project is as visionary, though far less innocent, than . . . an excursion to the moon in a cart drawn by geese."[273] Though a Federalist like Hamilton, Adams then accused him of using his position as titular head of the army to position himself as the leader of a British government for the United States of America.

The old Federalist Party was fast melting away, and with it a general breakdown in political civility. Roving gangs of Republicans and Federalists clashed in the streets of Philadelphia. Partisan newspapers were filled with so much venomous hyperbole that it was said they riled people to violence. At one point the Republican newspaper *Aurora,* whose publisher was Benjamin Franklin's grandson Benjamin Franklin Bache, was set upon by a band of furious Federalists. Windows were smashed, type was roughed up, and the elder Franklin's statue smeared with mud. Two congressmen, a Federalist and a Republican, engaged in a disgraceful brawl on the floor of the House of Representatives, one armed with a walking cane, the other with a pair of fireplace tongs.

Meanwhile, Hamilton's efforts to organize the new army were not going well. Recruitment was down to half of what was authorized, and morale was poor because many of the soldiers had not been paid in six months. Hamilton slowly began to discover that it was not only the inept secretary of war who was behind the trouble but President Adams himself, who could have helped matters by going directly to Congress for funds but did not. American citizens simply did not want their property taxes raised or loans taken out to support a large army, which so many thought unnecessary, especially as the French had thus far made no signs of invading the United States.

When Adams received word from France that a new Directory might be amenable to further negotiations with the United States, he decided to appoint another three-man commission to Paris. Hamilton was furious, because the move was abrupt and without consultation of the full cabinet. He went to see Adams in his boardinghouse and told the president that, as the head of an army designed to defend against a French invasion, he needed to parley with Adams on the peace mission to France. Adams took offense at this—in part because he thought the request a breach of etiquette, and in part because he had never wanted Hamilton in charge of the army in the first place and had appointed him only at Washington's insistence. The meeting got off to a poor start from the beginning. "I heard him with perfect good humor," Adams said, "though never in my like did I hear a man talk more like a fool."[274]

Hamilton proposed to Adams that the changes in the Directory likely meant that Louis XVIII would be put on the throne, and thus the old French war debts would again come due—an idea the president thought preposterous. (Louis XVIII was in fact restored to the throne but not until 1814.) Though Hamilton's three-hour meeting with Adams apparently did not involve shouting or harsh language, it ended all possibility of the two men working together cooperatively. And it did not persuade Adams to abandon his peace mission, which sailed the following month for France.

Hamilton's soured relations with Adams only complicated other problems in his life. The condition of the army weighed heavily on him, and at the same time his own finances were beginning to suffer. He found it impossible to run an army and conduct a lucrative law practice. He admitted to friends that his "mood was gloomy."

EVEN AS HAMILTON STRUGGLED THROUGH the final years of the eighteenth century, Aaron Burr added a further vexation by starting a bank. All banks, as well as many other corporations in New York, operated under charters handed out by the state legislature. Burr's reputation as a smooth and shady operator would probably not have qualified him to run a bank; he got around this problem by forming the Manhattan Company, with the stated goal of supplying clean water to the city. But somewhere in the fine print of the charter, the company was also granted the right to perform banking activities. When it opened for business, it quickly sold $2 million in stocks and spent $100,000 of that on the water company, which was quickly sold to the city. The remaining cash was used to open the bank.

The day after the bank opened, Hamilton was hit with personal news that shocked him: Aaron Burr and Hamilton's brother-in-law John Church had fought a duel. Burr had challenged Church after he learned that at a dinner party Church had accused him of bribery in connection with a Dutch real estate holding company. Church, never a man to refuse a challenge, got into a boat with Burr and rowed across the Hudson River in the late afternoon of September 2, 1799. There the two adversaries squared off, measured off ten paces, turned, and fired. Church's shot blew a button off Burr's coat, while Church found himself unscathed by Burr's discharge. As the seconds were reloading the pistols, Church told Burr that he had "been indiscreet and was sorry for it," at which feeble apology Burr declared that he was satisfied. The two duelists and their seconds were rowed back across the river, chatting amicably.[275]

THREE MONTHS LATER, on December 14, 1799, George Washington died at the age of sixty-seven. He had gone riding in a snowstorm to inspect his farm and had come down with a throat infection that killed him in two days.

It was devastating news to Alexander Hamilton. He had known Washington since he was twenty. They had fought their way through the Revolution, the tumultuous period afterward, and then the two terms of Washington's presidency. In the years following, they had grown even closer as Hamilton kept the former president apprised of the Federalists' fortunes and the politics roiling the country. Two days before Washington died, he had written a letter to Hamilton, responding enthusiastically to his idea for a military academy at West Point.

Writing to Washington's widow, Martha, Hamilton said, "No one, better than myself, knows the greatness of your loss or how much your excellent heart is formed to feel it in all its extent . . . I cannot say in how many ways the continuance of [Washington's] confidence and friendship was necessary to me in future relations."[276]

Jefferson, who had broken with Washington over his Federalist leanings, wrote his own homage: "His mind was great and powerful, but not of the first order; his penetration strong, tho[ugh] not so acute as that of a Newton, Bacon, or Locke . . . Hearing all suggestions, he selected whatever was best . . . He was incapable of fear, meeting personal dangers with the calmest unconcern.

"Perhaps the strongest feature of his character was prudence, never acting until every circumstance, every consideration was maturely weighed . . . His integrity was most pure, his justice the most inflexible ever known, no motives of . . . friendship or hatred, being able to bias his decision. He was indeed, in every sense of the words, a wise, a good, & a great man.

"His temper was naturally irritable and high toned; but reflection & resolution had obtained a firm and habitual ascendancy over it. If ever however it ever broke its bonds, he was most tremendous in his wrath.

"His character was . . . perfect, in nothing bad . . . never did nature and fortune combine more perfectly to make a man great."[277]

Two weeks after Washington's death Hamilton marched from Congress Hall in Philadelphia along with other present and former government officials, escorting the symbolic riderless white charger. Henry "Light Horse Harry" Lee, another veteran of the Revolution, famously eulogized his former commander and the first president as "First in war, first in peace, and first in the hearts of his countrymen."

Washington's death left the provisional army without an official commander. Hamilton expected Adams to name him in Washington's place. But the president failed to do so, leaving the post vacant. The next month, Congress halted recruiting for the army. News soon came from across the Atlantic that Napoleon Bonaparte had rid himself of the Directory and pronounced himself the dictator of France, fulfilling Hamilton's forecast that the French Revolution would end in despotism.

This also spelled the end of Hamilton's vision of leading a powerful army. In Congress's view, with France's revolutionary government eliminated, Napoleon posed no threat to America. A bill was passed giving Adams authority to disband the new army, which he did immediately. All of Hamilton's hard work and sacrifice were for naught.

Without George Washington's commanding presence, the fractious Federalist Party began to further fall apart. One of the first to realize this was the political intriguer Aaron Burr, who with the current turn of events saw a way clear not only to make Thomas Jefferson the next president, but to make himself vice president, with a good chance of becoming president one day. Adams had beaten Jefferson in the most recent presidential race by only three electoral votes. Burr schemed to turn New York's twelve electors to the Republican side by electing a Republican state legislature, which chose the electors. All other things being equal, there was an excellent possibility that Jefferson would win New York and become the third president of the United States, and in gratitude Burr would ride on his coattails into the second spot.

Throughout the late winter and spring of 1800 Burr campaigned relentlessly, holding sidewalk rallies, haranguing crowds with both Republican propaganda and what today is called a stump speech. He held meetings and informal gatherings, working tirelessly to persuade New Yorkers that Adams was an unfit president. Burr converted the fraternal Society of Saint Tammany, which had been a mostly Republican-leaning social organization, into a powerful political force that helped ensure New York's electoral delegates would vote Republican.

The Federalists, many of whom were also less than enthusiastic about the imperious-seeming Adams, were not as enthusiastic in their electioneering. Moving toward the impending election, Hamilton sensed that something was amiss and took to the streets himself, but Burr's damage had been done. On May 1 when the votes were tallied, the Republicans had swept New York City, meaning they would now control the state legislature, and Jefferson would receive all twelve of New York's electoral votes.

Burr was exuberant and taunted the downcast Federalists, saying they had lost to "superior management." In despair some of them, led by Hamilton, tried to get the outgoing Federalist legislature to change the way electors were chosen, but the effort failed. Hamilton was widely criticized for his attempt, even by members of his own party.

He compounded the damage by publishing an open "letter"—a fifty-five-page pamphlet chastising John Adams. Hamilton had taken umbrage at some remarks Adams had made describing him as leading a "British Faction" in America; in his pamphlet, he demanded that the president either present the evidence for the charge or refute it, couched in language that appeared to threaten a challenge to an affair of honor.

When Adams failed to respond, Hamilton began to seethe and brood, and he made the unwise decision to publish a highly uncomplimentary picture of Adams and his presidency. What damage this tirade did to Adams as a presidential candidate remains in dispute; he believed it did much harm, but others thought that Hamilton had hurt his own reputation more than the president's.

The election of 1800 played out better than Burr had anticipated and worse than Hamilton had feared. Despite his antipathy for Adams, Hamilton worried that in their dismay a number of Federalist congressmen planned to vote for Burr for president, rather than for the Republican Thomas Jefferson. By December political pundits who could count votes asserted that Jefferson and Burr were going to be even at seventy-three votes each—a tie that would have to be broken in the House—and that the other two candidates, Adams and South Carolinian Charles Pinckney, would get only sixty-three and sixty-four votes, respectively.

As much as Hamilton disliked Jefferson's beliefs in states' rights and a general populism over a strong central government, he responded to these rumors by sending a note to the staunch Federalist Secretary of the Treasury Wolcott: "As to *Burr,* there is nothing in his favor. His private character is not defended by his most partial friends. He is bankrupt beyond redemption except by the plunder of his country. His public principles have no other aim than his own aggrandizement. If he can he will certainly disturb our institutions to secure for himself *permanent power,* and with it *wealth*. He is truly the *Catiline* [a treacherous intriguer of ancient Rome] of America . . . But early measures must be taken . . . Burr will find partisans. If the thing be neglected he may possibly go far."[278]

As for Jefferson, Hamilton had considered the alternatives and concluded: "There is no doubt that upon every virtuous and prudent calculation Jefferson is to be preferred. He is by far not so dangerous a man and he has pretensions to character."[279]

The election was as predicted tied among electors and went to the House of Representatives, where Hamilton's efforts were rewarded. On the thirty-sixth ballot Jefferson prevailed, because Federalists from some states who had refused to vote at all rather than for Burr or Jefferson finally switched to the Sage of Monticello.

HAMILTON SUFFERED THROUGH the decline of his political fortunes by plunging himself into his law practice and his family. He commenced work on a country house at Harlem Heights, a comfortable two-story structure set on 35 acres of hardwoods, streams, gardens, and meadows, with views of both the Hudson and Harlem Rivers. The public rooms had, of all things, French windows and doors, and were appointed in Louis XVI–style furnishings. The house put Hamilton into debt, but he assumed that the income from his prospering law practice would soon enable him to pay off his loan. He called the house the Grange, after his grandfather's estate in Scotland.

Hamilton, now in his mid-forties, was looking forward to a comfortable old age with Eliza and the children in his fashionable new home; he had fought the British in that very area as a young lieutenant of artillery in the Continental Army. Now, Washington was gone and his own ambitions were quelled. He had no idea where events would carry him, but he felt confident that he could look forward to reaping the rewards of his hard-fought life.

While his law practice thrived, Hamilton faded from the public political scene as the Democratic-Republicans took over both Congress and the White House. Still, behind the scenes, he soldiered on in the dying Federalist Party. Jefferson's inaugural speech had struck a conciliatory tone, noting that despite party loyalties Americans were still Americans. Yet privately, Jefferson had promised to bury the Federalists forever. Called "one of history's most impressive image makers," the patrician Jefferson adopted a folksy, downhome style as president, often answering his own door wearing carpet slippers.

The new president relished his chance to put Hamilton away at last. He ordered his new treasury secretary, Albert Gallatin, to comb through Treasury Department files and find evidence of Hamilton's "blunders and frauds." In due time Gallatin appeared at the White House, where Jefferson eagerly demanded to know what he had found. "Mr. President," Gallatin replied, "I have as you directed made a thorough examination of all the books, accounts, and correspondence of my department. I have found the most perfect [financial] system ever formed. Any change that should be made in it would injure it. Hamilton made no blunders, committed no frauds. He did nothing wrong." Gallatin's praise for Hamilton, a bitter political enemy, was effusive. The president was crestfallen beyond disappointment.[280]

By 1801 many Federalist newspapers were struggling or had closed. To counter that, in November of that year, Hamilton and some friends founded the *New York Evening Post* (now the *New York Post* and the nation's oldest continually published newspaper). The paper quickly became a "mirror of Hamilton's mind" under his handpicked editor, William Coleman.

From the first month of publication, Hamilton began writing weekly essays under the pen name Lucius Crassus. He called his column "The Examination," and it vilified Jefferson and the Republicans for, among other things, unconstitutionally tampering with the federal judiciary and the midnight appointments that Adams had made in his final hours as president. Hamilton managed to retain his composure and publish these essays for eighteen consecutive weeks, despite the fact that the greatest tragedy in his life had occurred the month the *Post* published its first issue: his cherished first son, Philip, was involved in a duel concerning his father's reputation.

Philip was a handsome nineteen-year-old, who, like his father, had graduated with honors from Columbia College and was studying law. Hamilton expected Philip to accomplish great things in life and shepherded him along in an effort to keep him on a straightened path. If Philip had a fault, it was impetuosity.

During an elaborate 1801 Fourth of July celebration, amid the bands, church bells, marching, and cannon firing, a twenty-seven-year-old lawyer and militia captain named George I. Eacker, a dedicated Democratic-Republican, gave an oration to a crowd of Tammany Society members and other Republican partisans. In it, he berated the Federalists, and Hamilton by implication, for leading an army created under false pretenses that was aimed at suppressing the Democratic-Republicans. Philip Hamilton read the speech in the newspaper a few days later and brooded over the implications for his father.

Nearly five months afterward, on the eve of Thanksgiving, Eacker was attending a play at the Park Theatre in Manhattan. Young Hamilton was there as well with a former college mate,

Stephen Price. The two friends took notice of Eacker, entered his theater box, and began to ridicule him. When the scene drew the attention of the audience, Eacker asked the two men to step into the lobby, where he said, "It is too abominable to be publicly insulted by a set of rascals."

Quaint as the word "rascal" seems today, in those times it was a deep insult—"fighting words"—and a fight between gentlemen could be a deadly affair. A brief scuffle ensued, and the men decided to retire to a nearby tavern to sort things out. Hamilton and Price demanded to know which one of them was being called a rascal. Eacker replied he was referring to both. He then departed, saying he expected to hear from them. Hamilton and Price replied, "You shall."[281]

Later that night, Eacker received challenges to a duel from both men. He declined Hamilton's because Price's had arrived first but said that Hamilton should reissue his challenge after the first duel was done. Two days later, Eacker met Stephen Price at dueling grounds on a sandbar near Weehawken, New Jersey. Four shots were fired and no one was hit. Before a third round could begin the seconds intervened and the duel ended.[282]

With Hamilton's duel now on, his seconds tried desperately to arrange an "accommodation" with Eacker, but he refused to apologize in the least and demanded that the duel go forward. According to Henry Dawson, a former classmate of Philip's at Columbia and apparently one of his seconds, Alexander Hamilton learned of the impending duel and did not try to stop it. But he did intercede with the seconds to try for the "accommodation." When this failed, "General Hamilton . . . commanded his son when on the [dueling] ground to reserve his *fire* till after Mr. E[acker] had shot and then to discharge his pistol in the air," Dawson reported. According to the code duello, gentlemen would consider it murder to shoot an unarmed man.[283]

It was also considered cowardly to begin the duel by raising one's pistol in the air, so when the duel actually took place, Philip Hamilton went through the motions of all but the last command in "Ready, aim, fire!" Both men hesitated for a moment, then Eacker shot Hamilton in the abdomen. He lay wounded on the ground, "calm and composed beyond expression."

Philip was then "rowed with the greatest rapidity to the [New York] shore, where he was landed near the state prison. All the physicians in town were called for and the news spread like a conflagration." He was taken to the home of John and Angelica Church, and Dr. David Hosack, the Hamilton family physician, arrived shortly afterward. Philip seized his hand, exclaiming, "Doctor, I despair."

Alexander arrived and then Eliza, three months pregnant, rushed in. Their grief was unimaginable. Dawson described the scene: "On a bed without curtains lay poor Phil, pale and languid, his rolling, distorted eyeballs darting forth the flashes of delirium. On one side of him lay his agonized father, on the other, his distracted mother, around [him] were his numerous relatives and friends, weeping and fixed in sorrow."[284]

Philip died the next day at five in the morning. On a cold and rainy November morning he was buried in the Trinity Church cemetery in lower Manhattan, accompanied by a great crowd of mourners. His father had to be almost carried to the gravesite, so paralyzing was his grief. Afterward he sank into a deep despair that lasted months, similar to Jefferson's reaction to the deaths of his wife and his young daughter. Hamilton received a great many letters of condolence from friends, many of whom also remarked on the tragedy, inhumanity, and futility of dueling. A majority of newspapers did the same.

To Dr. Benjamin Rush, Hamilton wrote: "My loss is indeed great. The brightest, as well as the eldest, hope of my family has been taken from me . . . He was truly a fine youth." But, he added, "It was the will of heaven and he is now out of reach of the seductions and calamities of a world full of folly, full of vice, full of danger."

On June 2, 1802, the Hamilton's eighth and last child was born, a boy they named Philip, in honor of his slain brother. The birth event seems to have allayed Hamilton's troubled mind.

RESIGNEDLY, HAMILTON HAD CONCLUDED that in news reporting, as well as in society as a whole, there was a kind of political Gresham's law at work, in which "the base and spurious drove the genuine article out of circulation." Republican newspapers seemed to thrive on the sensational and the titillating, and while Hamilton was not in favor of imitating this, he cynically realized that the Federalists must engage in some sort of populism if they were to regain power.[285]

What he did not have in mind, however, was a story that broke in his own *Evening Post* on September 1, 1802. It was authored by the infamous James Callender, who had decamped from the Republicans after Jefferson would neither get him out of jail nor pay his fine for violating the Sedition Act. (And to add insult to injury, nor would Jefferson appoint Callender postmaster of Richmond, as he had requested.)

In vengeful retaliation for these omissions, Callender claimed that President Jefferson "keeps, and for many years has kept, as his concubine, one of his slaves." The article asserted, "There is not an individual in the neighborhood of Charlottesville who does not believe the story, and not a few who know it." Callender went on to identify the slave in question as "this wench Sally."

He was, of course, referring to Sally Hemings, who had escorted Jefferson's daughter Polly across the Atlantic to France and whom Jefferson presently employed as a housekeeper at Monticello. The story went on in detail, mentioning that Sally had five mulatto children, including one named Tom, who was known as "Yellow Tom" and looked very much like Thomas Jefferson.

The article "released a tornado of abuse" directed at both Callender and Alexander Hamilton for allegedly engineering its publication in his newspaper. Eventually, Hamilton apologized that the article violated the *Post's* motto of "temperate discussion and impartial regard to the truth." He reiterated his promise to avoid discussing "all personalities not immediately connected with public consideration." In other words, Hamilton, who himself had been dragged into a scandal by Callender, was not going to turn the *Evening Post* into a scandal sheet.[286]

By now, Hamilton and his family were living entirely at the Grange on Harlem Heights, nine miles from town and a three-hour-a-day ride to his Broadway office. According to his biographer Chernow, Hamilton had by then acquired the "uncomfortable status of a glorified has-been" in politics. But even if so, his mind seemed at ease and, aside from his law practice, his attentions turned to other projects to educate people. He made arrangements to publish *The Federalist Papers* in book form and planned to assemble an encyclopedic opus on the effects of government on human society. People who knew Hamilton then remember that he'd become more reflective and moderate, and that he lavished time on his wife and children—especially on little Philip, now two years old.

The Jefferson administration had begun punishing Federalist publishers under the Alien and Sedition Act, and Hamilton devoted a significant portion of his time to defending them. In one of the cases, a New York state publisher ran a story citing Callender's contention that Jefferson had paid him to write a story slandering both George Washington and John Adams. Hamilton was trying to get Callender to come to New York to put him on the stand when the drunken newsman drowned in Richmond, Virginia. Worse, the Republican judge in the case came up with a remarkable ruling, asserting that truth was no defense against seditious libel.

Hamilton appealed the ruling and made what many felt was his greatest legal performance ever. Appearing before a panel of Republican judges, he explained his arguments. Though the judges ruled against him, the 1805 New York legislature would take note of Hamilton's arguments and pass a new libel law allowing truth as a legitimate defense, as well as a stipulation that the intent in such libel cases had to be malicious.

AS THE PRESIDENTIAL ELECTION OF 1804 NEARED, Aaron Burr became certain that Jefferson would somehow deny him any chance at the presidency. Jefferson had come to see Burr as a schemer, a cad, and a liability to the Republican Party. Burr sought and received a brief audience with the president, asking if Jefferson would stipulate that he had been a good vice president. Jefferson demurred, saying he never interfered in elections. Burr decided to run anyway, for governor of New York. In so doing, he turned away from the Republicans, and toward the Federalists, for support.

In New England there had been much talk of forming a new confederacy of non-slaveholding states that would break away from the South: in other words, secession from the Union. Hamilton feared that if Burr were elected governor he might try to drag New York into the plot. In fact, Burr had already conducted clandestine meetings with various New England leaders at which the subject was raised; he had hinted strongly that New York should be against the "Virginia faction."

Burr was aware that Hamilton had opposed him in 1800, when some Federalists had suggested voting for Burr for president instead of Jefferson. But he had not known that during that election, in a note to Treasury Secretary Wolcott, Hamilton had assailed Burr's character and principles, calling him an "American Catiline": a traitor.

Burr learned of this three years later from the unscrupulous editor of the Republicans' New York mouthpiece the *American Citizen.* The editor, James Cheetham, had somehow obtained the contents of Hamilton's note and printed the information to goad Burr, whom he now hated because he had decamped from the Republicans back to the Federalists in his run for New York's governorship. Burr, Cheetham said, was "so degraded as to permit even General Hamilton to slander him with impunity." Of Hamilton, the editor wrote on January 6, 1804, "Yes, Sir, I dare assert that you attributed to Aaron Burr one of the most atrocious and unprincipled of crimes. He has not called upon you [to duel] . . . Either he is guilty or he is the most mean and despicable bastard in the universe."

A few weeks later, Burr filed a libel suit against Cheetham, who claimed that he was merely repeating what someone else had said. "General Hamilton believes him [Burr] guilty and has said so a thousand times." An old friend of Burr later said that Cheetham "had done everything in his power to set Burr and Hamilton to fighting."[287]

In late March 1804 Hamilton attended a dinner given by the Republican judge John Taylor. Among the other guests was a Dr. Charles D. Cooper, who also couldn't stand Aaron Burr. He was amused to hear Hamilton denounce Burr in the most virulent terms, calling him "a dangerous man and one who ought not to be trusted." Afterward, Cooper related this conversation in a letter to a friend, which was either opened or stolen. In any case, its contents appeared in Hamilton's own *New York Evening Post.*

Because Hamilton had "repeatedly declared his neutrality" in the state's governor's race, the *Post's* editor also published a rebuttal from Philip Schuyler, stating that Hamilton could never have said the things about Burr ascribed to him in the letter for this very reason.

Dr. Cooper, unhappy that Schuyler had seemingly impugned his honesty by asserting that Hamilton had not said the things Cooper attributed to him, wrote to Schuyler reasserting what he had witnessed. Not only that, he claimed to have been "unusually cautious" in composing his original letter, adding, "For really, Sir, I could detail to you a still more despicable opinion which General Hamilton has expressed of Mr. Burr." This letter also somehow appeared the next day in the *Albany Register.*

Burr, who had followed the original correspondence in the *Post,* was unaware of Dr. Cooper's April 24 letter in the *Albany Register* until six weeks later. By then, he had lost the governor's race in a landslide and knew he was done for politically. He also knew that in 1800 Hamilton had pulled strings in Congress to keep him from the presidency over Jefferson. Now, he blamed Hamilton for thwarting his run for governor, a post he had needed to sidestep his debts. For Burr, the "still more despicable opinion" alluded to in Cooper's letter was the last straw.

The normally placid, patrician aura that governed Burr's personality turned to rage. On June 18 he sent Hamilton a letter, carried to Hamilton's office by Burr's friend William P. Van Ness, demanding that Hamilton issue "a prompt and unqualified acknowledgment or denial" of anything Hamilton might have said about Burr that would have warranted Dr. Cooper's use of the word "despicable."

Hamilton saw the letter for what it was: the beginning of a challenge to a duel. He replied the next day, saying he could not exactly recall all of his conversation from three months ago and left it to Burr to put in writing "any particular expressions" that Hamilton might have used, in which case he would either "recognize or disavow them."[288]

Van Ness told Hamilton that his response was not adequate, and Hamilton replied that he had never seen Dr. Cooper's letter in the *Albany Register* and needed time to review it; he would get back to Burr later in the day. He then composed a reply in which he adopted the lawyerly tone of a busy man with other things on his mind, questioning the various shades of meaning of the word "despicable," which was not even his word, and closed with the hope that Burr would see it his way or, if not,

"I can only regret the circumstance and abide [by] the consequences."[289] Burr did not see it Hamilton's way. "Your letter has furnished me with new reasons for requiring a definite reply," Burr wrote.

Van Ness took Burr's letter to Hamilton's office and waited while he read it. Hamilton professed to be confounded that Burr continued to demand that he reply to unspecified remarks that he might or might not have made three months earlier. Van Ness, trying to resolve the situation, suggested that Hamilton reply that "he could recollect the use of no terms that would justify the construction made by Dr. Cooper." That would, Van Ness believed, result in an "accommodation."

Hamilton refused. There remained a brief war of words in letters exchanged between the two antagonists. On June 22 Burr responded to his most recent Hamilton letter, "I was greatly disappointed in receiving from you a letter which I could only consider as evasive . . . Thus, Sir, you have invited the course I am about to pursue." On June 27 he issued a formal challenge to a duel. No room was left for compromise. No further letters would be accepted.

Duels were usually fought soon after the challenge was accepted, but Hamilton asked that the meeting be put off until July 11. He had cases to argue for clients before the court: "I should not think it right . . . to withdraw my services from those who may have confided important interests to me."[290] Neither Elizabeth and the children nor Burr's daughter Theodosia knew any of this.

Hamilton decided in advance to throw away his first shot, as he had unfortunately advised his son Philip to do. The hope was that Burr would recognize this and not fire—or, if he did fire, would miss. Hamilton confided this plan to several people, all of whom tried to talk him out of it, to no avail. A few historians and psychobiographers have concluded from this decision that Hamilton was depressed and suicidal; most others think that Hamilton was willing to gamble that Burr would not shoot to kill, for it would have doomed him politically.

While Hamilton professed to loathe dueling, he had been involved as either a second or a participant in at least five duels during his lifetime. Dueling was a leftover from the medieval age of chivalry, when swords or other sharp weapons were the weapon of choice. But deadly pistols had come into use by the mid-eighteenth century. The practice was generally limited to a meeting between two "gentlemen," of which class Burr was a member by birth and Hamilton by marriage and earned position.

Hamilton and Burr met on at least one occasion before the duel, at a Fourth of July dinner banquet for the Society of the Cincinnati, held at Fraunces Tavern in New York City. Hamilton was president of the society, which had been started by Washington and was composed of Revolutionary War officers; Burr had joined the year earlier, when he was courting the Federalist vote for governor. Hamilton reportedly stood on the table at Fraunces and led the group in patriotic songs while Burr sat gloomily by.

Burr was said to have spent his spare time before the duel practicing his marksmanship. Hamilton drew up his will but otherwise went on with his life. A week before the duel he and Eliza threw an immense ball for seventy people, complete with orchestra and champagne. The day before the duel, Nathaniel Pendleton stopped by Hamilton's office to try and talk him out of holding his first fire. "My friend," Hamilton told him in a tone of finality, "it is the effect of a religious scruple and does not admit of reasoning. It is useless to say more on the subject as my purpose is definitely fixed."[291]

That night, Hamilton stayed at his New York town house and wrote to his wife. He asked her, among other things, to financially look after an aging cousin on St. Croix who had given him money to come to America and who had fallen on hard times.

Then he wrote: "The scruples of a Christian have determined me to expose my own life to any extent rather than subject myself to the guilt of taking the life of another. This must increase my hazards and redoubles my pangs for you. But you had rather I should die innocent than live guilty. Heaven can preserve me and I humbly hope will, but in the contrary event, I charge you to remember that you are a Christian, God's Will be done! The will of a merciful God must be good."[292]

At dawn on July 11, 1804, a mist hung over the Hudson River. Hamilton proceeded to a rowboat waiting at the docks. Many states, including New York and New Jersey, had outlawed dueling, but New Jersey was less strict about enforcing the ordnance. Most New York duels were fought across the Hudson on the New Jersey shore. With Hamilton that dawn was Pendleton, his second, carrying a polished felt-lined box containing the dueling pistols; and Dr. David Hosack, who had attended Hamilton's son Philip in his final hours. Boatmen rowed the three across to "a customary dueling ground"—a rock ledge above the Hudson in Weehawken, in an area known as the Palisades.

When they arrived at the site, the vice president was already there, and he and Hamilton exchanged the customary salutations. Their seconds, Van Ness and Pendleton, began measuring off the dueling paces and clearing some brush that had grown up in the way. The seconds then tossed a coin to see who would choose what position and whose second would give the signal to fire. Pendleton won both tosses. Both Burr and Hamilton seemed calm and deliberate.

The seconds explained the rules, which were simple. When the duelers had taken their positions ten paces apart (about 30 feet), Pendleton, the designated second, would ask, "Ready?" If the duelers responded with "Yes," Pendleton would give the order to "Present," at which the duelers would bring their pistols up, aim, and fire when they pleased. If one duelist fired before the other, and the other's pistol was still loaded, the second would say, "One, two, three, fire!" If the armed man failed to fire he lost his shot.

By dueling rules Hamilton, as the challenged party, could choose the weapons. He had chosen a fine pair of .54-caliber pistols owned by John Barker Church. They were large enough "for shooting horses" and contained a double trigger, the most forward of which had a hair-trigger device allowing the shooter to apply only a half pound of pressure instead of the regular 10 to 12 pounds to make it fire.[293]

The seconds indicated to the duelists to take their positions. Pendleton, amid much later criticism, chose to have Hamilton face the river, with the glare of the rising sun. Before Pendleton could call "Ready!" Hamilton said, "Stop. In certain states of the light one requires glasses." He reached into his coat pocket and put on a pair of spectacles. Then he took several sightings with his pistol before saying, "This will do. Now you may proceed."[294]

The seconds turned their backs on the duelists so that, in case they should be tried as accessories to murder, they could truthfully testify that they had not witnessed the duel. Pendleton called out, "Ready?" Both men said they were.

Pendleton then called out "Present!," the signal that the duelers should bring their pistols up, aim, and fire when ready. Hamilton apparently fired first. His shot went several feet wide of the vice president and struck a tree 20 feet off the ground. Then Burr fired. Hamilton dropped instantly. The ball had entered just above his right hip, torn through his liver and diaphragm, and lodged in a lower vertebra. He was instantly paralyzed. When Dr. Hosack got to him, he was "half sitting on the ground . . . His countenance of death I shall never forget. He had at that instant just [the] strength to say, 'This is a mortal wound, Doctor'; when he sunk away and became to all appearances lifeless."[295]

As the wounded man lay there, Burr "advanced toward Hamilton," making a sound and a gesture that sounded to Pendleton "expressive of regret." But he was quickly hustled away by Van Ness, shielded from sight by an umbrella provided by Van Ness, to the waiting rowboat. Again Burr tried, saying, "I must go and speak to him," but Van Ness explained it was impossible. They needed to cross the river quickly.[296]

Dr. Hosack lifted Hamilton's shirt to see the wound and concluded it was likely mortal. He felt for Hamilton's pulse and could find none. He bent his head to Hamilton's heart and could hear no beat; he didn't seem to be breathing. The doctor decided to get him back to New York as fast as possible.

The boatmen helped lift Hamilton's limp body and carry it down the narrow path from the ledge to the river. On the way Pendleton informed Hosack of Hamilton's pledge not to fire first at the vice president. Hamilton was laid in the bottom of the boat, and the doctor began furiously rubbing his hands, wrists, temples, and lips with spirits of hartshorn (an ammonia distilled from the horns and hooves of the male red deer that served as an early smelling salts). About 50 yards offshore Hamilton came to life again. He opened his eyes, which were "fixed," and a pulse returned. He was breathing again and able to speak. "My vision is indistinct," he said.

After a few minutes Hamilton's sight returned, and he noticed Church's pistol case lying in the bottom of the boat. "Take care of that pistol," he said, "it is undischarged and still cocked; it may go off and do harm." Trying to turn to Pendleton, who was behind him, Hamilton said, "Pendleton knows I did not intend to fire at him." Pendleton responded that he had already told Hosack about that. The doctor, trying to ascertain the extent of injuries, asked Hamilton how he felt—dizzy, nauseous? Hamilton said he had no feeling in his legs or anything below the waist. The doctor tried to turn Hamilton's legs but he was still paralyzed. Hamilton, Hosack said, "manifest[ed] in me that he entertained no hopes that he should long survive."[297]

As they neared the docks in Greenwich Village, Hamilton asked the doctor to send for his wife, but not to tell her that he was dying. When they reached the dock, Dr. Hosack arranged for Hamilton to be taken to the home of William Bayard, a prominent New York banker and friend of Hamilton's who lived close by. A leading physician from Columbia College had been sent for, but he could only confirm Dr. Hosack's fatal diagnosis. The French consul sent surgeons from two warships in the harbor, as they had expertise in gunshot wounds. After an examination, they sadly shook their heads.

Hamilton asked that Dr. Benjamin Moore, an Episcopal bishop and president of Columbia College, come to him. When he arrived, Moore was shocked that Hamilton had been wounded in a duel, an activity he thought immoral. When he learned that Hamilton had never been baptized and wished to be, the bishop refused, saying that Hamilton needed "time for reflection." Hamilton then sent for his friend the Reverend John M. Mason, of the Scottish Presbyterian Church, but was told that church policy dictated communion could be taken only at the altar of the church during its Sunday ceremony.

Eliza arrived around noon, believing from the message given her that her husband was not badly hurt. She soon discovered otherwise and became wild with anguish. Hamilton told her to remember she "[was] a Christian." Dr. Moore returned and Hamilton told him "with the utmost calmness and composure . . . 'My dear Sir, you perceive my unfortunate situation, and no doubt have been made acquainted with the circumstances that led to it. It is my desire to receive the communion at your hands. I hope you will not conceive there is any impropriety in my request.'"

The bishop, referring to "the delicate position in which I have been placed," made Hamilton promise that if he got well he would never duel again, to which Hamilton replied, "That, sir, is my deliberate intention," adding, "I have no ill will against Col. Burr. I met him with a fixed resolution to do him no harm. I forgive all that happened." Bishop Moore then administered the rite of communion.[298]

That evening Eliza brought the seven Hamilton children to the bedside of their dying father. Hamilton saw them, then closed his eyes until they had left, unable to bear their tearing faces. Eliza was dumbstruck in grief. To lose a husband, as she had her eldest son, in such a jolting, vain, unnecessary manner was beyond all comprehension.

The next morning Hamilton's condition remained the same but his life was slipping away. Friends came and went, including Nathaniel Pendleton, Angelica Church, and Hamilton's good friend Gouverneur Morris. Bishop Moore returned and stayed by the bedside. At 2 p.m. Hamilton died. He was roughly fifty years old (his exact birth year has never been conclusively determined).

Burr, who had holed up in his home, had sent a note that morning to Dr. Hosack, inquiring after Hamilton's condition and his chances of survival. There is no record that the doctor answered. Burr also sent a note to Van Ness, his second. Burr had no doubt picked up information and rumors about the consequences of the duel, including that Pendleton was telling people Hamilton had thrown away his first shot. This, Burr told Van Ness, "must be forthwith contradicted." Burr knew there would be trouble over what had happened, but he was beginning to suspect it would be far greater than he imagined.[299]

News of Hamilton's death spread through New York like a contagion. People mourned and wept in the streets. Oliver Wolcott Jr. told his wife, "The feelings of the whole community are agonized beyond description."

The nation's loss was observed with pomp and ceremony. The city council of New York agreed to shut all businesses on the day of Hamilton's funeral and asked ship's captains in the harbor to lower their flags to half-mast. Church bells, which by city ordnance were not supposed to be rung at funerals, were allowed to chime as Hamilton's services were conducted. Cannons in the Battery boomed for hours. All New Yorkers were asked to wear a black crepe armband for thirty days in honor of the "Integrity, Virtues, Talents, and Patriotism of General Hamilton."

Hamilton's great friend Gouverneur Morris was chosen to give the oration at the funeral service. A friend of Morris had said of the fatal duel, "If we were truly brave we would not accept a challenge. But we are all cowards." Morris replied that the friend was one of the bravest men alive, but he doubted that he would "so far brave public opinion as to refuse a challenge."[300] For the eulogy, Morris decided to ignore the matter of the duel altogether, as he feared he would lose his composure and also provoke the mourners. "Their Indignation amounts almost to a frenzy already," he said.

Burr, for his part, was furiously trying to change a joint statement by the seconds of the events of the duel. He was particularly incensed "at the falsehood that H fired only when falling and without aim," which "has given rise to very improper suggestions," he wrote to Van Ness. In the same note Burr (always short of money) then tried to borrow a thousand dollars from Van Ness, evidently in contemplation of making an escape from the authorities.

At noon on Saturday, July 14, Hamilton's friends who were serving as pallbearers carried his mahogany coffin down the steps of the John B. Church home and into the street, where a regiment of militia waited with their rifles reversed in mourning. The "Dead March" from Handel's *Saul* was played by a military band. Next came the members of the Society of the Cincinnati, followed by the coffin and pallbearers. On top of the casket lay Hamilton's crossed swords and hat.

Hamilton's gray charger with the general's spurred boots reversed in the stirrups was led by two black servants wearing white turbans. Next came the carriage of Gouverneur Morris. Members of the New York Bar were followed by the students and teachers of

Columbia College. Behind them was the Tammany Society, followed by many thousands of the general public. Multitudes lined the streets and crowded windows and rooftops as the somber procession slowly made its way through the streets. One person likened the mourning over Hamilton's sudden demise to that of the death of Washington.

The procession marched through the hot July streets to Broadway's Trinity Church, where a raised platform had been constructed at the entrance for Morris to speak. Seated on the platform in silent tears were four of Hamilton's boys, ages six to eighteen.

Morris began with Hamilton's youth, when he left college to join the army. "Such was his zeal, and so brilliant his service that we heard his name before we knew his person." He was pure at heart, Morris said, and often his opinions were misrepresented. When President Washington was looking for cabinet officers, he wanted "splendid talents," "extensive [knowledge]," and, above all, "incorruptible integrity—All these he found in Hamilton," Morris told the mourners. When the recent provisional army was formed, Washington selected Hamilton as second in command, because "He thought the sword of America might safely be confided to the hand which now lies cold in that coffin . . . Bear this testimony to the memory of my departed Friend," Morris said, "I charge you to protect his fame—It is all he has left."

When Morris finished, the pallbearers carried the coffin to the small graveyard at the side of the church for the burial service. The life of Alexander Hamilton was over. But his imprint on America was just beginning.[301]

CHAPTER NINE

On March 4, 1801, Thomas Jefferson was sworn into office as the third president of the United States. It had taken seven days and thirty-six different ballot counts in the House of Representatives before the tie with Aaron Burr ended in Jefferson's favor. Burr had maneuvered disgracefully to challenge Jefferson, but in the end that had worked against him. Still, Aaron Burr would be the country's vice president. At the time, no one could possibly have anticipated that three years later he would murder Alexander Hamilton in a duel.

In his inaugural speech Jefferson sought to unite the divided nation. "We are all republicans, we are all federalists," he said, addressing a joint session of Congress and a multitude of guests at the half-finished Capitol building. "Every difference of opinion is not a difference of principle . . . Let us restore to social intercourse that harmony and affection without which liberty, and even life itself, is but a dreary thing."[302] It was a fine speech and set a new, hopeful tone for a country not yet fifteen years old but already exhausted by vicious partisan politics. Now it had elected the first Republican president and Congress.

Though he fashioned himself a man of the people, he had brought many elegant objects from Monticello with him to furnish the house, along with a voluminous quantity of books. As he had no wife, Jefferson sometimes called on his daughter Patsy to serve as hostess, but he also relied on Dolley Madison, James Madison's vivacious wife, to fill that role. As his politically savvy "chargé d'affaires," she orchestrated presidential dinners and events, official and unofficial.

One of Jefferson's first priorities during his initial month in office was to work to rescind the Judiciary Act of 1801. A second was to commute the sentences of all Democratic-Republican editors imprisoned by the Federalists under the Sedition Act and to shepherd a bill through Congress to pay their fines from public funds. Third, he began pressing for the arrests and trials of Federalist editors under various state libel laws, as the Alien and Sedition Acts had mostly expired by the end of Adams's term. Jefferson had long supported the First Amendment protections for freedom of the press, but enduring the slings and arrows of Federalist newspapers had changed his mind.

Jefferson's next action reached further afield—he started a war with the Barbary states of North Africa: Tripoli (now Libya), Tunis (now Tunisia), Morocco, and Algiers (now Algeria). Ever since he had served in Paris after the Revolution he had been in favor of military action against the state-supported piracy that was savagely waged in the Mediterranean unless enormous bribes were paid for protection. If they were not, ships of non-Muslim countries were seized, their goods taken, and their surviving crews and passengers sold into slavery.

The United States had not had a navy capable of extended operations abroad in its first decades, but the previous Congress had appropriated money for six new twenty-two-gun frigates, as well as the creation of a marine corps. Once Jefferson was inaugurated, the pasha of Tripoli issued a demand for a bribe of $3.4 million from the U.S. government. The total projected treasury revenues for 1801 was only $10 million, so the demand encompassed more than a third of the nation's revenue.

Jefferson ignored the pasha, instead asking and receiving authorization from Congress to take military action. He dispatched three frigates and a sloop into the Mediterranean Sea to seek out and destroy the pirate ships and blockade the port of Tripoli, a walled fortress city containing 25,000 Muslim soldiers and bristling with artillery. Commanding the expedition was Commodore Richard Dale. He was sent forth with a variety of expensive gifts for the Barbary sultans and the pasha of Tripoli. A letter to the pasha explained that the American naval squadron was there "to protect American commerce."

The gifts were never delivered. On May 4, 1801, the pasha declared war on the United States, not by sending a formal declaration but by the quaint custom of chopping down the American flagpole in front of the U.S. consulate in Tripoli. When Dale learned of this he reciprocated. From July through September, Tripoli was blockaded by the American navy and mortar shells were fired into the city. During that time, marines aboard the USS *Enterprise* scored a resounding naval victory. At a cost of no casualties to themselves, they fended off an attacking ship, killing thirty Tripolitan pirates, wounding thirty more, and capturing another three, including the commander. But the pasha remained safe behind the walls of his fortress, plotting his next move.

EVEN AS THE PASHA WAS PLOTTING, America was growing. In early 1802 Congress passed an act authorizing "The inhabitants of [Ohio] . . . to form for themselves a constitution and a state government," and admission of Ohio to the union of states. The Enabling Act set the procedures and conditions for territories to apply for statehood. A few weeks afterward, the Jefferson government paid Georgia around $1.5 million for the vast Yazoo lands that today comprise the states of Alabama and Mississippi. For a decade, those territories had been the subject of a major scandal, because they had been sold by Georgia to land speculators under a statute that was later rescinded by a different state government. Jefferson also had his eye on Spanish-held lands, including Florida and Louisiana.

In addition to his plan for territorial acquisition, Jefferson was also reconsidering his earlier push to have Federalist editors and journalists persecuted for printing "libelous" statements. Writing to his attorney general, Jefferson said, "I would wish much to see the experiment tried of getting along without public prosecutions for libels. I believe we can do it. Patience and well-doing, instead of punishment, if it can be found sufficiently efficacious, would be a happy change in the instruments of government."[303]

In another year, Jefferson would have reason to change his mind yet again when James Callender turned on him and began publishing his series of salacious stories about Jefferson and Sally Hemings in the *Richmond Recorder*. Callender also accused Jefferson of bribery and improper advances on the wife of a neighbor, and claimed that Jefferson had paid him to write attacks on the Federalists for Republican newspapers. Callender produced letters from Jefferson that referenced sums of money and discussed various topics he could write about. (In his defense, Jefferson said he was merely trying to help Callender, an indigent refugee who was the father of three motherless boys.)

Callender's explosive charges were reprinted in papers throughout the country, resulting over the next year and more in indignant letters to the editor, widespread guffawing at Jefferson's expense, and further elaboration on the story by rumormongers. Frances Trollope, an English writer living in the United States (and mother of the novelist Anthony Trollope), wrote that Jefferson had fathered children by almost all of his female slaves.[304] Ribald songs were published, including one to the tune of "Yankee Doodle" whose refrain asked: "What wife were half so handy/To breed a flock of slaves for stock/A blackamoor's the dandy."

By early 1803 Jefferson seems to have had enough. In February he wrote to Pennsylvania's governor Thomas McKean, accusing the Federalists of "pushing its licentiousness and its lying [of the press] to such a degree of prostitution as to deprive it of all credit . . . This is a dangerous state of things, and the press ought to be restored to its credibility if possible. The restraints provided by the laws of the states are sufficient for this . . . Not a general prosecution, for that would look like persecution; but a selected one."[305]

Callender went to his grave that summer, after falling drunkenly from a riverboat into three feet of mud and water in the James and drowning. But his sensational story regarding Sally Hemings did not die with him. In 1998 DNA tests were undertaken on the remains of Eston Hemings, Sally's youngest son. The tests showed definitively that he was related to someone in the Jefferson line. In 2000 a committee appointed by the Thomas Jefferson Foundation, which owns and operates Monticello, announced its belief that Jefferson fathered not only Eston but most probably all of Sally Hemings's six children.[306]

As 1803 began Jefferson had more than just Callender's accusations to deal with. At the end of February the Supreme Court at last handed down a decision in *Marbury v. Madison,* which had been rolling through the courts since Jefferson's inauguration in 1801. Marbury, one of John Adams's "midnight judges," had been denied his commission by Secretary of State Madison. The court ruled against Marbury, but the case had much more far-ranging implications. In the written decision Chief Justice John Marshall established for the first time the concept of judicial review. In its decision-making capacity, the Supreme Court could rule on the constitutionality of laws passed by Congress, as well as rules passed by other branches of government.

Jefferson was furious at the decision, because he saw it as the Supreme Court's usurping the powers of the other two branches—in particular the executive, his own. In letters written to friends and associates Jefferson decried *Marbury v. Madison* as judicial overreach and suggested that each of the three branches should be able to supervise its own laws and rules. As a lawyer Jefferson should have understood the judicial conflicts that might arise if there were no single body to resolve them—but in any case he learned to live with the decision.

In the spring of 1803, the reversals that had plagued Jefferson earlier in the year suddenly turned around when he received news that would forever change his presidential legacy. It came from an unlikely quarter: Napoleon's France.

Jefferson had been keeping a wary eye on the general-turned-ruler and his obvious ambitions of empire. In 1802 the president learned that two years earlier Napoleon had persuaded Spain to cede the Louisiana Territory back to France. The vast area included New Orleans and the expansive wilderness west of the Mississippi, extending from the Gulf of Mexico to Canada and as far west as present-day Montana. Spain had acquired this territory at the end of the Seven Years' War, but now it was again under France's dominion.

That alarmed Jefferson and others, particularly people in the western states and territories who feared losing their trade down the Mississippi and into the Gulf of Mexico at New Orleans. The British minister to the United States correctly assessed Americans' attitude when he wrote that he had met "scarcely any member of either party who would not prefer almost anybody to the French as neighbors." An anxious Secretary of State Madison predicted that in case of a French occupation of the area "the worst events are to be anticipated," and a war would likely result.

In truth, Napoleon had harbored plans of establishing a grand French empire in the New World, but those hopes had recently been dashed. Almost two-thirds of a 20,000-man French force dispatched to quell a slave rebellion on the Caribbean Island of Saint-Domingue had been lost, mostly to yellow fever. The loss left Napoleon saddled with heavy debts, a war with Britain on the horizon, and an enormous new territory to administer and defend in North America.

So he was delighted when James Monroe and Robert Livingston—American envoys Jefferson had dispatched—offered to buy New Orleans for as much as $10 million.

Against the advice of the long-serving foreign minister Talleyrand, Napoleon countered by offering the whole 828,000-square-mile Louisiana Territory for $15 million, or three cents an acre. Even though it was more than they were authorized to spend, the two dumbfounded envoys quickly signed the papers. When word of the acquisition reached Jefferson on July 3, 1803, he was both flabbergasted and delighted. It was the most tremendous news he would receive in either of his two terms; acquisition of the Louisiana Territory effectively doubled the size of the United States.

The president quickly spread word of the purchase. On the Fourth of July the Washington paper the *National Intelligencer* ran it boldly on the front page. There was great rejoicing in most quarters, but in Federalist enclaves the response was muted. Alexander Hamilton's *New York Evening Post* concluded that "Every man . . . will readily acknowledge that the acquisition has been solely owing to a fortuitous concurrence of unforeseen and unexpected circumstances, and not to any wise or rigorous measures on the part of the American government." Most newspapers, however, stressed the blessings of peace and security that the purchase brought, rather than seeing it as a mere acquisition of land. Jefferson wrote to his son-in-law that the purchase "removes from us the greatest source of danger to our peace."[307]

Jefferson had wanted to acquire the Spanish Floridas almost since he took office. When the first treaty documents for the Louisiana Purchase were examined by Livingston in Paris, he determined that at least West Florida was included, and his findings were confirmed by one of the French negotiators.

The 50-mile-wide strip along the Gulf Coast extended from Alabama west to New Orleans and included all of the thriving ports in between. Monroe went further in searching documents and ferreted out obscure papers from the original division of Florida by the British after the Seven Years' War. Those documents showed that West Florida included not only Mobile but a boundary about 50 miles farther east at the Perdido River. Jefferson would have liked to acquire both West and East Florida, from the Florida panhandle at Pensacola all the way to Key West. But he concluded that the East Florida peninsula would probably have to be taken by force "at some future time."

Jefferson's next big hurdle was to get the acquisition through Congress; even some members of his own party were heard to grumble that nowhere in the Constitution was a president given power to purchase land. Treasury Secretary Gallatin, however, delivered a legal opinion on the question that seemed to satisfy the constitutional requirements. He argued that the nation had an inherent right to acquire territory, and that when such an acquisition was by treaty, the same constituted authorities in whom the treaty-making powers were vested had a constitutional right to sanction the acquisition—in this case, the president and the Senate. Gallatin also averred that whenever territory was acquired, Congress had the power of admitting it into the Union as a new state, or states.

Jefferson, ever fearful of loose interpretations of the Constitution, decided it would be best to enshrine Gallatin's legal opinion in a constitutional amendment. Congress, however, disagreed and voted Jefferson's proposed amendment down. Nevertheless, the Senate ratified the Louisiana Purchase agreement as a treaty on October 20, 1803.

Ironically, neither the Spanish, the French, nor Jefferson knew exactly what the purchase consisted of: its exact boundaries, who and what lived there, and, most important, if any navigable rivers flowed through the new territory to the Pacific. Jefferson decided that in order to find out what lay in the sweeping territory, a party of exploration should cross it all the way to the Pacific and report back on its findings. He wanted an accurate map of the country, showing its rivers, mountains, plains, deserts, and other geographic features. He wanted a catalogue of each of the Native American tribes encountered, as well as the trees and other plants and animals. He also wanted to understand the commercial and military advantages of the new land.

Happily, Jefferson had someone in mind to lead the expedition: his young friend and Albemarle neighbor Meriwether Lewis, to whom he had written when he first learned he had won the presidency. Jefferson had told Lewis then that he needed a secretary, "not only to aid in the private concerns of the household, but also to contribute to the mass of information which it is interesting for the administration to acquire." Even then, Jefferson was thinking of expansion beyond the Alleghenies: "Your knowle[d]ge of the Western country, of the army and all of its interests & relations, has rendered it desirable . . . that you should be engaged in that office." Jefferson added that Lewis would live in the President's House with full pay and promotions, and that the appointment "would make you know & be known to characters of influence in the affairs of our country, and give you the advantage of their [wisdom]." The new president further explained that the job would be "more in the nature of an aid de camp than a mere secretary."[308] Lewis had been stunned and overjoyed when he received the letter and wrote back that he would rush to Washington to serve.[309]

Born in 1774, Lewis was from one of Virginia's most distinguished families, but his father had died when he was still young. His mother remarried an army captain, and the family moved to the Georgia mountains—frontier country—when the boy was eight or nine. Meriwether flourished in that environment, hunting, fishing, hiking, camping, exploring. As a young man he had returned to Virginia to run the plantation he had inherited from his father, but the life of a planter bored him. When calls went out for militiamen to put down the Whiskey Rebellion, Lewis joined up and later enlisted in the regular army, where he thrived.

When the Quasi-War with France began and Congress voted to greatly enlarge the regular army, Lewis was promoted to first lieutenant and made paymaster for the First Infantry Regiment. His duties included traveling through the Northwest—Kentucky, Indiana, Illinois, Ohio, Michigan, Wisconsin—to carry banknotes to soldiers and officers in far-flung army outposts. In that capacity, Lewis learned the skills of a waterman and became something of an expert on the people and natural resources of the large territory. In 1800 he was promoted to the rank of captain and given command of a rifle company in Pittsburgh, which is where he was posted when he received Jefferson's letter.

The first task the president had in mind for his new secretary was a daunting one, but it was one of the main reasons Jefferson had chosen him. Now that the country was at peace again, Jefferson was determined to reduce the size of the army, particularly of Federalist-leaning officers appointed by Adams in his final days as president. Jefferson wanted the army to be led by the most competent men of the best quality—meaning Republicans. Lewis began a thorough assessment and, at his recommendation, the best of the Federalists officers were retained, despite Jefferson's inclinations.

Jefferson became Lewis's mentor, encouraging him to delve into the books in his own extensive library and serving as a writing coach by helping Lewis eliminate much of the verbosity that had marred his earlier letters. The rapport between the two men built until they were extremely close. As Jefferson put it, "Capt. Lewis and I are like two mice in a church."

In the summer of 1802 Jefferson took Lewis with him to Monticello, where he began tutoring him in botany as they walked in the woods and fields. He also taught the young army captain the rudiments of astronomy and navigation, as well as how to use the telescope, sextant, and theodolite he had purchased long ago in London. The two pored over maps in Jefferson's library, perhaps the finest geographic collection in North America. Jefferson talked of his desire to send an expedition across the country, to explore the upper reaches of the Missouri River, which flowed into the Mississippi at St. Louis, and to find out if any direct continuous water route existed to the Pacific Ocean. Lewis was excited by the prospect and indicated that he would very much like to lead such an expedition. This was precisely what Jefferson had in mind.

He had become increasingly anxious to get American explorers moving West, particularly after the publication in England of a book by the fur trader and explorer Alexander Mackenzie. Mackenzie had advanced out of Canada to the Pacific Northwest and laid claim for Britain to some land there, in what is now Washington State. In his book Mackenzie suggested a number of commercial uses that the region could sustain—uses that would be exclusively British if Jefferson did not move fast.

Thus the Corps of Discovery was born. It would explore and map the Louisiana Purchase to the headwaters of the Missouri, then continue to the Pacific and claim that land for the United States. Lewis would head the corps, because, as Jefferson explained, "It was impossible to find a character who [possesses] a compleat [knowledge of] science in botany, natural history, mineralogy &

astronomy, joined with the firmness of constitution & character, prudence, habits adapted to the woods, & familiarity with the Indian manners & character requisite for this undertaking. All the latter qualification Capt. Lewis has."[310]

Congress agreed to a two-year expedition with an allocation for about twelve men to make the trip. Lewis figured the entire cost to be no more than $2,500—about $3.42 per day. But before he could set out, Jefferson sent him to study under America's leading scientists in Philadelphia, then the nation's seat of higher learning.

While there, in the early summer of 1803, Lewis sent a letter to his old army commander Capt. William Clark, inviting him to join his Corps of Discovery as a co-captain. Lewis had served under Clark in the Chosen Rifle Company, a group of sharpshooters, but he had not seen Clark in seven years. A Virginian then living in Indiana Territory, Clark was the younger brother of Gen. George Rogers Clark, who had scored a major victory in the Revolution and was a great friend of Jefferson.

Lewis explained to Clark that he intended for the expedition to take a keelboat (in this case a 55-foot square-rigged rowing-sailing vessel) down the Ohio River to the Mississippi, then up the Mississippi to the Missouri River at St. Louis. After St. Louis the corps would hunt their own food, bringing along presents—bead necklaces, mirrors, needles, scissors—for the Indian tribes they would encounter. The expedition would follow the Missouri as far west as it was navigable by keelboat. Then they would make canoes and continue on to the Missouri's source, thought to be somewhere in the Rocky Mountains. Once that had been located, they would continue west across the mountains, searching for a navigable waterway to the Columbia River and follow it to the Pacific.

The twenty-nine-year-old Lewis said he envisioned a party of twelve stout, healthy, unmarried men, who were good hunters and woodsmen "capable of bearing bodily fatigue of a pretty considerable degree." Lewis also said he expected to find at least some of these men at a military post at Kingsport, Tennessee, and asked Clark, thirty-three, to scout his neighborhood for others.

Waiting for Clark's answer, Lewis spent his time acquiring supplies of all sorts. He had spent a year of study in Philadelphia, and before he left the storied city he bought a hundred dollars' worth of "portable (dried) soup," which was to prove a godsend later. From the government arsenal at Harpers Ferry, Lewis got the latest model army rifles and kegs of powder. He had ordered a keelboat built in Pittsburgh, and while there he received a response from Clark, accepting the invitation with pleasure.

On August 31 the keelboat was at last finished, and by ten in the morning Lewis had it loaded and was on his way down the Ohio to Clark. Progress was slow as the river was low—lower than anyone remembered. On the trip downriver, Lewis dismissed several men who had come with him whose work or behavior was unsatisfactory. Finally, on October 14 in Clarksville, Indiana, Lewis reunited with Clark. He had a fairly large ensemble of men waiting with him, as word had gotten out that men who completed the journey would receive a government land grant—as precious as gold to a western backwoodsman. Although the secretary of war had authorized only twelve men for the party, Jefferson had told Lewis to select as many men as he believed he needed.

Lewis and Clark chose sixteen men, and their Corps of Discovery set off down the Ohio and then battled up the Mississippi. At Fort Kaskaskia, on the Illinois side of the river, they recruited perhaps another dozen men to the expedition. On December 7 they arrived in Cahokia, across the river from Spanish-held St. Louis.

The next day, Lewis met with the Spanish governor, who told him that until the transfer of the Louisiana Purchase was formalized the corps could go no farther. Given the lateness of the season and the need for more supplies Lewis did not protest. The captains put the party in winter camp across the river from St. Louis.

THE BARBARY WARS WERE NOT GOING WELL for Jefferson by the end of that year. Americans had grown weary of paying the taxes necessary to conduct a conflict several thousand miles away, even though Jefferson had managed to save a considerable amount of expenditures through cost-cutting measures. Chief among them was dry-docking naval warships not in use, rather than keeping them in the water with full crews; even some Federalists branded this idea as "brilliant." But the blockade of Tripoli's harbor had been evaded by at least six pirate ships, because there were too few naval vessels to both blockade and effectively patrol. Pirates resumed raiding U.S. ships and those of other countries, but Jefferson could not bring himself to make what he felt were dishonorable payments to ensure protection in the Mediterranean.

On October 31, while chasing a pirate vessel, the USS *Philadelphia* struck an uncharted reef two miles outside Tripoli Harbor and was grounded. Her captain, Edward Preble, who was also the new commodore of the Mediterranean squadron, tried desperately to refloat her but to no avail. Rather than have the ship, its cargo, and armaments captured by the pirates, Preble ordered holes drilled in the hull to sink the vessel. Her crew of 307 officers and men were taken prisoner and held for ransom; if it was not paid they would be sold into slavery.

The pirates managed to refloat and repair the *Philadelphia* and anchored her in Tripoli Harbor. On the night of February 16, 1804, U.S. Navy Lieutenant Stephen Decatur Jr. and a party of seventy-five volunteers brazenly sailed a captured Tripolitan ketch into the harbor. With enemy gunboats anchored all around, they boarded the *Philadelphia,* overcame several dozen Arab guards in a brief swordfight, then loaded each of the ship's thirty-four cannons. That done, Decatur and his men set fires that entirely consumed the ship. They made a successful getaway as the fires reached the guns and set them off one by one, creating a stunning spectacle as the furious Arabs looked on in frustration. When Lord Horatio Nelson, the most celebrated seaman of his time, heard of Decatur's exploit, he called it "the most bold and daring act of the Age."[311] For his part, Jefferson strengthened the American squadron in the Mediterranean, doubling its size.

That autumn Jefferson was reelected president in a landslide. Not so his vice president, Aaron Burr, who had gone into hiding after being indicted by grand juries in both New York and New Jersey for murdering Hamilton. But on February 4, 1805, members of the Senate were shocked to see Burr sitting calmly in the vice president's chair, ready to preside over the impeachment of Federalist Supreme Court justice Samuel Chase, accused by Republicans of making improper political statements to juries. The trial lasted several days, resulting in Chase's impeachment in the House; to Jefferson's displeasure

Chase was acquitted by the Senate, despite the fact that it too was Republican-dominated.

After the presidential inauguration on March 4 Burr relinquished his office to the new vice president—Hamilton's longtime nemesis George Clinton of New York. Burr then fled to Louisiana Purchase lands and conceived a vague scheme of conquest to take over the remaining Spanish territories in the West—in Texas and in the vast New Mexico Territory. When the murder charges against him for Hamilton's death were dropped, Burr returned to Ohio and western Virginia to organize a force of fewer than a hundred men for his conquest. Gen. James Wilkinson, head of the army, was in on the plan. He was later found to have been a highly paid spy for Spain.

THE EARLY MONTHS OF JEFFERSON'S second term proved historic. On June 4 the pasha of Tripoli, seeing that the tides of war had turned against him, signed a Treaty of Peace and Amity with the United States, ending the First Barbary War. Weeks earlier, in mid-May, the Louisiana Purchase had become official and Lewis and Clark had resumed their expedition. By autumn their Corps of Discovery had pushed upstream and, with great exertion, through what are now the states of Missouri, Kansas, Nebraska, South Dakota, and North Dakota.

It was an exciting and dramatic journey. Along the way they met various bands of warlike Sioux Indians, who were nonetheless generally friendly to the men of the corps. In South Dakota they saw their first large herds of American bison, or buffalo, and camped for the winter in North Dakota near a village of friendly Mandan Indians. While there, they met several French Canadians who had lived and traded with the Indians for years; they hired these trapper-traders as interpreters and guides. The corps also managed to catch a prairie dog, which no one from the East had seen before. They sent it back to Jefferson with a party of trappers headed downriver. Remarkably, it arrived at the President's House alive.

Through the spring and summer of 1805, Lewis and Clark pushed ever west, taking astrological readings and measurements as well as collecting and recording the rocks, geography, and flora and fauna as they went. They had given up their keelboat in favor of six canoes and two pirogues and had taken on a guide: Sacagawea, a seventeen-year-old Shoshone girl, and the eight-week-old baby she carried in a papoose on her back.

On August 12, they at last reached the headwaters of the Missouri. By mid-September the corps was struggling across the steep peaks and ravines of the Bitterroot Mountains, made almost impassable by fallen timber. It was the worst ordeal they had faced. Surviving on horseflesh and the portable soup that Lewis had purchased in Philadelphia, they were nearly starving when they reached the Lolo Trail in northern Idaho. By October they were on the Clearwater River, which took them to the Snake, then into the Columbia and downriver to its mouth.

Finally, on November 7, 1805, Jefferson's Corps of Discovery reached the Pacific. "Ocian in view! O! the joy," Lewis wrote in his journal. The men built a winter camp—Fort Clatsop—on an inlet of the Columbia near present-day Astoria, Oregon. They had hoped to return east on a merchant vessel, but those proved extremely rare. Dangerous shoals and the huge surf that built up when the Columbia emptied its full force into the Pacific had sunk many sailing ships. The men of the corps would have to return the way they came—overland—when spring made travel possible.

As the men of the corps battled their way west, Jefferson had been distracted by the first serious threat to the new republic. The British and French had begun capturing American merchant ships, treating them and their cargoes as contraband of war and selling them on the open market. Hungry for manpower, Britain had also seized thousands of American sailors and impressed them into its own navy, arguing that once a man was a British subject he was forever a British subject—even if he had since become an American citizen. British impressment had many Americans clamoring for war, but Jefferson instead attempted a diplomatic solution, sending James Monroe to England to convince the British to stop their harassment of American ships and impressment of American seamen.

In late October 1806, under this threatening cloud of war, Jefferson received news that brought him "unspeakable joy." Word reached him that the previous month the Lewis and Clark expedition had returned "in good health to St. Louis." The Corps of Discovery had traveled 8,000 miles through the new Louisiana Purchase territory, encountered some seventy Indian tribes and bands, obtained specimens of nearly two hundred plants previously unknown to science, and produced more than a hundred maps documenting the trails they took to the Pacific coast and back. They had lost only one man, Sgt. Charles Floyd, to appendicitis. On New Year's Eve at the President's House, Lewis presented Sheheke, one of the principal chiefs of the Mandan people, to Thomas Jefferson, the president of the United States.

Some months earlier, responding to continued provocations on the part of Great Britain, Congress had passed and Jefferson signed the Non-Importation Act, prohibiting many British imports. Soon thereafter, Britain, certain it had the military might to bully its former colonies, issued Orders in Council, forbidding the neutral United States from trading with France unless it first paid a tribute to Britain. In turn, Napoleon issued an edict ordering the seizure of all U.S. vessels paying tribute to England.

Jefferson had had enough of Britain's seafaring ravages and France's depredations. He pushed Congress to pass a retaliatory act that would halt U.S. trade with any other country in the world. In December 1807, the much-debated Embargo Act was passed.

It proved to be an imprudent measure. Cargo of all sorts began to pile up in American ports and rot on wharfs. The wharfs, too, and the ships tied up in berths began to rot. Seeing their large fleet of merchantmen idle, New Englanders, many of whom had been unsettled ever since Jefferson's election, held a meeting in Hartford and once again threatened to secede from the union. A second embargo act was even worse than the first, but Jefferson was determined to do everything possible to avoid war with Britain and France and their powerful navies.

Jefferson also wanted to limit slavery, and at his urging Congress passed a law prohibiting the importation of slaves into the United States after January 1, 1808—this, despite a new invention that had created a vast new need for slaves in the upland South.

To date, the only commercially viable cotton in the United States was so-called long staple cotton, grown on the sea islands of Georgia and South Carolina. Short staple cotton could be grown all over the South, but its dense seeds and husks had to be removed by hand, rendering it virtually valueless. Then, in 1793, inventor Eli Whitney came up with a mechanical cotton gin machine that could easily "gin out" the detritus. Suddenly, almost the entire southland was ripe for producing cotton for the clothing mills that had sprung up with the industrial revolution in England and France. Southern cotton, grown mostly by the labor of slaves, soon became the chief export of the United States.

In the meantime, dark rumors from the Southwest had begun to drift back to Washington: Aaron Burr had recruited a force of men and intended to invade the Southwest and make it a separate country, with himself as leader. Jefferson issued a public statement warning citizens not to become involved in any plot to invade or annex Spanish territory. Meanwhile, Gen. James Wilkinson, who had been corresponding with Burr in his schemes, had gotten cold feet and relayed to Jefferson that he had evidence about Burr's subversive plot.

Jefferson immediately issued an arrest warrant for Burr, who attempted to flee to Spanish Florida. Apprehended by soldiers in what is now Washington County, Alabama, he was taken to a circuit court in Richmond, Virginia, where he was tried for treason. He was acquitted, however, after General Wilkinson was forced to admit he had forged a letter from Burr outlining his whole plan. The letter was the state's sole physical evidence in the case, and Wilkinson's credibility as a prosecution witness was destroyed.

A freed Burr sailed for England to escape his creditors. He later returned to New York, the practice of law, and his tangled ways.

His beloved wife Theodosia had died in 1794, and on his return to New York he briefly remarried a wealthy woman who quickly discovered that he was stealing much of her money and was a serial adulterer. He died in 1836, never having repented his role in Hamilton's death.

IN 1808, JEFFERSON FOLLOWED Washington's lead and refused to run for a third term. His close ally and secretary of state, James Madison, was elected the nation's fourth president. Three days before Jefferson left office, Congress repealed the Embargo Act and replaced it with the Non-Intercourse Act, under which U.S. ports were closed to ships of Britain and France until those countries agreed to respect the rights of U.S. ships and citizens. The situation only worsened, and President Madison faced continued aggressions by Britain.

After eight years in Washington, Jefferson at last went home to Monticello. His chief interest during his final decades lay in establishing Central College, now the University of Virginia. Jefferson had conceived of the college during his first term in the presidency and used his influence to obtain state funds for it. It was built on land owned by James Monroe, who was himself the American president when the college was established in 1819. Jefferson personally oversaw the college's visionary approach to teaching and subject matter, which broke with adherence to religious doctrine. He also designed its grounds, including the enticing serpentine walls that framed formal gardens; and its redbrick buildings, including the student quarters, called the Range; and the massive heart of the college, the Rotunda.

During his later years, Jefferson maintained a voluminous correspondence with many of the major figures of his day, both at home and abroad. He also entertained a host of distinguished guests at Monticello—presidents and former presidents, Lafayette and other European royalty, Indian chiefs, artists, musicians, and scientists in every field of study and discipline. He continued to write often to Madison encouragingly as war with Britain became inevitable. In late June 1812 he wrote, "The declaration of war . . . is entirely popular here . . . The federalists indeed are open mouthed against the declaration[,] but they are poor devils here, not worthy of notice."

By August 1814 the British had invaded Washington, burning the Capitol, the Library of Congress, and the White House. The following year, Jefferson sold his precious personal library to Congress to replace the volumes the British had burned.

Jefferson enjoyed his life at Monticello. Its Great Hall was museum-like, decorated with his collection of Indian weapons and artifacts, plant and mineral specimens, fossils, and sculpture. Two busts facing each other in the entranceway to the hall had extra significance. One was a terra-cotta image of Jefferson by the French artist Houdon, whom Jefferson had sat for during his Paris days. It portrayed him focused on a distant point, "sensitive, intellectual, aristocratic" and with "an almost knowing half-smile."[312] The white marble bust opposite also captured an aristocratic, intelligent, firm character with a half-smile on his face: Alexander Hamilton, placed there respectfully by Jefferson after Hamilton's death. The two men were opposites to the end.[313]

That was not so with John Adams. He and Jefferson reconciled by letter in 1811, and their frequent correspondence over the remaining years of their lives was respectful, affectionate, and contemplative. Jefferson once remarked that Adams had done only one thing to anger him: making the last-minute judicial appointments, which Jefferson felt saddled him with a court system run by his enemies.

The two founders died within hours of each other on the Fourth of July, 1826. Neither knew the other had reached the end; the eighty-three-year-old Jefferson preceded ninety-year-old Adams by a few hours. The next afternoon, Jefferson was buried next to his wife, Martha, in the family cemetery at Monticello. It was a simple Episcopal ceremony attended by a few dozen family friends and slaves. A much larger funeral procession walking up from Charlottesville had been organized, but due to a delay it missed the burial service by a few minutes.

Ever the writer and planner, Jefferson had left precise orders for the inscription on his tombstone to record the things for which he wished "most to be remembered": "Here was buried/Thomas Jefferson/Author of the Declaration of American Independence/ of the Statute of Virginia for religious freedom/& Father of the University of Virginia."

EPILOGUE

The men we call Founding Fathers had no idea what life—and history—had in store for them. As young men, Alexander Hamilton, John Adams, and Thomas Jefferson lived safe within the confines of the world's great empires. All three were driven by their own passions and particular genius, and when in the course of human events they saw a new fate opening for America they chanced their fortunes and futures on creating a more just and promising world.

Alexander Hamilton was an eighteenth-century version of a Horatio Alger story—a boy from humble beginnings helped by a wealthy man (in Hamilton's case, several). He used their assistance wisely, and with courage, honesty, and determination he managed to leave behind the West Indies of his boyhood to pursue a more promising life in America. But Hamilton succeeded far beyond the typical Alger hero, gaining both fortune and the apex of fame as one of America's leading voices.

Hamilton always approached life fearlessly. From the age of eighteen he risked his neck to free America from the British yoke, and by the time he left the Continental Army after the Yorktown victory his name had become a household word. With the revolution won, Hamilton felt strongly that the still amorphous United States needed a government that could control the passions of the people; if left unchecked, those passions, he believed, could lead to anarchy and ruin. The constitution he diligently worked to help draft still frames the rules that govern the nation today. Hamilton also conceived of and wrote the bulk of *The Federalist Papers,* a stroke of genius that explained what the U.S. Constitution would mean in the lives of ordinary people.

Hamilton's commitment to a strong central government led to his becoming the undisputed leader of the Federalist faction. He was accused of advocating for a royal government with a king and an aristocracy, but in truth he did not want anything like that. Instead, he was convinced that the federal government must be powerful if it was to govern the country effectively and to defend it from all threats, including internal ones.

Hamilton faced many threats himself, including from his own demons. Had he taken the counsel of Proverbs—"Pride goeth before destruction"—his life might not have ended on the banks of the Hudson on a hot July morning in 1804. But pride, dueling, and fearlessness were features of his life, and the combination brought him to an untimely death.

Alexander Hamilton was not a heralded founder until early in the present century, when Ron Chernow's bestselling biography resurrected public interest in him. Then, in 2015, Lin-Manuel Miranda's wildly successful musical *Hamilton* premiered on Broadway. Since then, he has reigned as the Founding Father of the hour.

A man of courage, brilliance, and vision, Hamilton remains the youngest treasury secretary in American history; his face has been on the ten-dollar bill for almost a century. Yet even before that, his *Federalist* essays and arguments were often cited in courtrooms and in Congress. Moreover, the U.S. financial and banking system, including the Federal Reserve, is largely the brainchild of Alexander Hamilton.

JUST AS HAMILTON WAS FORMED by his West Indian childhood, John Adams was a product of his New England upbringing. Though he came from humble circumstances, his opportunities were more promising than Hamilton's. He graduated high in his class at Harvard, read the law well, hung out his shingle, and soon became a leading lawyer in Massachusetts. He married Abigail Smith, a strong, earnest, witty woman who was both his full partner and his wife.

In the face of strong anti-British sentiments Adams was both secure and brave enough to defend in court the British soldiers accused in the Boston Massacre. Yet he also worked tirelessly to ensure that America continue to function during the long and bitter Revolutionary War. As a congressman during its precarious early years, he knew his own fate lay in the balance if America lost the war. As minister to France in the final years of the Revolution, he secured vital loans to continue the fight and persuaded the French to send forces across the Atlantic, ultimately leading to the British surrender at Yorktown. Through all those years, he chronicled in his letters and journals the momentous events unfolding around him with a keen insight and wry humor.

After the war Adams suffered through eight years as the first vice president of the United States. He was vice president when the French Revolution broke out, and as it progressed he correctly predicted it would come to a bad end. The lesson he took away was the notion that when the general populace was given too much power, sooner or later it would abuse that power. That belief drove him into the camp of Hamilton's Federalists.

As the nation's second president, John Adams governed well and made few mistakes. The greatest mark against his presidency were the ill-conceived sedition laws; they were a keen example of giving government too much power. He managed to negotiate the abominable Quasi-War with a petulant France and, through skillful diplomacy, to keep his young country out of a full-fledged conflict, simultaneously building an army and a navy in case of war. Owing to a variety of factors, chief among them the uproar over the Alien and Sedition Acts and the dissolution of the Federalists as a viable party, Adams was not reelected to a second term. But as he told a friend, he left the country with its coffers full, at peace with the world, and its commerce flourishing.

Adams was a man of strong character, earnest faith, and good intentions. Though he did not have the far-ranging vision of Hamilton or Jefferson, he took great care to see that his governing was done correctly, giving room for the nation to prosper and progress. In the centuries that followed his death, he was mostly overlooked as a Founding Father; no significant memorial in Washington celebrates his memory. Then, in 2001 the popular historian David McCullough wrote a bestselling biography of Adams, and for a time John Adams's name was on everyone's lips. In 2008, an enormously popular miniseries based on McCullough's book was released, and Americans began to appreciate anew this querulous but exceptional man of deep character and insight.

AFTER GEORGE WASHINGTON, Thomas Jefferson has historically been the most well known of the nation's founders. His most vaunted legacy will always be the resounding thoughts and words of the Declaration of Independence. Those words reflect his passion as a natural philosopher who contemplated long and hard how a free, republican government should function and defended that vision throughout his life. Jefferson was a man of liberty, and anything that threatened liberty was to him simply wrong. He saw shoals and dangers in the Federalist government of George Washington, and though he believed in the U.S. Constitution he pressed for amendments to ensure freedom of speech, of the press, of religion, of the right of assembly, and protection from unreasonable searches and seizures.

Yet Jefferson, along with others, also worked to enshrine the right to own slaves in the Constitution. Like many of his fellow southerners he had inherited slaves. Northern heirs generally inherited bonds, or gold, or stocks, or buildings, or factories; that was their capital. In the South of Jefferson's era slaves were capital, just as land was; without slaves, it was believed, larger tracts of land could not be worked profitably.

Jefferson's feelings and writings about slavery are difficult for the modern American to understand. He wrote that he detested the institution of slavery, seeing it as degrading to both slave and master and a threat to the nation. As president, he eagerly signed into law a bill making it a crime to import slaves. But he also believed that if the slaves were set free, they must be deported to Africa or the Caribbean, as free blacks and whites could not peacefully live together. Most of his contemporaries agreed; they felt that American slavery was equivalent to riding a tiger but saw no way to get off. It has long been an axiom among historians that a man deserves to be judged by the times in which he lived: Jefferson was a man of his time, although his time was consumed by one of the great evils of history.

Jefferson's greatest accomplishment as president was acquiring the geographic heart of America—the lands that angle up from Louisiana through the Plains and into the Mountain West. Owing to his vision, Lewis and Clark undertook an unprecedented expedition of scientific exploration and foreign policy. Their presence in the west of the new Louisiana Purchase territory established America's rights to it. Also on the foreign policy front, Jefferson sent the U.S. Navy to clear the Mediterranean Sea from the scourge of the Barbary pirates, and he kept America out of war with Britain—but at a great cost to the economy. His Embargo Act created serious financial strain and failed to prevent the British from continuing their depredations on American shipping and seamen.

Yet Jefferson also left the country with one of its leading state institutions, the University of Virginia. The "academical village" he designed for it along with his nearby Monticello residence remain recognized architecturally and are honored throughout the world. His love of neoclassical architecture is echoed in the Jefferson Memorial, which graces the shores of the Tidal Basin in the nation's capital, while his words echo around its walls.

Beyond his role as a founder, Thomas Jefferson was an extraordinary man—a musician, scientist, philosopher, lawyer, architect, and cultivator of the soil. He loved his country deeply, and gave up much that he loved to serve it.

As a result of his early death Hamilton remained frozen in middle age, but Jefferson and Adams lived to old age. Despite their political differences—and surely because of their shared love of country and their personal history together—Adams and Jefferson reconciled in their last years. They lived to see the age of the steamboat and steam locomotive railways, the invention of tin cans and the rise of canneries, and the use of natural gas to light city streets and factories. By their deaths in 1826 there were twenty-four stars on the American flag.

Each of these three founders had his foibles. But those foibles pale beside their accomplishments and characters. These men loved with an abiding perseverance the new country they had helped create, and each made deep personal sacrifices to ensure their dream of an ever free United States of America. Each also had strong ideas on how the government would function best, and feared that any other approach might lead to despotism and ruin. After all, the republican government that held together the barely united states was at that time an experiment no nation had tried before. And yet thanks to them these United States have held together for more than two centuries.

Hamilton, Jefferson, and Adams made the country what it is today, and their dust still sparkles like stars in the minds of their fellow Americans.

ACKNOWLEDGMENTS

As in all my histories I must first acknowledge all those historians who have persevered through the years to chronicle the characters and events of this fraught and critical period in American history. To you I owe undying thanks. I also owe an enormous gratitude to the persons—both in the academic and administrative worlds—who created the marvelous resource Founders Online at the National Archives. Here one can bring a quote—or even a piece of quote—from whatever sources, and the Founders Online site will almost invariably match it to the original correspondence between the individual quoted and his correspondent, providing the full context of the letter or other document, the date issued, and other vital information. It is one of the wonders of the Internet age—unerring and trustworthy.

I must send my everlasting thanks to the splendid Lisa Thomas, my longtime editor and now the publisher and editorial director of National Geographic Books. Her faith in me has known no bounds. Also to the kind, dogged, and dependable Hilary Black, now my editor, who reads with a perfect eye to make the book as smooth and accurate as possible. And to Karen Kostyal for her own careful and thoughtful editing. And to senior editorial project editor Allyson Johnson, I owe much for always seeing that all aspects of the bookmaking process run smoothly as prescribed. Once again my enduring gratitude must go to my longtime copy editor Don Kennison, who has saved me from myself more times than I can recall. To each and every one of these talented persons, my sincere thank you.

Winston Groom
Point Clear, Alabama
March 18, 2020

SELECT SOURCES

Adams, Abigail. "To Thomas Jefferson from Abigail Adams, 27 June 1787." *Founders Online,* National Archives. Accessed March 17, 2020. https://founders.archives.gov/documents/Jefferson/01-11-02-0420.

Adams, Abigail Smith. "From Abigail Smith Adams to Mary Smith Cranch, 21 November 1800." *Founders Online,* National Archives. Accessed March 17, 2020. https://founders.archives.gov/documents/Adams/99-03-02-0794.

——. "From Abigail Smith Adams to Cotton Tufts, 28 November 1800." *Founders Online,* National Archives. Accessed March 17, 2020. https://founders.archives.gov/documents/Adams/99-03-02-0799.

——. "From Abigail Smith Adams to Thomas Boylston Adams, 3 January 1801." *Founders Online,* National Archives. Accessed March 17, 2020. https://founders.archives.gov/documents/Adams/99-03-02-0842.

——. "From Abigail Smith Adams to Thomas Boylston Adams, 3 February 1801." *Founders Online,* National Archives.

Accessed March 17, 2020. https://founders.archives.gov/documents/Adams/99-03-02-0883.

Adams, Charles Francis, ed. *The Works of John Adams,* vol. VIII. Boston: Little, Brown, 1856.

Adams, John. "[A Letter to Richard Cranch about Orlinda, a Letter on Employing One's Mind, and Reflections on Procrastination, Genius, Moving the Passions, Cicero as Orator, Milton's Style, &c., October–December 1758.]" *Founders Online,* National Archives. Accessed March 17, 2020. https://founders.archives.gov/documents/Adams/02-01-02-0010-0001-0003.

——. "John Adams to Abigail Adams, 6 January 1794." *Founders Online,* National Archives. Accessed March 17, 2020. https://founders.archives.gov/documents/Adams/04-10-02-0008.

——. "John Adams to Abigail Adams, 5 March 1797." *Founders Online,* National Archives. Accessed March 17, 2020. https://founders.archives.gov/documents/Adams/04-12-02-0005.

——. "Letter from John Adams to Abigail Adams, 19 December 1793." *Adams Family Papers: An Electronic Archive,* Boston, Massachusetts Historical Society. Accessed March 17, 2020. https://www.masshist.org/digitaladams/archive/doc?id=L17931219ja.

——. "Letter from John Adams to Abigail Adams, 13 June 1800." *Adams Family Papers: An Electronic Archive,* Boston, Massachusetts Historical Society. Accessed March 17, 2020. http://masshist.org/digitaladams/archive/doc?id=L18000613ja&hi=1&query=November%201800&tag=text&archive=letters&rec=6&start=0&numRecs=141.

——. "John Adams to Thomas Pickering." Quoted in John Ferling. *Setting the World Ablaze: Washington, Adams, Jefferson, and the American Revolution*. New York: Oxford University Press, 2000.

——. "From John Adams to William Tudor, Sr., 13 December 1800." *Founders Online,* National Archives. Accessed March 17, 2020. https://founders.archives.gov/documents/Adams/99-02-02-4711.

——. "To Thomas Jefferson from John Adams, 4 April 1794." *Founders Online,* National Archives. Accessed March 17, 2020. https://founders.archives.gov/documents/Jefferson/01-28-02-0047.

——. John Adams to Dr. Benjamin Rush, August 21, 1798

Biddle, Charles. *The Autobiography of Charles Biddle, Vice-President of the Supreme Executive Council of Pennsylvania*. Philadelphia: E. Claxton, 1883.

Bowen, Catherine Drinker. *John Adams and the American Revolution*. Old Saybrook, Conn.: Konecky & Konecky, 1979.

——. *Miracle at Philadelphia: The Story of the Constitutional Convention*. Boston: Little, Brown, 1986.

——. *The Most Dangerous Man in America: Scenes from the Life of Benjamin Franklin*. Boston: Little, Brown, 1974.

Brodie, Fawn McKay. *Thomas Jefferson: An Intimate History*. New York: Norton, 1974.

Brookhiser, Richard. *Alexander Hamilton, American*. New York: Free Press, 1999.

Burr, Aaron. "Aaron Burr to Joseph Alston, November 20, 1815." *Founders Online*, National Archives.

Butterfield, L. H., ed. *The Adams Papers: Diary and Autobiography of John Adams,* 4 vols. New York: Atheneum, 1961.

——. *The Book of Abigail and John: Selected Letters of the Adams Family, 1762–1784*. Cambridge, Mass.: Harvard University Press, 1975.

Callender, James. *The History of the United States for 1796; including a Variety of Interesting Particulars Relative to the Federal Government Previous to that Period*. Philadelphia: Snowden & M'Corkle, 1797. Retrieved from Evans Early American Imprint Collection, University of Michigan Library. Accessed March 17, 2020. https://quod.lib.umich.edu/e/evans/N24129.0001.001?rgn=main;view=fulltext.

Century Illustrated Monthly Magazine 34 (May 1887).

Chernow, Ron. *Alexander Hamilton*. New York: Penguin Press, 2004.

Coleman, William, ed. *A Collection of the Facts and Documents, Relative to the Death of Major-General Alexander Hamilton: With Comments, Together with the Various Orations, Sermons, and Eulogies, that have Been Published or Written on His Life and Character*. New York: Printed by Hopkins and Seymour for I. Riley and Co., 1804.

Cook, Don. *The Long Fuse: How England Lost the American Colonies*. New York: Atlantic Monthly Press, 1995.

Cosway, Maria. "To Thomas Jefferson from Maria Cosway, [20 September 1786]." *Founders Online,* National Archives. Accessed March 17, 2020. https://founders.archives.gov/documents/Jefferson/01-10-02-0267.

——. "To Thomas Jefferson from Maria Cosway, [5 October 1786]." *Founders Online,* National Archives. Accessed March 17, 2020. https://founders.archives.gov/documents/Jefferson/01-10-02-0298.

Emery, Noemie. *Alexander Hamilton: An Intimate Portrait*. New York: Putnam, 1982.

Ferling, John. *John Adams: A Life*. Knoxville: University of Tennessee Press, 1992.

——. *Setting the World Ablaze: Washington, Adams, Jefferson, and the American Revolution*. New York: Oxford University Press, 2000.

Fleming, Thomas. *Duel: Alexander Hamilton, Aaron Burr, and the Future of America*. New York: Basic Books, 1999.

Flexner, James Thomas. *The Young Hamilton: A Biography*. New York: Fordham University Press, 1997.

Gelston, David. "David Gelston's Account of an Interview Between Alexander Hamilton and James Monroe, 11 July 1797." *Founders Online,* National Archives. Accessed March 17, 2020. https://founders.archives.gov/documents/Hamilton/01-21-02-0093.

Hamilton, Alexander. *Alexander Hamilton: Writings*. New York: Library of America, 2001.

——. "From Alexander Hamilton to Angelica Church, 23 October 1794." *Founders Online,* National Archives. Accessed March 17, 2020. https://founders.archives.gov/documents/Hamilton/01-17-02-0324.

——. "From Alexander Hamilton to Elizabeth Hamilton, [10 July 1804]." *Founders Online,* National Archives. Accessed March 17, 2020. https://founders.archives.gov/documents/Hamilton/01-26-02-0001-0262.

——. "From Alexander Hamilton to James Monroe, [10 July 1797]." *Founders Online,* National Archives. Accessed March 17, 2020. https://founders.archives.gov/?q=Volume%3AHamilton-01-21&s=1511311112&r=100.

——. "From Alexander Hamilton to James Monroe, [22 July 1797]." *Founders Online,* National Archives. Accessed March 17, 2020. https://founders.archives.gov/documents/Hamilton/01-21-02-0110.

——. "From Alexander Hamilton to Martha Washington, 12 January 1800." *Founders Online,* National Archives. Accessed March 17, 2020. https://founders.archives.gov/documents/Hamilton/01-24-02-0140.

——. "From Alexander Hamilton to Oliver Wolcott, Junior, 16 December 1800." *Founders Online,* National Archives. Accessed March 17, 2020.

——. "From Alexander Hamilton to Theodore Sedgwick, 2 February 1799." *Founders Online,* National Archives. Accessed March 17, 2020. https://founders.archives.gov/documents/Hamilton/01-22-02-0267.

——. "From Alexander Hamilton to Timothy Pickering, [22 March 1797]." *Founders Online,* National Archives. Accessed March 17, 2020. https://founders.archives.gov/documents/Hamilton/01-20-02-0351.

——. "From Alexander Hamilton to Timothy Pickering, 17 March 1798." *Founders Online,* National Archives. Accessed March 17, 2020. https://founders.archives.gov/documents/Hamilton/01-21-02-0217.

——. "The Warning no. I [27 January 1797]." *Founders Online,* National Archives. Accessed March 17, 2020. https://founders.archives.gov/documents/Hamilton/01-20-02-0315.

——. "The Warning no. II [7 February 1797]." *Founders Online,* National Archives. Accessed March 17, 2020. https://founders.archives.gov/documents/Hamilton/01-20-02-0324.

Hopkinson, Francis. "To Thomas Jefferson from Francis Hopkinson, 1 December 1788." *Founders Online,* National Archives. Accessed March 17, 2020. https://founders.archives.gov/documents/Jefferson/01-14-02-0106.

Hosack, David. "David Hosack to William Coleman, 17 August

1804." *Founders Online,* National Archives. Accessed March 17, 2020. https://founders.archives.gov/documents/Hamilton/01-26-02-0001-0280.

——. "The Hamilton-Burr Duel." 1804. *Digital History.* Accessed March 17, 2020. http://www.digitalhistory.uh.edu/disp_textbook.cfm?smtID=3&psid=1071.

Jefferson, Isaac. *Memoirs of a Monticello Slave: As Dictated to Charles Campbell in the 1840s by Isaac, One of Thomas Jefferson's Slaves.* Edited by Rayford W. Logan. Charlottesville: University of Virginia Press, 1951.

Jefferson, Thomas. "III. First Inaugural Address, 4 March 1801." *Founders Online,* National Archives. Accessed March 17, 2020. https://founders.archives.gov/documents/Jefferson/01-33-02-0116-0004.

——. "Autobiography by Thomas Jefferson: 1743–1790." The Avalon Project, Yale Law School Lillian Goldman Law Library. Accessed March 17, 2020. https://avalon.law.yale.edu/19th_century/jeffauto.asp.

——. "From Thomas Jefferson to Benjamin Smith Barton, 27 February 1803." *Founders Online,* National Archives. Accessed March 17, 2020. https://founders.archives.gov/documents/Jefferson/01-39-02-0499.

——. "From Thomas Jefferson to Edward Rutledge, 27 December 1796." *Founders Online,* National Archives. Accessed March 17, 2020. https://founders.archives.gov/documents/Jefferson/01-29-02-0189.

——. "From Thomas Jefferson to George Washington, 23 May 1792." *Founders Online,* National Archives. Accessed March 17, 2020. https://founders.archives.gov/documents/Jefferson/01-23-02-0491.

——. "From Thomas Jefferson to Horatio Gates, 3 February 1794." *Founders Online,* National Archives. Accessed March 17, 2020. https://founders.archives.gov/documents/Jefferson/01-28-02-0015.

——. "From Thomas Jefferson to James Madison, 25 April 1786." *Founders Online,* National Archives. Accessed March 17, 2020. https://founders.archives.gov/documents/Jefferson/01-09-02-0360.

——. "From Thomas Jefferson to James Madison, 20 December 1787." *Founders Online,* National Archives. Accessed March 17, 2020. https://founders.archives.gov/documents/Madison/01-10-02-0210.

——. "From Thomas Jefferson to James Madison, 9 June 1793." *Founders Online,* National Archives. Accessed March 17, 2020. https://founders.archives.gov/documents/Jefferson/01-26-02-0219.

——. "From Thomas Jefferson to James Madison, 17 November [1798]." *Founders Online,* National Archives. Accessed March 17, 2020. https://founders.archives.gov/documents/Jefferson/01-30-02-0392.

——. "From Thomas Jefferson to John Adams, 30 August 1787." *Founders Online,* National Archives. Accessed March 17, 2020. https://founders.archives.gov/documents/Jefferson/01-12-02-0075.

——. "From Thomas Jefferson to John Jay, 23 April 1786." *Founders Online,* National Archives. Accessed March 17, 2020. https://founders.archives.gov/?q=Volume%3AJefferson-01-09%20john%20jay&s=1511311112&r=28.

——. "From Thomas Jefferson to Levi Lincoln, 24 March 1802." *Founders Online,* National Archives. Accessed March 17,

2020. https://founders.archives.gov/documents/Jefferson/01-37-02-0092.

——. "From Thomas Jefferson to Maria Cosway, [5 October 1786]." *Founders Online,* National Archives. Accessed March 17, 2020. https://founders.archives.gov/documents/Jefferson/01-10-02-0297.

——. "From Thomas Jefferson to Maria Cosway, 25 July 1789." *Founders Online,* National Archives. Accessed March 17, 2020. https://founders.archives.gov/documents/Jefferson/01-15-02-0291.

——. "From Thomas Jefferson to Meriwether Lewis, 23 February 1801." *Founders Online,* National Archives. Accessed March 17, 2020. https://founders.archives.gov/documents/Jefferson/01-33-02-0048.

——. "From Thomas Jefferson to Peter Carr, 19 August 1785." *Founders Online,* National Archives. Accessed March 17, 2020. https://founders.archives.gov/documents/Jefferson/01-08-02-0319.

——. "From Thomas Jefferson to Peter Minor, 20 July 1822." *Founders Online,* National Archives. Accessed March 17, 2020. https://founders.archives.gov/documents/Jefferson/98-01-02-2966.

——. "From Thomas Jefferson to Thomas McKean, 19 February 1803." *Founders Online,* National Archives. Accessed March 17, 2020. https://founders.archives.gov/documents/Jefferson/01-39-02-0461.

——. "From Thomas Jefferson to Thomas Paine, 11 July 1789." *Founders Online,* National Archives. Accessed March 17, 2020. https://founders.archives.gov/documents/Jefferson/01-15-02-0259.

——. "From Thomas Jefferson to William Cocke, 21 October 1796." *Founders Online,* National Archives. Accessed March 17, 2020. https://founders.archives.gov/documents/Jefferson/01-29-02-0154.

——. "From Thomas Jefferson to William Short, 3 January 1793." *Founders Online,* National Archives. Accessed March 17, 2020. https://founders.archives.gov/documents/Jefferson/01-25-02-0016.

——. "From Thomas Jefferson to William Short, 12 June 1807." *Founders Online,* National Archives. Accessed March 17, 2020. https://founders.archives.gov/documents/Jefferson/99-01-02-5747.

——. "From Thomas Jefferson to William Stephens Smith, 13 November 1787." *Founders Online,* National Archives. Accessed March 17, 2020. https://founders.archives.gov/documents/Jefferson/01-12-02-0348.

——. "Notes on Conversations with John Adams and George Washington, [after 13 October 1797]." *Founders Online,* National Archives. Accessed March 17, 2020. https://founders.archives.gov/documents/Jefferson/01-29-02-0439.

——. June 9, 1814. Washington, Jefferson& Madison Institute. http://wjmi.blogspot.com.

——. "Thomas Jefferson's Memorandum of Conversations with Washington, 1 March 1792." *Founders Online,* National Archives. Accessed March 17, 2020. https://founders.archives.gov/documents/Washington/05-10-02-0004.

——. "Thomas Jefferson to Benjamin Rush, 16 January 1811." *Founders Online,* National Archives. Accessed March 17, 2020. https://founders.archives.gov/documents/Jefferson/03-03-02-0231.

——. "Thomas Jefferson letter to William Gordon, 16 July 1788." Quoted in Dumas Malone, *Jefferson and His Time,* vol. I: *Jefferson the Virginian*, Boston: Little, Brown, 1948.

——. "To James Madison from Thomas Jefferson, 8 January 1797." *Founders Online,* National Archives. Accessed March 17, 2020. https://founders.archives.gov/documents/Madison/01-16-02-0313.

Kranish, Michael. *Flight from Monticello: Thomas Jefferson at War.* New York: Oxford University Press, 2010.

Lewis, Meriwether. "To Thomas Jefferson from Meriwether Lewis, 10 March 1801." *Founders Online,* National Archives. Accessed March 17, 2020. https://founders.archives.gov/documents/Jefferson/01-33-02-0196.

Mackenzie, Alexander Slidell. *Life of Stephen Decatur, a Commodore in the Navy of the United States.* Boston: Charles C. Little and James Brown, 1846.

Madison, James. "James Madison to Thomas Jefferson, January 24, 1790." *The Writings of James Madison,* vol. V. New York: G. P. Putnam's Sons, 1900.

——. "From James Madison to James Monroe, 4 December 1794." *Founders Online,* National Archives. Accessed March 17, 2020. https://founders.archives.gov/documents/Madison/01-15-02-0306.

Malone, Dumas. *Jefferson and His Time,* vol. I: *Jefferson the Virginian.* Boston: Little, Brown, 1948.

——. *Jefferson and His Time,* vol. II: *Jefferson and the Rights of Man.* Boston: Little, Brown, 1951.

——. *Jefferson and His Time,* vol. III: *Jefferson and the Ordeal of Liberty.* Boston: Little, Brown, 1962.

——. *Jefferson and His Time*, vol. IV: *The President: First Term 1801–1805*. Boston: Little, Brown, 1970.

Massachusetts Historical Society, Boston. "Adams Papers Digital Edition." Accessed March 17, 2020. https://www.masshist.org/publications/adams-papers

McCullough, David. *John Adams*. New York: Simon and Schuster, 2001.

McHenry, James. "Enclosure: James McHenry to John McHenry, Junior, 20 May 1800." *Founders Online*, National Archives. Accessed March 17, 2020. https://founders.archives.gov/documents/Hamilton/01-24-02-0422-0002.

Meacham, Jon. *Thomas Jefferson: The Art of Power*. New York: Random House, 2012.

Miller, John C. *Alexander Hamilton: Portrait in Paradox*. New York: Harper and Brothers, 1959.

——. *Alexander Hamilton: Portrait in Paradox*. Whitefish, Montana: Literary Licensing LLC, 2012.

Mitchell, Broadus. *Alexander Hamilton: A Concise Biography*. New York: Oxford University Press, 1976.

——. *Alexander Hamilton: Youth to Maturity, 1755–1788*. New York: Macmillan, 1957.

Monroe, James. "To Alexander Hamilton from James Monroe, 21 July 1797." *Founders Online*, National Archives. Accessed March 17, 2020. https://founders.archives.gov/documents/Hamilton/01-21-02-0109.

——. "To Alexander Hamilton from James Monroe, 27 November 1797." Quoted in "To Alexander Hamilton from James Monroe, 2 December 1797." *Founders Online*, National Archives. Accessed March 17, 2020. https://founders.archives.gov/documents/Hamilton/01-21-02-0176.

———. "To Alexander Hamilton from James Monroe, 6 August 1797." *Founders Online,* National Archives. Accessed March 17, 2020. https://founders.archives.gov/documents/Hamilton/01-21-02-0127.

Moré, Charles-Albert. *A French Volunteer of the War of Independence [by] Chevalier de Pontgibaud.* Translated and edited by Robert B. Douglas. New York: *New York Times,* 1969.

Moore, Benjamin. "Benjamin Moore to William Coleman, 12 July 1804." *Founders Online,* National Archives. Accessed March 17, 2020. https://founders.archives.gov/documents/Hamilton/01-26-02-0001-0268.

Moten, Matthew. *Presidents and Their Generals: An American History of Command in War.* Cambridge, Mass.: Belknap Press, 2014.

New York Evening Post. "The Funeral [14 July 1804]." *Founders Online,* National Archives. Accessed March 17, 2020. https://founders.archives.gov/documents/Hamilton/01-26-02-0001-0271.

Philbrick, Nathaniel. *Bunker Hill: A City, a Siege, a Revolution.* New York: Viking, 2013.

Pierson, Hamilton W. *Jefferson at Monticello: The Private Life of Thomas Jefferson*. New York: C. Scribner, 1862.

Randall, Henry S. *The Life of Thomas Jefferson,* vol. I., 1858. Reprint, Philadelphia: J. B. Lippincott, 1865.

Syrett, Harold C., ed. *The Papers of Alexander Hamilton,* vol. 3, *1782–1786.* New York: Columbia University Press, 1962.

———. *The Papers of Alexander Hamilton,* vol. 4, *January 1787–May 1788.* New York: Columbia University Press, 1962.

Trollope, Frances. *Domestic Manners of the Americans.* New York: Alfred A. Knopf, 1949.

Washington, George. "From George Washington to Charles Mynn Thruston, 10 August 1794." *Founders Online*, National Archives. Accessed March 17, 2020. https://founders.archives.gov/documents/Washington/05-16-02-0376.

——. "From George Washington to Thomas Jefferson, 21 January 1790." *Founders Online,* National Archives. Accessed March 17, 2020. https://founders.archives.gov/documents/Washington/05-05-02-0019.

——. "From George Washington to Thomas Jefferson, 1 January 1794." *Founders Online,* National Archives. Accessed March 17, 2020. https://founders.archives.gov/documents/Washington/05-15-02-0001.

NOTES

1 Broadus Mitchell, *Alexander Hamilton: A Concise Biography*, New York 1975.
2 Ibid.
3 Ibid.
4 Noemie Emery, *Alexander Hamilton: An Intimate Portrait*, New York 1982.
5 Charles-Albert Moré, *Chevalier de Pontgibaud*, New York 1969.
6 Ron Chernow, *Alexander Hamilton*, New York 2004.
7 Ibid.
8 Ibid.
9 Mitchell op cit.
10 Richard Brookhiser, *Alexander Hamilton, American*, New York 1999.
11 James Thomas Flexner, *The Young Hamilton: A Biography*, New York 1997.
12 Ibid.
13 Chernow op cit.
14 Mitchell op cit.

15 Ibid.

16 Flexner op cit.

17 Brookhiser op cit.

18 Flexner op cit.

19 Chernow op cit.

20 Emery op cit.

21 Ibid.

22 Flexner op cit.

23 John C. Miller, *Alexander Hamilton: Portrait in Paradox,* New York 1959.

24 David McCullough, John Adams, New York 2001.

25 John Adams to Thomas Pickering, quoted in John Ferling, *Setting the World Ablaze,* New York 2000.

26 McCullough op cit.

27 Ibid.

28 John Ferling, *John Adams: A Life,* Knoxville, Tenn. 1992.

29 L. H. Butterfield, ed., *The Adams Papers: Diary and Autobiography of John Adams,* 4 vols., New York 1961; Ferling, ibid.

30 Ferling, *World Ablaze* op cit.

31 Ibid.

32 Ferling, *Adams* op cit.

33 Ibid.

34 Ibid.

35 Catherine Drinker Bowen, *John Adams,* Old Saybrook, Conn. 1979.

36 Ibid.

37 Ibid.

38 Ibid.

39 Ibid.

40 Catherine Drinker Bowen, *The Most Dangerous Man in America: Scenes from the Life of Benjamin Franklin,* Boston 1974.

41 Bowen, *Adams* op cit.

42 Ferling, *World Ablaze* op cit.

43 Bowen, *Adams* op cit.

44 Ibid.

45 Don Cook, *The Long Fuse: How England Lost the American Colonies,* New York 1995.

46 *Adams Papers* op cit.

47 Ibid.

48 Ibid.

49 Ibid.

50 *Adams Papers* op cit.

51 Cook op cit.

52 Ibid.

53 Nathaniel Philbrick, *Bunker Hill,* New York 2013.

54 Ibid.

55 Ibid.

56 Bowen, *Adams* op cit.

57 *Adams Papers* op cit.

58 Bowen, *Adams* op cit.

59 Ibid.

60 *Adams Papers* op cit.

61 Philbrick op cit.

62 Ibid.

63 Ferling, *World Ablaze* op cit.

64 Bowen, *Adams* op cit.

65 Adams letter to Thomas Pickering, quoted in Ferling, *World Ablaze* op cit.

66 Ferling, *World Ablaze* op cit; Bowen, *Adams* op cit.
67 *Adams Papers* op cit.
68 Ibid.
69 Ibid.
70 Ibid.
71 Ibid.
72 Ibid.
73 Ibid.
74 Ibid.
75 Ibid.
76 Ibid.
77 Dumas Malone, *Jefferson and His Time,* vol. I, Boston 1948.
78 Henry S. Randall, *The Life of Thomas Jefferson,* vol. I, Philadelphia 1865.
79 Malone, vol. I op cit.
80 Malone, vol. 1 op cit.
81 Malone, vol. 1 op cit.
82 Malone, vol. I op cit.
83 Ibid.
84 Randall op cit.
85 Malone, vol. I op cit.
86 Ibid.
87 Ibid.
88 Randall op cit.; Malone, vol. I op cit.
89 Malone, vol. I op cit.
90 Jefferson op cit.
91 Ibid.
92 Ibid.
93 Jon Meacham, *Thomas Jefferson: The Art of Power*, New York 2012.

94 Jefferson op cit.
95 Ibid.
96 Ibid.
97 Malone, vol. I op cit.
98 Jefferson letter to Dr. Benjamin Rush, July 16, 1788, quoted in Malone ibid.
99 Randall op cit.
100 Ibid.; Michael Kranish, *Flight from Monticello: Thomas Jefferson at War,* New York 2010.
101 Malone, vol I op cit.
102 Fawn Brodie, *Thomas Jefferson: An Intimate History,* New York 1974.
103 Ibid.
104 Hamilton W. Pierson, *Jefferson at Monticello: The Private Life of Thomas Jefferson,* New York 1862.
105 Chernow op cit.
106 Flexner op cit.
107 Harold C. Syrett, ed., *The Papers of Alexander Hamilton,* New York 1962.
108 Ibid.
109 Chernow op cit.
110 Dumas Malone, *Jefferson and His Time,* vol. III, Boston 1962.
111 Ferling, *Adams* op cit.
112 Alexander Hamilton, *The Writings of Alexander Hamilton,* New York 1961; Chernow op cit.
113 Catherine Drinker Bowen, *Miracle at Philadelphia: The Story of the Constitutional Convention,* Boston 1986.
114 Ibid.
115 Mitchell op cit.

116 Miller op cit.
117 Ibid.
118 Chernow op cit.
119 Miller op cit.
120 Ibid.
121 Ibid.
122 Mitchell op cit.
123 Miller op cit.
124 Mitchell op cit.
125 Ibid.
126 Broadus Mitchell, *Alexander Hamilton: Youth to Maturity,* New York 1957.
127 Ibid.
128 Emery op cit.
129 Ibid.
130 *The Writings of Alexander Hamilton,* New York 2001.
131 Emery op cit.
132 Ibid.
133 *Adams Papers* op cit.
134 L. H. Butterworth, ed., *The Book of Abigail and John: Selected Letters of the Adams Family, 1762–1784*, Cambridge, Mass. 1975.
135 *Adams Papers* op cit.
136 Ibid.
137 Ibid.
138 *Adams Papers* op cit.
139 Ibid.
140 Ibid.
141 Ibid.
142 *Adams Papers* op cit.

143 Ibid.

144 Ibid.

145 Ibid.

146 Ferling, *Adams* op cit.

147 Ibid.

148 Ibid.

149 McCullough op cit.

150 *Adams Papers* op cit.

151 Ibid.

152 Ibid.

153 Ferling, *Adams* op cit.

154 *Adams Papers* op cit.

155 Ibid.

156 Ibid.

157 Charles Francis Adams, ed., *The Works of John Adams,* vol. VIII, Boston 1856.

158 Ibid.

159 Ferling, *Adams* op cit.

160 Charles F. Adams op cit.

161 McCullough op cit.

162 Ibid.

163 Charles F. Adams op cit.

164 Adams Family Papers. Boston, Massachusetts Historical Society Online.

165 Ibid.

166 Ibid.

167 Ibid.

168 Randall op cit.

169 Dumas Malone, *Jefferson and His Time,* vol. II, Boston 1951.

170 Ibid.

171 Ibid.

172 Thomas Jefferson to John Jay, 23 April 1776, *Founders Online,* National Archives.

173 Ibid.; Malone, vol. III op cit.

174 Randall op cit.

175 Thomas Jefferson to James Madison, 24 April 1776, *Founders Online,* National Archives.

176 Malone, vol. III op cit.

177 Ibid.

178 Thomas Jefferson to Maria Cosway, 9 October 1786; Maria Cosway to Thomas Jefferson, 9 October 1786, *Founders Online,* National Archives.

179 Randall op cit.

180 Ibid.

181 Thomas Jefferson to John Adams, 30 August 1787, *Founders Online,* National Archives.

182 Randall op cit.

183 Ibid.

184 Abigail Adams to Thomas Jefferson, 27 June 1787, *Founders Online,* National Archives.

185 Meacham op cit.

186 Thomas Jefferson to William Smith, 13 November 1787; Thomas Jefferson to James Madison, 20 December 1787, *Founders Online,* National Archives.

187 Thomas Jefferson to James Madison, 20 December 1787, *Founders Online,* National Archives.

188 Francis Hopkinson to Thomas Jefferson, 1 December 1788, *Founders Online,* National Archives.

189 Thomas Jefferson to Francis Hopkinson, 13 March 1789, *Founders Online,* National Archives.

190 Thomas Jefferson to Thomas Paine, 1 July 1789, *Founders Online,* National Archives.

191 Thomas Jefferson to Maria Cosway, 25 July 1789, *Founders Online,* National Archives.

192 Malone, vol. III op cit.

193 Ibid.

194 George Washington to Thomas Jefferson, 21 January 1790, *Founders Online,* National Archives.

195 Malone, vol. III op cit.

196 Thomas Jefferson to James Madison, 9 June 1793, *Founders Online,* National Archives; Malone ibid.

197 James Madison to Thomas Jefferson, 24 January 1790, *The Writings of James Madison,* New York 1900.

198 Thomas Jefferson to Benjamin Rush, 16 January 1811, *Founders Online,* National Archives.

199 Ibid.

200 Ibid.

201 Ibid.

202 Ibid.

203 Thomas Jefferson, *Memorandum of Conversations with Washington,* 1 March 1792, *Founders Online,* National Archives.

204 Ibid.

205 Ibid.

206 Ibid.

207 Ibid.

208 Ibid.

209 Thomas Jefferson to George Washington, 23 May 1792, *Founders Online,* National Archives.

210 Ibid.

211 Ibid.

212 Ibid.

213 Ibid.

214 Ibid.

215 Thomas Jefferson to William Short, 3 January 1793, *Founders Online,* National Archives.

216 Ibid.

217 Randall op cit.

218 George Washington to Thomas Jefferson, 1 January 1794, *Founders Online,* National Archives.

219 John Adams to Abigail Adams, 6 January 1794, *Founders Online,* National Archives.

220 Thomas Jefferson to Horatio Gates, 3 February 1794, *Founders Online,* National Archives.

221 Thomas Jefferson to Peter Minor, 22 July 1822, *Founders Online,* National Archives.

222 Thomas Jefferson to Peter Carr, 19 August 1785, *Founders Online,* National Archives.

223 Isaac Jefferson, *Memoirs of a Monticello Slave,* Charlottesville, Va. 1951.

224 Ibid.

225 John Adams to Thomas Jefferson, 4 April 1794, *Founders Online,* National Archives.

226 Thomas Jefferson to William Cocke, 21 October 1796, *Founders Online,* National Archives.

227 Ibid.

228 Thomas Jefferson to James Madison, 17 December 1796, *Founders Online,* National Archives.

229 Thomas Jefferson to Edward Rutledge, 27 December 1796, *Founders Online,* National Archives.

230 Ibid.

231 John Adams to Abigail Adams, 5 March 1797; Thomas Jefferson to James Madison, 8 January 1797, *Founders Online,* National Archives.

232 Thomas Jefferson, *Notes on Conversations with John Adams and George Washington,* [after] 13 October 1797, *Founders Online,* National Archives.

233 Letter from John Adams to Abigail Adams, 19 December 1793, Boston, Massachusetts Historical Society.

234 Letter from John Adams to Dr. Benjamin Rush, 21 August 1798, *Founders Online,* National Archives.

235 Thomas Jefferson to William Short, 12 June 1807, *Founders Online,* National Archives.

236 McCullough op cit.

237 Ibid.; James McHenry to John McHenry Jr., 20 May 1800, *Founders Online,* National Archives.

238 John Adams to Abigail Adams, 13 June 1800, *Founders Online,* National Archives.

239 Ibid.

240 John Adams to William Tudor Sr., 13 December 1800, *Founders Online,* National Archives.

241 Abigail Adams to Mary Smith Cranch, 21 November 1800, *Founders Online,* National Archives.

242 Ibid.

243 Abigail Adams to Cotton Tufts, 28 November 1800, *Founders Online,* National Archives.

244 Ibid.

245 Abigail Adams to Thomas Boylston Adams, 3 January 1801, *Founders Online,* National Archives.

246 Abigail Adams to Thomas Boylston Adams, 3 February 1801, *Founders Online,* National Archives.

247 *Century Illustrated Monthly Magazine* 34, May 1887.

248 George Washington to Charles Mynn Thruston, 10 August 1794, *Founders Online,* National Archives.

249 Alexander Hamilton to Theodore Sedgwick, 2 February 1799, *Founders Online,* National Archives.

250 Alexander Hamilton to Angelica Church, 23 October 1794, *Founders Online,* National Archives.

251 James Madison to James Monroe, 4 December 1794, *Founders Online,* National Archives.

252 Ibid.

253 Hamilton to Angelica Church op cit.

254 Ibid.

255 James T. Callender, *History of the United States for the Year 1796,* Philadephia 1797, *Founders Online,* National Archives; Chernow op cit.

256 Alexander Hamilton to James Monroe, 10 July 1797, *Founders Online,* National Archives.

257 "David Gelston's Account of an Interview Between Alexander Hamilton and James Monroe, 11 July 1797," *Founders Online,* National Archives.

258 Ibid.

259 Ibid.

260 Ibid.

261 Ibid.

262 Ibid.

263 Ibid.

264 Ibid.

265 James Monroe to Alexander Hamilton, 15 June 1797, *Founders Online,* National Archives.

266 James Monroe to Alexander Hamilton, 6 August 1797,

Founders Online, National Archives.

267 James Monroe to Alexander Hamilton, 7 November 1797, *Founders Online,* National Archives.

268 Aaron Burr to Joseph Alston, 23 September 1815, *Founders Online,* National Archives.

269 Alexander Hamilton, "Warning no. I," "Warning no. II," *Gazette of the United States,* 27 January, 7 February 1797, *Founders Online,* National Archives.

270 Alexander Hamilton to Timothy Pickering, 22 March 1797, *Founders Online,* National Archives.

271 Alexander Hamilton to Timothy Pickering, 17 March 1798, *Founders Online,* National Archives.

272 Ibid.

273 Chernow op cit.

274 Ibid.

275 Ibid.

276 Alexander Hamilton to Martha Washington, 12 January 1800, *Founders Online,* National Archives.

277 Thomas Jefferson, June 9, 1814. Washington, Jefferson & Madison Institute. http://wjmi.blogspot.com.

278 Alexander Hamilton to Oliver Wolcott Jr., 16 December 1800, *Founders Online,* National Archives.

279 Ibid.

280 Chernow op cit.

281 Ibid.

282 Ibid.

283 Ibid.

284 Ibid.

285 Miller op cit.

286 Ibid.; Brodie op cit.

287 Thomas Fleming, *Duel: Alexander Hamilton, Aaron Burr, and the Future of America,* New York 1999; Charles Biddle, *The Autobiography of Charles Biddle,* Philadelphia 1883.

288 Fleming ibid.

289 Chernow op cit.

290 Ibid.

291 Fleming op cit.

292 Alexander Hamilton to Elizabeth Hamilton, 10 July 1804, *Founders Online,* National Archives.

293 Ibid.

294 Ibid.

295 Dr. David Hosack, "Statement on the Duel and Death of Alexander Hamilton 1804," *Founders Online,* National Archives.

296 William Coleman, ed., "A Collection of Facts and Documents Relating to the Death of Alexander Hamilton 1804," *Founders Online,* National Archives.

297 Hosack op cit.

298 Rev. Benjamin Moore to William Coleman, 12 July 1804, *Founders Online,* National Archives.

299 Fleming op cit.

300 Ibid.

301 Gouverneur Morris's oration is contained in *New York Evening Post,* "The Funeral [14 July 1804]," *Founders Online,* National Archives.

302 Thomas Jefferson, "First Inaugural Speech, 3 March 1801," *Founders Online,* National Archives.

303 Thomas Jefferson to Levi Lincoln, 24 March 1802, *Founders Online,* National Archives.

304 Dumas Malone, *Jefferson and His Time*, vol. IV, Boston 1970. Cites Frances Trollope's *Domestic Manners of the Americans* (1832).

305 Thomas Jefferson to Gov. Thomas McKean, 19 February 1803, *Founders Online,* National Archives.

306 Thomas Jefferson's Monticello (Online).

307 Thomas Jefferson to Thomas Mann Randolph, September 20, 1803, *Founders Online,* National Archives.

308 Thomas Jefferson to Meriwether Lewis, 23 February 1801, *Founders Online,* National Archives.

309 Meriwether Lewis to Thomas Jefferson, 10 March 1801, *Founders Online,* National Archives.

310 Thomas Jefferson to Benjamin Smith Barton, 27 February 1803. *Founders Online,* National Archives.

311 Alexander Slidell McKenzie, *The Life of Stephen Decatur,* Boston 1846.

312 Ibid.

313 Ibid.

INDEX

ILLUSTRATIONS CREDITS

Front cover: (Hamilton), Francis G. Mayer/Corbis/VCG via Getty Images; (Jefferson), Donaldson Collection/Getty Images; (Adams), Courtesy National Gallery of Art, Washington, D.C.; (flag), Mark Thiessen, NG Staff. Back cover: (LE), GraphicaArtis/Getty Images; (CTR), VCG Wilson/Corbis via Getty Images; (RT), Bridgeman Images.

1 (UP), GraphicaArtis/Getty Images; 1 (LO LE), Photo Josse/Leemage/Corbis via Getty Images; 1 (LO RT), History and Art Collection/Alamy Stock Photo; 2 (UP LE), Bridgeman Images; 2 (UP RT), Bridgeman Images; 2 (LO), Smith Collection/Gado/Getty Images; 3 (UP), Yale University Art Gallery; 3 (LO), Bettmann/Getty Images; 4 (UP), Peter Newark American Pictures/Bridgeman Images; 4 (LO), Michael Neelon (tourism)/Alamy Stock Photo; 5, Bridgeman Images; 6, MPI/Getty Images; 7, Bridgeman Images; 8, Peter Newark American Pictures/Bridgeman Images; 9, Museum of Fine Arts, Boston, MA, Bequest of Charles Francis Adams/Bridgeman Images; 10, mambo/Alamy Stock Photo; 11 (UP), GraphicaArtis/Getty Images; 11 (LO), ©Thomas Jefferson Foundation at Monticello. Gift of the Gilder-Lehrman Collection of New York, and its principals, Richard Gilder and Lewis E. Lehrman; 12 (UP), De Agostini Picture Library/M. Seemuller/Bridgeman Images; 12 (LO), Monticello: 1st version (elevation), probably before March 1771, by Thomas Jefferson (N48;K23). Courtesy of the Massachusetts Historical Society; 13, VCG Wilson/Corbis via Getty Images; 14, Nawrocki/ClassicStock/Getty Images; 15 (UP), Academic Village Engraving by W. Goodacre, ca 1831. Special Collections, University of Virginia Library; 15 (LO), Print Collector/Getty Images; 16 (UP LE), F&A Archive/Art Resource, NY; 16 (UP RT), Photo © Christie's Images/Bridgeman Images; 16 (LO), Bridgeman Images.